MR.
MINDBOMB

MR.

Eco-Hero and Greenpeace Co-founder Bob Hunter

MINDBOMB

A LIFE IN STORIES

Edited by **BOBBI HUNTER**

CO-FOUNDER OF GREENPEACE

Introduction by **CAPTAIN PAUL WATSON**

Afterword by **ELIZABETH MAY**

RMB

For information on purchasing bulk quantities of this book, or to obtain media excerpts or invite the author to speak at an event, please visit rmbooks.com and select the "Contact" tab.

RMB | Rocky Mountain Books Ltd.
rmbooks.com
@rmbooks
facebook.com/rmbooks

Cataloguing data available from Library and Archives Canada
ISBN 9781771606240 (paperback)
ISBN 9781771606257 (electronic)

Design: Lara Minja, Lime Design

Printed and bound in Canada

We acknowledge the financial support of the Government of Canada through the Canada Book Fund and the Canada Council for the Arts, and of the province of British Columbia through the British Columbia Arts Council and the Book Publishing Tax Credit.

Disclaimer

The views expressed in this book are those of the author and do not necessarily reflect those of the publishing company, its staff, or its affiliates.

Mindbomb:
an image that sends a collective shock
through the world and leads to action;
the 1970s version of "going viral."

CONTENTS

FOUR: SOLIDIFYING

ROBERT HUNTER
The Mind Bomber

by Dr. Stephen Scharper

STORIES OF GREENPEACE CO-FOUNDER Robert Hunter could fill a book, and now, happily, they do. This volume is a "story quilt," with colourful swatches from Robert Hunter's remarkable life, collected, arranged and woven together by his cosmic co-conspirator, Bobbi Hunter.

Framed by fellow Canadian environmental paladins Paul Watson of the Sea Shepherd Conservation Society and the Hon. Elizabeth May, MP, of the Green Party, these vibrant vignettes from friends, family and colleagues reveal an expansive soul who was of and for the Earth. As a result, Bob was deeply at home wherever he found himself and wherever the Earth found him. And the Earth did find him.

A high school dropout from a broken home in rural Manitoba, with a derelict dad and an overworked mom, Bob became a Governor General Award–winning author, a pre-internet, mind-bombing media Einstein, and co-founder of Greenpeace, one of the largest and most effective environmental organizations in the world. But his amazing sojourn on this planet was also filled, as these rich stories attest, with humour, love, joy, *wild* adventures and profound relationships with fellow humans – as well as with flowers, whales and rainbows.

I first found Bob, not in person, but on television. While visiting family in Toronto in the early 1990s, I recall turning on the TV one morning and seeing a middle-aged, pony-tailed hippie in a housecoat, sitting in what looked like his office. With a stentorian voice and calm, conversational manner, he carefully went through highlighted sections from Toronto's daily newspapers, the *Toronto Sun,* the *Toronto Star,* and *The Globe and Mail,* showing how each paper's bias shaped their stories about the environment and other key issues.

This guy is way *cool,* I thought, *and sharp.* Bob's morning talks were my first introduction to what came to be known as media studies.

LINES OF THE SPIRIT

Years later, I met Bob as a guest on his whimsically monikered CityTV program, *Hunter's Gatherings.*

He had invited me to talk about religion and ecology, an intersection I was working on as a newly minted professor at the University of Toronto. What impressed me was not only his kindness but also his insight into the deep sacral dimension of all reality. Although at this point he was an eco-icon, he treated me as an equal, an experience shared by many in this volume, and welcomed me to the set with warmth, humour and gentle hospitality.

Though marked by intrepid eco-showdowns, shrewd tactical acumen and brilliant writing, Bob's story is as much about spiritual connection as environmental activism.

In our later conversations, we spoke about Pierre Teilhard de Chardin, SJ, the Jesuit paleontologist whose works, though initially banned by the church, later became celebrated for showing how the divine Spirit was at work in the unfolding of the cosmos. These ideas were picked up and advanced by cultural historian and "geologian" Thomas Berry, CP, author of *The Dream of the Earth,* who proposed that *the universe is a communion of subjects, not a collection of objects.* In other words, all reality has a psychic-spiritual dimension. Bob intuited this, and his life was guided by it. He was raised Roman Catholic, and his early years entailed the sacramental, spiritual cosmology and social justice teachings of that tradition, giving rise within him to what liberation theologian

Leonardo Boff would later articulate as listening to the "cry of the poor and the cry of the Earth." Bob's deeply rooted sense of social justice and communion with the more-than-human-world and his affinity for the thought of Teilhard de Chardin and Thomas Berry are linked to this spiritual lineage, leading him later to use, with favour, the intriguing term "eco-Catholicism."

Like Thomas Berry, Bob had a deep sense of awe and reverence for the mystery and beauty of the natural world. As he wrote during one of his Greenpeace actions, "This protest is somehow connected with the nerve centre of what is thought of as religion…the emotion we know as 'awe.' From awe one moves to reverence…. And the feeling of awe fills the boat, it fills our heads."

Whether diving into frigid waters off a Greenpeace vessel to catch a rainbow where it met the sea, or lying in his backyard with daughter Emily asking her to reflect on the wisdom of trees, Bob Hunter had a deeply felt innate and joyful sense of the inscrutable wonder of the world. As Emily notes, he never felt alone or afraid in the wild. Rather, he felt at home there, and protected. If, as celebrated American naturalist Henry David Thoreau declared, "In wildness is the preservation of the world," for Bob Hunter, in wildness was the preservation of his home – and his being.

LINES OF THE HEART

A pulsating motif in Bob's spiritual connection with nature is love. As these fascinating stories reveal, Bob had the rare ability to be fully present to any given moment. Media sage Marshall McLuhan, a fellow Canadian who influenced Bob's thought, reputedly once observed that an artist is able to be fully present in and to any given moment. Bob, I think, was such an "artist," and, as a result, was able to be in love with the people, places and more-than human-realities that also co-inhabited any given moment with him.

This aura-like love surrounding Bob was a discovery made by Jerry Rothwell, director of the 2015 film about Greenpeace, *How to Change the World*. After the Toronto premiere, Jerry mentioned to me that one thing all the people he interviewed for the film shared was "a love of Bob Hunter," despite wide ideological and political differences. Perhaps it was Bob's non-ego-driven, self-critical and compassionate approach that enabled him to bring such diverse people – and species – together for a common purpose.

AN AUTHENTIC HUMILITY

A further dimension of Bob's spirit and spirituality was a deep humility. Many contributors, like myself, were gobsmacked by Bob's prodigious achievements, yet Bob knew that proper awe was reserved for the Universe, not, as in my first encounter, for a gifted, middle-aged environmental *merde* disturber. Bob did not want to be a star; rather, he wanted all of us to have the ability, *sans* air and light pollution, to see and be inspired by *the* stars.

Robert Hunter, as these bountiful stories attest, manifests that the loves we share – among ourselves and with all the species with whom we co-inhabit this planet – are in each of us and have been all along.

The Earth is a far better place because Robert Hunter had the courage, not only of his convictions, but also of his loves.

PREFACE

by Bobbi Hunter

BOB HUNTER WAS MY HUSBAND. We both put our bodies in front of deadly whaling harpoons to protect whales and to bring attention to the slaughter of these incredible creatures. Together we opened the first and second Greenpeace offices. We gathered the friends who formed the core community of activists that boldly set out to alter the path of destruction being taken against the world's whales and seals. We put up family finances to provide the footing for two of the largest environmental organizations in the world – Greenpeace and the Sea Shepherd Conservation Society. Together we travelled for campaigns, for lectures and for support. We raised a family, loved, and lived every day to the fullest. For over 30 years we walked the course of life together until Bob's course ended.

It has been 16 years since his passing, and although many honours were bestowed upon Bob during his time with us and after he died, there has not yet been a book dedicated to documenting this legendary man, his life's passion and his ecological legacy. Bob is celebrated as the visionary and catalyst for the environmental movement in Canada, and is studied in universities and colleges, so I decided this book was a necessary and timely way to entertain the armchair reader looking for real-life adventure, and to inspire the next generation of environmental activists.

Bob's influence touched countless people, so I decided to reach out to as many of them as I could and ask for their stories! This is an unusual – and challenging – approach to a biography, and yet it has worked well.

When I approached the contributors, both well known and unknown, to write a chapter for a specific time period or event in Bob's life, the response was resoundingly positive. Time spent with Bob was not only memorable but life altering.

Some of the over 40 pieces recount well-known exploits viewed from new perspectives, and some are being told here for the very first time. As you progress through Bob's history of shared experiences, a common voice emerges, a voice of awe and appreciation for a man who embodied and communicated the important things in life.

The ecology movement today is tethered to many and varied roots, but one of the primary taproots of the movement is the life and teachings of Bob Hunter, an unassuming Canadian whose life story proves that, regardless of background or experience, any one person can do something HUGE in their own unique way to make a difference to the health of our planet. As you read each contribution and discover how things evolved, you'll understand that it wasn't a straight line. It was an unpredictable line that sometimes connected the right people at the right time. Bob's story and connections with the contributors reveal, encourage, and even demand that, if you follow your heart and start walking in any direction, change will happen. Despite setbacks and disappointments, Bob didn't give up. He just found another direction, another solution and, most importantly, he never forgot who he really was and what his heart desired: ecological health and fairness.

Bob's message is reflected through the voices in this book because many live by it: any single person can make a difference. Just do something.

THE MAN, THE LEGEND

by Captain Paul Watson

BOB HUNTER once famously remarked that a Greenpeace founder could be found in any beer parlour on the west coast of Canada; there were many who claimed the title, a few with some self-justified validity, but most without. There were plenty of co-founders, but only one man truly deserving of the title of founder. Robert (Bob) Lorne Hunter is "the" founding father of Greenpeace. The first clue may be that his official membership number was 000.

But of course it is far more complex than that.

Bob told us many times of the Cree legend of the Warriors of the Rainbow. It foretold of a time when the Earth was in peril due to the destructive power of greed, but it was also a time when people of all races would band together to protect the planet, our common Mother. He was passionate about the need for the environmental movement to form a powerful alliance with Indigenous Peoples.

Bob not only understood it was time, he also took action, and he led the way. He understood how to become an environmental strike force for planetary salvation.

It was Bob who made the decision for Greenpeace to take on the whalers, and it was Bob who engineered the creation of Greenpeace International. I am quite confident that if not for those two defining decisions, Greenpeace would not exist today, and we can only imagine the state of our ecosystem without the activists who have been, and will be, motivated to act on its behalf.

Bob saw the future, and he acted to address it by focusing on taking action in the present. He knew that what we do in the present defines what the future will be. When he saw a need, he always seized any opportunity to take any action that presented itself to address that need.

In 2003, Bob published his book *2030: Thermageddon*, to address climate change with a plea for action that our time on Earth is running out. He wrote: "What a waste if we continue the plunge into the chaos and suffering of a world aflame or flooded or crushed under ice! What a waste of an excellent planet and a species with greatness in it!.... It's not the Fall of Man we are talking about any longer; it's the Fall of Eden."

However, the mainstream environmental groups were not ready for his message on climate change, and Greta Thunberg had not yet been born. What set Bob apart from most environmentalists was that he was a passionate and courageous visionary with a boundless imagination for impossible solutions.

In 1971, when we set off for Amchitka, Nelson Mandela was in prison. The very idea that Mandela would one day be president of South Africa was unthinkable, impossible. Yet the impossible became reality. You do not sail into the teeth of a nuclear weapons test believing you can shut it down unless you're willing to attempt the impossible.

Bob saw the formidable obstacles before us and, when faced with impossible problems, he worked to find impossible solutions, because he knew within his heart that impossible problems could be overcome.

The early success of Greenpeace came, in part, from Bob's understanding of the nature and power of media. He was an adept "Master of Media" strategist. He knew how to create a story and how to keep the story energized and relevant, and he had absolutely no qualms about inserting himself into the narrative. He was an absolute master of gonzo journalism.

Bob coined the term "mindbomb," which was the 1970s equivalent of "going viral."

He was the right person for the right job at the right time: a counterculture activist, journalist and philosopher who both thought and lived outside the box. He also had an amazing ability to work with people across the political and cultural spectrum.

All of us who knew him, campaigned with him, worked with him and debated him were influenced and emboldened by him. Many of us stood side by side with him and laughed in the face of the dangers we shared with him.

Together Bob and I blocked a Soviet harpoon vessel in the North Pacific, and a year later stopped a Norwegian sealing ship in the ice off the coast of Labrador. Together we chased Spanish trawlers from the Grand Banks of Newfoundland. Together we led a band of Indigenous Peoples from British Columbia to intercept the re-enactment voyages of the *Nina*, *Pinta* and *Santa Maria* off Puerto Rico. Together we confronted drift netters in the North Pacific, and together we opposed the plans by the Makah Tribe to kill whales in the waters off Washington state.

Following the guidance that Bob had provided during my days with Greenpeace, I built Sea Shepherd up from an organization to a global movement, and I was happy when many of my former Greenpeace colleagues joined my crew.

The Greenpeace Foundation exists today primarily because of one exceptional man but, as you will see, that is not the whole story of Bob Hunter's influence. It's far more multi-dimensional than that.

You are about to take a ride through the life and times, adventures and accomplishments of a fascinating and remarkable man. Contributions by activists, cohorts, colleagues, offspring and family give you their perspective on some of the wildest and most profound actions in the ongoing work of defending this extraordinary jewel of a planet.

You will experience not just an understanding of Bob Hunter but also a foundation for hope and action. Because, more than anything, Bob's message was that each and every one of us has the power and the ability to change the world, to save a species, to defend an ecosystem, and to lay down the stepping stones for a brighter, greener, kinder and more progressive future.

ONE
EMERGING

FORESTS AND FIGHTERS

by Dr. Myron MacDonald

BOB HUNTER was a complex and wonderful man. I think to understand him we need to delve a little into the roots of his lineage.

One could say Robert Lorne Hunter was a perfect example of the Canadian settler state – half French Canadian and half Scots-Irish. Anyone who knew Bob might be surprised to find there are no great leaders, no scholars, no clergymen and no social activists to be found in his ancestry! Both sides of his family were simple folk: labourers, farmers, mechanics, waitresses, hairdressers and homemakers. Can looking at his background even begin to answer the question of how this great man came to be? To answer that question, I have stitched together a bit of the fabric of Bob's direct heritage.

Robert Lorne Hunter was born on October 13, 1941, in St. Boniface, Manitoba, to Andrew Lorne Hunter and Augustine Bernadette Gauvreau.

The first Hunter in Bob's lineage to come to Canada was Bob's great-great-grandfather, William Hunter. He and his wife Rachel made their passage to Canada from Ireland and settled in Ontario. William is listed as a Presbyterian and a labourer. Their son Mathew and his bride Mary Ann Miller had Robert Henry Hunter, Bob's grandfather, in 1873. By the age of 27, Robert Henry Hunter, a Presbyterian and a beauty engineer (the title for a cosmetics chemist at the time), had made his way to Manitoba. There he met and wed Harriet Jane Boyd. Between 1902 and 1917, Robert Henry and Harriet Jane Hunter had seven children: five boys and two girls.

Andrew Lorne Hunter, the last of the seven children born to Robert Henry and Harriet Jane, was Bob's father. Born in 1917 at Haliburton, Ontario, he was always referred to simply as Lorne. Soon after his birth, Lorne and family resumed living in Manitoba. Lorne later became a mechanic. The Hunter family history was typical of the times: large families, hard-working pioneers who often married in their early 20s.

The first direct Gauvreau ancestor to come to Canada was Bob's great-great-great-great-grandfather, Etienne Gauvreau. Born in 1683 in St-Hilaire, Poitou, France, he came to Canada in his early 20s and died in Quebec in 1765. His family stayed on in Quebec until 1909, when Bob's grandfather Louis Wenceslas Gauvreau ventured to Manitoba.

Louis is listed as a general bookkeeper. He married Marie Eugenie Bernadette Schwarz, possibly of German background, on February 1, 1910, in St. Boniface, Manitoba. Louis Gauvreau and Bernadette Schwarz had five daughters and four sons between 1913 and 1928. Bob's mother Augustine Bernadette, born on May 28, 1913, in Dunrea, Manitoba, was the first of the nine children.

Bob's parents could not have come from more different worlds. His father was the youngest of seven children of Scots-Irish descent, with a mix of Presbyterian and Catholic faith, while Bob's mother was the oldest of nine children of a French Canadian Catholic family. It was a coming together of vastly different upbringings, but Bob's parents would also find their marriage was not entirely accepted, not only for the cultural and religious divide but also because Bob's mother was older than his father – quite an anomaly for that time.

Bob's only sibling, Donald Hunter, was born on September 21, 1943, in St. Thomas, Ontario. Sadly, Lorne and Augustine's marriage ended in divorce, and Augustine became a waitress to support her two sons.

The unhappiness of Bob's parents' marriage might account for some of the depth of Bob's character. He was given a broader scope as to what families could look like from an early age. He was not restricted to one doctrine or another. His mother raised him as a French Canadian Catholic after the divorce, but the awareness of his father's culture was always with him. His world could be viewed through two quite different lenses, giving him a broader base of experience upon which to draw than per-haps most young people of that era.

In later years Bob travelled to Scotland with his family – wife Bobbi, and youngest children Will and Emily. It was by great luck that they were welcomed onto the Hunterston Castle lands, which were owned by the current family of the laird of the Hunter clan. There they camped in an ancient walled garden and slept in the manor house. Bob felt a great affinity to Scotland and briefly researched his clan history through the Hunter Clan Office of Canada.

Bob discovered that he was descended from a long line of men of the forest, hunters and soldiers. In the halls of the castle of Hunterston there is a bust of a laird of the clan, Robert Hunter, from the 15th century. That Robert Hunter bore an uncanny resemblance to our Robert Hunter. The roots of our identity are much deeper than we realize.

CURSUM PERFICIO

by Donald Hunter

HITLER INVADES RUSSIA, the Blitz intensifies against Britain's cities, and Japan attacks Pearl Harbor. It is 1941 and my brother, Robert Lorne Hunter, is born in Winnipeg, Canada.

Our father had enlisted with the RCAF, but rather than being posted in Europe, he was assigned as ground crew at a flight-training base near St. Thomas, Ontario. He kept the Harvard trainers flying here in Canada.

In 1945, two years after I was born, Dad was discharged, and we returned to Winnipeg. Dad got a job with North Star Oil delivering oil drums to gas stations and repair shops around rural Manitoba. He was rarely home. When he was, he would hang a white sheet in the living room and project 16mm black-and-white films recorded by cameras on Allied warplanes. For Bob and me this was the beginning of our interest in action movies. During the summer, Dad would occasionally take Bob or me on the road with him to a town called Alonsa, near a sandy beach on Lake Manitoba.

I was too young to realize at the time, but many were aware that Dad had a drinking problem. Not only that, but he was also living in two worlds: one with his wife and kids in Winnipeg and another with Lila, in Alonsa. Eventually, Dad just stopped coming home.

During the 1950 "Flood of the Century" that devastated Winnipeg, the Red and Assiniboine rivers spilled their banks overnight. Our house sat between the two rivers. Dad appeared in the company truck to evacuate

Mom, Bob and me to the home of an elderly woman in Teulon, who became our "Aunt Elma." After that, Dad left and never lived with us again.

Teulon's main street consisted of a single grain elevator and rail line on one side, with a general store and gas station on the other. When I look back to that first spring and summer in Teulon, I believe that's when Bob and I bonded for life. We spent most of our time exploring. There was a scrap metal yard with a large water-filled ditch. The roof of a sedan, cut from a scrapped car, was partly submerged – perfect as our vessel. In our secret summer we were Huckleberry Finn and his adventurous friend Tom. Bob wrote the plays, and I performed with him – a budding young playwright and his extra.

We were sad to move back to Winnipeg, but the Manitoba government had paid to repair our "waterlogged, not destroyed" home. Mom had found full-time work at a restaurant, so Aunt Noella, Mom's sister, and her husband, Dave, moved in to mind us. Another room had been added on the back of our house during the repairs. Mom slept there in the poorly insulated room, heated only by a small space heater. The Winnipeg winters are cold, but Mom managed. She always managed.

By the summer of 1952, Mom had become the manager of the restaurant. Uncle Dave held down a union job with the CNR. Mom took us on vacations for two weeks at Grand Beach on Lake Winnipeg, where we would spend the entire day camped on the sandy beach. With two household incomes, luxuries like television, and even new bicycles, were possible. Life was so good that Mom bought a two-storey house in a well-established neighbourhood.

By now, Bob and I were teenagers with heady opinions of our own. It was not long before our newfound taste in music and entourage of lively friends escalated into a fight with Uncle Dave. He slapped me, and Bob jumped on his back and pounded on his head. Noella broke up the fight, but not long after that they moved out. Mom, adaptable as ever, turned our home into a boarding house. A cousin, also named Bob Hunter, moved in, as did a University of Manitoba student. Cousin Bob, or "Cuz," became the "other" brother. He was older than Bob by five years and a plumber. He had a motorcycle, a Model A Ford and another more practical car. He also kept a case of beer in the basement and did not mind if Bob and I helped ourselves from time to time.

Our teen years were happy. Mom kept things lively – she was a talker who often started her stories with "to make a long story short," then continued on a monologue lasting half an hour, without taking a breath. We were the captive audience required for her stories about her workday or family hijinks. Bob, a chip off the old block, could also capture the attention of people around him. The big difference was that Bob's stories were funny, interesting and more to the point. I think he learned the art of storytelling by improving on Mom's style.

As we each had our own room, Mom slept on a fold-up cot in the dining room, sacrificing to make our lives better. But she had firm house rules. Bob respected that his girlfriend Margaret was not allowed to stay all night, but they sure spent a lot of time in Bob's room with the door closed. Bob loved to read, write and paint, even creating his own sci-fi comic books. He was a reader from an early age. Even though he was only 5, when Mom temporarily lost her sight after surgery for a tumour, he'd read the newspaper to her every evening until her sight returned. Could have been the start of Bob's interest in becoming a newsman.

Mom, whom everyone called Stein, was outgoing and loved to meet new people. Her first date after Dad left was with Andy, a nice man who looked somewhat like our father. However, the relationship didn't last.

Her next date was with Austin, a widower with two boys the same ages as Bob and me. Austin was a man of means who wanted a wife at home and a mother for his boys. It wasn't a love affair – it was practical. The proposal was made, Bob and I were all in, and Mom turned him down.

Mom's next gentleman friend, Lyle Potter, looked like a good catch. Owning a garage and car dealership in Carman kept him busy and his visits occasional. When he did visit, he would always arrive in a different car.

Before long, Lyle proposed. We were thrilled that Mom accepted. We had enough time to sell our house and finish the school year before leaving Winnipeg to settle in Carman. When weeks went by and Lyle did not show up, we became suspicious. When Lyle finally came by, Bob kept him talking while I snuck out to check the registration papers for the Ford he had arrived in. The car belonged to a rental company. Mom was devastated by his lie, but not shocked. With our house already sold, and Lyle gone again, we moved in with Uncle Freddy, Mom's youngest brother. Soon after Lyle's vanishing act, Uncle Freddy took us out to Carman.

There was indeed a Potter Garage, but it was Lyle's cousin who owned it. There was no car dealership – never had been. Lyle's cousin said Mom was not the first woman to come looking for Lyle.

Happily, much later, when Bob and I had grown up, Mom met a wonderful, decent man named Fred Stein. After a proper courtship, they married, and our mom humorously became Stein Stein.

On Bob's first day of high school, he met Peter French. Peter went on to study nuclear physics, followed by a career at the Pickering Nuclear Power plant. By the end of the first day, they were best friends. Meanwhile, by coincidence, at the local junior high school I met Peter's younger brother, Rodney. We too became lifelong friends.

In 1957, the Russians launched Sputnik, the first satellite to orbit the Earth. Peter thought Canada should have been first – it was so easy, even he could build a rocket. Of course, Bob encouraged him. There was an old garage at the back of the Frenches' home. The scientific team of French and Hunter went to work. By the summer of 1958, the rocket was ready to fly. We took it out late one evening, the fuse was lit, and with a blast of flames, up, up, up it went! Sirens were heard, and shortly after a fire engine and police car arrived. Rocket Man, his accomplice and their awestruck brothers watched from a distance.

When Bob and Pete were 18, they set off to see the world, choosing the farthest possible destination – Australia. However, they stopped off in Las Vegas, thinking it would be a memorable start. It was. Peter lost so much money that he was forced to return home. Bob headed for Vancouver, where Mom's brother, Uncle Art, and his wife, Julie, took him in. Bob stayed there for quite some time, exploring the Pacific coast and nearby mountains. He was in heaven – an experience that clearly stayed with him.

At the age of 21, Bob was still restless and itching to see the world. Mom and I were comfortably settled in a new house in Winnipeg, so Bob packed his bag once again and said goodbye.

From Montreal, Bob found a Baltic cargo ship, which cost far less than the passenger liners. The final destination was Italy, with a stopover in Cuba. It was 1962, and Bob was already on the ship celebrating his 21st birthday when news broke of the Cuban Missile Crisis. Bob did not know why American warships met the freighter and turned it away from Cuba, but they then stayed the course for Italy.

As soon as Bob disembarked in Genoa, Italy, he was arrested. It was a case of mistaken identity, and he was released after a few nights of free room and board in an Italian jail. He took a bus to Rome and thumbed his way to London.

Eight months later, Bob arrived back in Winnipeg. The letters from London had not told it all. He arrived with his new love – a very pregnant Zoe.

By 1964, I was living the bachelor life, renting a modern apartment. Bob meanwhile was deeply distressed because Zoe had run off to Vancouver with their baby, Conan. Bob had to stay for his job at the *Winnipeg Tribune*. He was not taking care of himself, drinking and smoking too much. I convinced him to come and stay with me. After a week or so, he decided to get on a plane to Vancouver, find Zoe and Conan, and reconcile.

Two weeks later I still had not heard from him. I couldn't sleep. I kept thinking about Bob. For reasons I can never explain, I got out of bed, got in my car, and drove to the Winnipeg airport. There was a flight arriving from Vancouver. I went to the gate, and Bob was there! He spotted me and gave a sigh. He was so happy, as he did not have the cash for a taxi, or even a bus.

That was my brother. Time and time again, what shouldn't be, was; what couldn't happen, did; what was logical, didn't matter.

BEATNIK BOB

by Jim Deacove

IT WAS EARLY YEARS in Winnipeg, and my new neighbour Bob appeared to be a charming, casual and certainly not suit-and-tie person, as most reporters of that era were. For some interviews, he did manage a shirt and open suit jacket, but his heart and soul were those of the Beat Generation. It must have been the late 1950s when Bob first introduced himself to me.

I lived in my art studio on the second floor of a rooming house, and Bob had his writer's pad in the third-floor garret. Our Victorian rooming house was located near the Red River in the older part of the 'Peg, kitty-corner to a Franciscan monastery. My studio was a large, expansive room in full view of a home for "wayward" girls across the alley. These unruly "Misses" lived up to their reputation. It was quite the eclectic mixture of humanity in a compact area, and this variety of beings was great fodder for the cache of images that Bob filed in his mind for later stories.

To keep paints on my palette, I worked nights at the bus depot restaurant, which was part of an extremely popular chain named Salisbury House. When it was quiet, Bob would drop by to shoot the shit after filing his stories at the *Winnipeg Tribune*. He was an aspiring reporter, consistently taking every assignment on offer. Human interest, crime, theatre – they were all grist for his eloquent use of his typewriter. At the restaurant, I would apprise him of my nocturnal and often strange customers, and he in turn would update me on the stories he was writing.

They varied greatly, but he knew how to make them all interesting. He was learning not only the craft of newspaper reporting but also the art of creative writing. He was immersed in the School of Life, gathering information, absorbed as a word artist for the purpose of writing his first novel, *Erebus*.

Bob would take me along on his more offbeat assignments – ones that were sure to have an unusual twist, such as interviewing the white witch from the US, here to neutralize the black witch who was apparently spreading evil throughout Winnipeg. Some believed the black witch had possessed the minds of those in power. Bob had a good time with that one, saying to me, "Why the fuss, man, aren't all politicians possessed to begin with?" Then he laughed that infectious laugh.

Bob told me about a complicated and tedious trial he had to cover, where the accused was defended by renowned lawyer Harry Walsh. After many long days, Bob was literally awakened by the sounds of the vacating courtroom as the trial wound up. Had it been a murder trial he would have been on high alert, but financial fraud was totally boring to a high-energy guy like Bob. Nevertheless, he had a deadline, so he scrambled to interview anyone left in the courthouse for usable quotes. It seems some of the cleaning staff became the story's "reliable sources." The next day, Bob was called in to his editor's office to face the ire of Mr. Walsh himself, who was threatening legal action for major flaws in the story. Bob, who was close to fainting, uttered a humble apology as the editor promised a retraction. As Walsh left the office, he poked Bob in the ribs, smiled and gave him a wink. It was a lesson in legal theatre.

In reality, that piece was an exception. Bob was not a lax reporter, and he took the craft very seriously. I recall that Bob took a long time to probe, investigate and marshal well-documented facts about some political corruption in the city's government circles. He submitted reams of work and waited expectantly for a response. When summoned to the chief editor's office, he was congratulated for his fine substantive work before watching it all, promptly and unceremoniously, being dropped into the wastebasket. We shared a few beers that night, commiserating over a hard lesson learned about bucking the inner circles of power and position.

He was determined to write "real stuff," and, man, could he deliver, in torrents. He would write on a roll of newsprint, tacking the night's work on my doorframe for me to comment on. In the morning, I would open my studio door and get tangled up in a head-to-toe roll of writing. I knew of no one then, and know no one now, who can pour out such wonderful work with such apparent ease.

I vividly recall Bob coming into the restaurant, simply burbling with childlike excitement. It was the annual Press Club Beer and Skits Night, and Bob had delivered a skit. He could not believe how much applause and laughter he had received from the veteran reporters. Bob had just discovered more of what he would become. He was mastering the written word in his creative writing, and now he was finding his strong speaking voice.

We regularly gathered with like-minded friends at local pubs where we dissected and examined the great writers. We would pontificate on the meaning of Joyce's more obscure novels and discuss Henry Miller, a American ex-pat who inspired many of that pub group to head for Europe. Bob succumbed to the lure, taking a freighter from Montreal to Italy.

Bob had been gone for almost a year when he flew back home from London with his new bride, Marion, who later changed her name to Zoe. Bob was but 21, and she was 23 – and pregnant. She had introduced Bob to a new world in London, taking him to listen to historian and political and social activist Bertrand Russell. Bertie spoke on a soapbox at Hyde Park and expounded on his call for nuclear disarmament. This hit Bob like a lightning bolt, and the encounter was the catalyst for much of Bob's life trajectory.

Soon after Zoe arrived, she experienced the freezing cold of a Winnipeg winter; she was pregnant and suffering from culture shock. Within a short time, she had delivered their baby son, Conan, and she and Bob entered the world of many new parents – a colicky baby and sleep deprivation. His meagre reporter salary was barely sustainable for one person, let alone three. Zoe had made Bob's world larger, but it seemed he was making her world smaller.

As always, in order to cope, Bob retreated to his writing. I particularly remember the startlingly beautiful descriptions of nature that adorned the stories that flowed from him. He was always in a state of observing and recording.

I wrote a little, but each word and sentence was like carving in concrete. My passion is art. I still have the paintings I did of Bob, always marked "Not for Sale" at my exhibitions. I can see why he easily charmed the ladies. He was so handsome and rugged, and radiated such a larger-than-life soul that it still hovers around.

A painting of a striding Bob with a backpack and bedroll about to enter the dark woods on the way to Elk Island portrays a typical Bob. Leading. Fearless. His back to the world. Alone. Searching. Which is why I call the painting *In Search of an Island*. But I want to be clear. Even though there were pub nights full of questioning what we were doing, and hours spent staring at a blank sheet in the typewriter, or a blank canvas on the easel while "real" life went on all around us, we were not floundering. We were not searching for the meaning of life, because the work itself was the meaning. The search was for identity, for who we were. *In Search of an Island* was a search for that strong, secure sense of who we were. So, when someone asked, "Who are you?" Bob could answer, "I'm a Writer!" Meaning and identity all wrapped up together.

As for our Elk Island trips, visualize, if you will, two unkempt guys, unshaven, messy hair. Me, in used army surplus garb, bag on my back with a ground sheet, sleeping bag, food, hunting knife, easel, sketchpad and paints, and Bob, with the same basic supplies but with more exotic food items and a small portable typewriter. Off we'd go to find the shifting sandbar that would be our road to Elk Island. Stripping to bathing suits, gear held over our heads, we'd carefully slither along the sandy tightrope to cross the channel to the island. Bob was a maximum risk taker who also introduced me to the nurturing quality of nature.

On one particular trip, we had travelled separately, and I was late getting to the crossing. I had decided to wait for Bob when I saw the flicker of a small fire far across the water. Damn! Bob was already on the island. It was a tough, cold crossing, with the wind whipping and the sandbar shifting, but knowing I would find Bob and a warm fire kept me going. It was a joyful reunion!

Moving on, we came across an abandoned fishing settlement – a ghost village with everything just left behind: cabins with clothing, food, firewood and even an old car. The most astonishing find was a couple of old, yellowed *Winnipeg Free Press* news pages with headlines about Hitler invading Poland. Only Bob could bring to words how we felt at that moment.

The war had had a huge negative effect on Bob's parents' marriage, leading to their difficult divorce. Bob reflected on all the needless wars and the destruction of innocent human life in foreign lands, as well as the pernicious damaging impact war had on generations close to home.

Back on the shore, Bob waded out and perched on a large rock. While I sketched him, he meditated with his usual unshakeable ability to sink into some kind of deep inner reality. He continued meditating while the sky darkened, and the Northern Lights flared around him. I captured that moment on canvas, and it remains on my wall to this day. I titled it *Hunter's Point*. I look at it now and Bob is with me.

This was Bob's way — a deep regard for nature combined with a sense of humour in which nothing really mattered, but yet everything mattered at the same time. This philosophy gave him the great sense of freedom to experience what it means to be a human being. He maintained that we are all here as spiritual creatures to experience what it means to be human. Not the other way around.

Dear Bob, will there be anything natural and wild left for us to explore when the wheel of life spins around again, and we once again hook up for more adventures? It will be tough to be a spirited renegade again. I hear that even Elk Island has been made into a provincial park.

HEADLONG EXHILARATION

by Walt Patterson

MY FIRST MEETING with Bob was clearly not propitious. It was 1962, and I was in London, England, earning a pittance at private tutoring and living frugally in a one-room bed-sitter in Bayswater.

I was late for what I hoped would be a promising first date. As I shot down the stairs in my building, mid-leap I suddenly had to seize the banister to stop myself from plummeting feet first into the grimace on the bearded face of the tall rucksack-toting figure confronting me! As I regained my balance, the grimace turned into a crinkled grin. "Hi! I'm Bob Hunter."

"Hi, Bob. Look, I'm in a helluva hurry. If you head to Terry and Chloe's at 52 Gloucester Terrace, I'll meet you there later."

I sprinted past him and leapt onto the bus, only to realize I'd given him the wrong address. I'd garbled the Gloucester Terrace address of Canadian friends, Terry and Chloe Clark, with other Canadian friends, Al and Jackie Clarke.

I met my date at Piccadilly Circus, excusing myself repeatedly to make futile phone calls. At last, I got through to Al and Jackie and alerted them to look for Bob and tell him to meet me at my place. Needless to say, the date fizzled out. At last, I could rush back to Bayswater to find Bob, but he was not sitting on the steps of my bedsit, nor was he in the building. I tried Terry and Chloe, suddenly genuinely worried. No Bob. I searched past the Albert pub, scene of nightly bull sessions in the saloon bar, down another side street and around the corner toward Al and Jackie's.

In a moment, a lanky Al materialized at the door. "Yeah, I found 'im. Guess where?" I followed Al through the hallway, mumbling in relief. Al chortled, "Yeah. The Albert. Didn't take him long to get his card punched."

As I entered the room, Bob arose from the armchair, turned ominously, and glowered at me through his shrubbery. Before I could voice a sheepish apology, he growled, "Welcome to London!" and burst out laughing. Jackie poured me a mug of coffee. Four hours later, back in my bedsit, I knew that we had hardly begun to talk.

Thus began my friendship with Bob, the closest and most intense friendship I have ever had, apart from the one with my beloved late wife, Cleone. Bob moved into the bed-sitter above mine. We found ourselves becoming part of a small colony of bohemian Canadians: Bob and I, Terry and Chloe, Al and Jackie, Dave Berner and Stan Eby, all variously aspiring writers and would-be deep thinkers. We convened almost every evening in the Albert pub, on Praed Street across from Paddington Station, sitting around a table discussing life, the universe and everything. We called ourselves the Bayswater Group, since it sounded classier than Paddington.

The discussions were unlike any I have known since. Leaning on elbows, setting aside a pint of Guinness, one of us would discourse uninterrupted for perhaps five minutes, the others paying rapt attention. Then another would take up the theme, probably for another five minutes; and so on, until chucking-out time. Bob, Dave and I probably took up most of the discussion, but it was wide ranging and thoughtful. We discussed James Joyce, Henry Miller and Lawrence Durrell, and at the time it seemed very meaningful and significant.

Even in those days, Bob was a virtuoso storyteller, with a vast repertoire, a rich and resonant speaking voice and impeccable timing. On one memorable night, the discussion ranged far and wide until Bob at last leaned forward and said, "But seriously, you guys, when you get right down to everything..." I cannot now recall whether that cracked everyone up, but it remained with me. It became the epigraph of what I call my statutory unpublished novel.

Bob became my closest confidant. In late 1962, I went on a solo hitchhiking trip to the Lake District. It turned into what was, for me, a horror story culminating in a panic attack that became the penultimate sequence in my novel. At last, scared and shaking, I made it back home. It was Bob who brought me through, calmed me down and stayed with me until the panic subsided.

The early months of 1963 were like a Winnipeg winter, except that every winter always takes the English by surprise. All the pipes froze. People had to get water from a standpipe at the end of Porchester Square. Bob and I had a brilliant idea and made our coffee from the water we scooped out of the loo cistern.

None of us had any idea how to cook. Bob, in the bed-sitter above mine, decided to make porridge for us on his gas ring stove. He chose a random amount of water and an equally random amount of porridge oats. When the resulting consistency proved unsatisfactory, he added more porridge oats, then more water, then more porridge oats, until the pot was a solid mass of inedible wodge.

Al and Jackie found a corner flat with a full-size pool table in the middle of the room. One morning around Christmas time, Bob and I, Terry and Chloe, and Stan dropped in. Other itinerant Canadians also joined us. We sat around the pool table at nine on a Sunday morning drinking the duty-free Advocaat liqueur the visitors had brought – gooey yellow intoxicating glup, memorably inappropriate at that – or any – time of day.

We were all smokers, though I fancied a pipe rather than cigarettes. In our penury, we collected cigarette butts and fashioned them into rollups.

Bob bought a cheap guitar and undertook to play it for us. Unfortunately, he proved to have neither an ear for music nor any skill as a guitarist. We referred to it unkindly as Bob's concrete guitar.

In 1963, in the middle of the night, I got a phone call from my parents in Winnipeg. My younger brother Fent had been badly hurt in a motorcycle accident. Bob stayed with me, helping me to hold it together while I booked a flight to Winnipeg and organized the trip. By the time I reached Winnipeg, Fent had died – one of the worst days of my life. But I have always remembered and cherished how Bob steadied me and helped me do what had to be done.

By 1963, the Bayswater Group was no more. Terry and Chloe had long since returned to Canada, followed by Al and Jackie, Dave, and Stan.

Bob had departed for Winnipeg with his new lady, Zoe. Although we remained in tenuous contact by letter, I didn't see Bob again for five years.

In the meantime, I met the best thing to ever happen to me, my beloved Cleone; and in February 1968, I finished the novel, typed on my battered Royal Portable with five carbons. I sent one carbon to Bob, who was by then a columnist for the *Vancouver Sun*.

A few weeks later, I was standing by our Land Rover at the Tower Hill filling station in Chipperfield when a Green Line bus stopped, and who should get off but Bob. He had read the novel and decided to come for a visit. He did not know where we lived, and he had not bothered to tell us he was coming. How he happened to find the right bus, and how I happened to be standing by the Land Rover when the bus stopped in Chipperfield where he saw me, we will never know. That was typical Bob, and typical Bob karma.

With considerable apprehension, I took Bob back to my first home with Cleone, The Folly in Commonwood. Despite our long separation, I still thought of Bob as my closest male friend; and Cleone was already my closest friend of all. Two very high-definition individuals – what if they hated each other? I introduced Bob to Cleone and discreetly left them together while I adjourned to the Coach and Horses pub down the road and slowly nursed a long, uneasy pint. When at last I warily ventured back to The Folly, I found Bob and Cleone were far from coming to blows. They had checked each other out and decided they were both on the same page. Cleone later told me that if she had not found me, she would undoubtedly have chosen Bob.

Bob stayed with us at The Folly for two weeks. At the time he was seriously into karate and spent many happy hours in his white robe in the garden practising, shouting "Hun TAH!" as he chopped down invisible attackers. He later told me he had to ease up on the karate, because he found himself in elevators wanting to assault someone. But he also told us, with thrilling and alarming detail, about something happening on the west coast of Canada and the US, concern about something called the "environment."

By the time Bob departed, he had turned Cleone and me into that strange new thing, "environmentalists." Soon we were reading Paul

Ehrlich, Barry Commoner and other commentators, learning about air pollution, water pollution and all the other dreadful things we humans were doing to our only planet. In 1970, I joined three poets to write and publish the UK's first environmental magazine. In 1972, I attended the UN Conference on the Human Environment in Stockholm. I was working with the newly formed Friends of the Earth (FoE), to produce an independent daily newspaper at the conference. On my return, FoE invited me to join their tiny, ill-paid London staff. Cleone, a hard-working dentist, said, "It needs to be done, and you can do it. If you want to, I'll back you." And she did. I became FoE's first "Energy Campaigner," using my university training in nuclear physics to focus particularly on the UK's extravagant plans for nuclear power.

Before long I was a full-time and high-profile environmental campaigner, not only in the UK but also in many other countries – all because Bob had triggered the spark that ignited Cleone and me. Bob's influence – not only the information and insight he provided but also the burning ardour and headlong exhilaration he brought with it – became a unifying principle throughout the rest of our lives. Thenceforth, every time our paths crossed, my meetings with Bob reinforced our joint commitment to making the world a better place.

BE WHERE YOU ARE

by Dave Berner

HUNTER WAS REALLY FUNNY. Falling down funny. Sure, he was witty and clever and capable of some great verbal hijinks, but, like any great comedian, he was not averse to some Three Stooges–style slapstick, bad puns and filthy, tasteless jokes. Bless him.

Of course, it didn't take much time in his presence to find out that he was made of incredibly special stuff indeed.

Hunter and I met in our hometown of Winnipeg when I was about 17. Hunter and most of our gang were a year or two older than me. We belonged to a loose association of young men with the customary obsessions. We also shared one peculiar quirk.

We were all literature freaks.

Each of us had an area of "expertise." Bobby Lithown worshipped Faulkner. Nick had read Proust's masterwork several times in French and later wrote a dissertation on the French symbolist poets. Willie could tell the Hemingway story inside and out several times over. I loved Joyce, Beckett and Henry Miller.

Hunter had a unique perspective. He loved almost anything in print, especially science fiction, mystery and oddness.

I still remember vividly the afternoon I called Bob with wild excitement. I was now all of 19 and had just returned from a short stay in Europe. "Bob! Bob! I'm reading the letters between Henry Miller and

Lawrence Durrell! It is so wonderful! See you at the Abby at seven!" The Abby being our favorite watering hole. I knew he'd show up.

Another time, I got so tired of waiting for him to show up for beers at the Aberdeen that I wandered over to his home. Bob was living in a square-turreted room at the top of a lovely old heritage house just down the street from the provincial legislature. That makes two Golden Boys on one tree-lined avenue. As I climbed the endless set of stairs to his lair, I could hear the keys tapping away on his portable typewriter. I called his name repeatedly. Soon I was standing about two feet away from him. He sat cross-legged on the floor as he wrote. Years later, I would interview a famous classical pianist. The man was intelligent and communicative...until he decided to illustrate a point about the music. His head bent down. His hands hovered for just a moment over the keys, and he was gone. For that man, at that moment, there was no room, no street outside the windows, no television cameras and no David. Only music. Chopin. For Hunter, writing was the same. Only the story. Only the beginning, a middle and an end.

Today, everyone and his Aunt Tessie carry on about something called mindfulness. Hunter was there long before the art of showing up became an industry. Present. In the exact place where he was. Attentive to the pulse of life around him. And loving every breath.

Everything is amazing. Everything will make you laugh and cry. Everything will send you to tear strips of paper off the walls in rage and indignation at our own cruelties and iniquities. I never knew Bob to critique another soul without also demanding of himself to do better. Be better.

In the 1960s, when we were both living in Vancouver, Bob gently elbowed me in the direction of better. He was by then a well-recognized writer for the *Vancouver Sun* daily newspaper. I was a taxi driver.

"You know, David, you should go check out the Company of Young Canadians."

"Excuse me?"

"Yah. You know the American Peace Corps, right? They send kids with a bit of university on volunteer missions all over the world to help people who are struggling with one thing or another. Well, then they created a domestic version called Vista. Our prime minster, Lester Pearson, kind of liked this whole idea, so he opened the Company of Young Canadians. I think they give people money to go do interesting goofy things, sort of like the Canada Arts Council."

Well, Hunter didn't exactly get that right, but no matter. I went, I got involved and began working with two Indigenous men who had recently been released from a BC penitentiary. They had a dream for a kind of halfway house, a safe place where men like them could transition from the traumatizing nightmare of prison to this baffling confusion called society. Four years later, we had 125 men, women and children living and working in X-Kalay, Canada's first residential treatment centre for addicts, alcoholics, ex-cons and others. Our Winnipeg site opened the next year, and soon we had over 250 resident clients in two provinces, and we were running half a dozen small businesses. Now, some 55 years later, that Winnipeg facility is still running and still proudly turning out clean and sober citizens every day.

Hunter participated in our very first attempt to do group therapy, conducted by one of the best clinical psychologists of the day. The exercise was a 24-hour non-stop encounter group, no holds barred. The good doctor insisted that this was the most dramatic group he had ever experienced. Of course, Bob threw himself wholeheartedly into this frightening process. I still recall the moment when some guy was so enraged at Hunter that he stood up and heaved a plate of fried chicken in Hunter's face.

If Bob had not casually said to me, "You know, David, you should go check out the Company of Young Canadians," thousands of people would not have made the arduous, miraculous journey that leads to reclaiming their citizenship and dignity.

In September 1971, Bob Hunter and a group of inspired, lunatic, courageous shit disturbers sailed a boat to Alaska, destined for the middle of a site intended by the United States to be ground zero for yet another atom bomb test. Thus, Greenpeace was born. Photos of Bob Hunter on the ship, looking like a pirate and laughing madly, were in every paper and on every TV set on Earth.

At our treatment centre, we threw an Amchitka Watch Party. Hundreds of guests arrived in the early evening and stayed until six in the morning. Jazz combos, priests, rabbis, guitar players, poets and actors took the stage while our kitchen kept the whole affair going with delicious food. Almost 500 people signed the telegram that we sent to these early eco-warriors – Hunter, of course, at the centre of it all.

One of the things I always loved about Bob, however, was that on a personal level, he was an argumentative, agreeable, silly and urgent vaudeville act. With one throwaway sentence he sent me off in a direction that changed my life – and the lives of many others. I will forever be grateful to him for that.

Otherwise, he was just another agonized clown with a straw hat and a cane, playing to the cheap seats.

I am one in a crowd of many who miss him and remember him fondly.

From Bob I learned to see, hear and listen.

Be where you are.

FRACTURED FAMILY

by Justine Hunter

IN 1967, Bob and Zoe headed down the west coast from Vancouver to Mexico in a Volkswagen van. Looking at the few photos of the trip that have made their way into my collection, I can never get my head around what would propel them on a Kerouac-fantasy adventure with a baby and preschooler in tow.

One photo shows Zoe next to the van pulled off on the side of the road, a cooler at her feet. No palm trees or beaches – there is nothing to see but desert and the road disappearing way off on the horizon.

I was the baby on this journey, so I've no direct memories of this trip. The journey was recounted as a series of amusing near-misses: That time my older brother, Conan, mistook a tarantula for a squirrel and tried to pet it. When Bob got stopped for having Canadian licence plates on the van, it was clear the penniless gringo in bare feet had no way to pay a fine. Conan remembers our father sleeping in a hammock during a hurricane while the wind buffeted the van. My mom would tell me how beautiful I was as a baby – with my skin tanned brown enough to match the locals', but my hair bleached white by the Mexican sun. She and Bob lost track of me – more than once – when one of the locals wandered off with me to show off this funny blond baby. In the retelling, Zoe seemed remarkably nonchalant about losing the baby.

Finally, the whole lot of us heading north for home, every one of us sick with dysentery. At the border between the US and Mexico, the van was pulled apart by suspicious border guards. Conan's last memory of Mexico was the chrome trim of the headlights sitting on the dusty ground.

Zoe was born in Swansea, Wales. She didn't share much about her childhood but did recall those moments, as a very young child during the Second World War, when she had to retreat to bomb shelters carting an ill-fitted gas mask. The bombing of Swansea would have left deep emotional trauma for her and her family, but she only spoke of the singing in the shelters as people tried to keep their spirits up.

A BBC report provides a snapshot of the world she was born into. Thirty thousand bombs were dropped on Swansea over the span of three days in 1941. The town buried 37 children because of that raid.

Whatever misery came out of her childhood, Zoe Rahin, with her porcelain skin and East Indian name, left home as a teenager and went to London, demonstrating an independent streak that has always defined her.

Bob and Zoe met in London. He was a Canadian from the prairies, working as a reporter at the *Winnipeg Tribune*. She introduced Bob to the peace movement. They participated in the Aldermaston marches against the Atomic Weapons Research Establishment – a precursor to Bob's involvement in the Amchitka anti-nuclear protest.

Bob brought his bohemian bride to Winnipeg in 1963 to live with her new mother-in-law; Zoe was five months pregnant with Conan.

I rely again on family lore here – Zoe endured just a few Winnipeg winters, bloodthirsty mosquitoes, and the tea served in mugs, before she'd had enough. In 1966, pregnant with me, she packed up Conan and got on a train bound for the west coast, where the weather felt more like home.

Eventually, Bob followed.

On the coast, Bob reinvented himself. The former clean-cut newspaper reporter from Winnipeg now sported long hair and a beard, promoted on billboards as the *Vancouver Sun's* counterculture columnist. Some nights he would bring me to the loading docks, the smell of fresh newsprint in the air, to grab the paper hours before delivery.

———

Bob and Zoe's East Vancouver home was one of the meeting places for the early Don't Make a Wave Committee that would later morph into Greenpeace. The gatherings could be intense, but often evolved into loud parties, accompanied by the smell of cigarettes, marijuana and beer.

Us children were mostly feral – no regular bedtimes and routines. We formed our own pack of similarly dishevelled and often interesting kids.

We didn't appreciate it at the time, but we had front row seats as a small group of people set out to change the world. When some musician backstage at a Greenpeace fundraiser handed me his guitar pick as a souvenir, I was oblivious to the fact that I'd just met some rock royalty. I lost the pick within minutes.

"Not only were they going to change the world, but they were also forming the club that would do it. What had been a Mad Hatter's tea party now had rules and needed to be aligned to a greater cause, and Bob ran the meetings," Conan recalls.

Bob and Zoe were being pulled apart, and the movement that Bob was growing was at the centre of it.

Conan is now a grandfather, and with the insight of his own parenting experience, he sees the oddity of our childhood. "There were always signs, placards, lying around the yard as other homes had bicycles and badminton rackets," Conan said. "It's hard to fix in my mind a picture of our parents together in the same room, never mind as a couple. And it's not because they were so different from each other or had radically different views – they were more similar than dissimilar."

Conan saw the tension building while I was too young to figure out what was going on. I don't recall asking why it was our father on stage speaking to ever-growing crowds, while Zoe was nowhere in sight.

Zoe wanted to stage sit-ins, wave signs and make impassioned pleas to whoever got close enough to be handed a leaflet. But Bob had found his calling, and his drinking and drug use was part of the package as he dealt with the pressure. To Zoe, it was self-indulgence. "She quite explicitly and repeatedly accused him of ego-tripping, and that really was the centrepiece of all arguments that I recall," Conan says.

After our parents' divorce, Bob carried on with Greenpeace while Zoe worked on environmental and human rights campaigns, marching for peace and justice and Pride. She even, eventually, spoke at rallies with a bullhorn – something I thought I would never see.

As a teen, I remember sitting one evening in Bob's basement office, with its floor-to-ceiling shelves stacked with books, as well as knick-knacks from his travels, including a white statue of the Buddha. Bob was holding forth on the one topic Zoe would never discuss: her family history. I was eager for the stories – her reticence only stoked my curiosity. The conversation ended abruptly when the Buddha toppled off a high shelf for no apparent reason. Bob concluded that it was a sign that we were offside, and we dropped the topic for good. I spent hours reassembling the porcelain figure with glue.

It took me a long time to work through my grief after Bob's death. As Alzheimer's gradually robs Zoe of her memories, I am grieving in a different way. But I understand that I will not reassemble her story.

PRESS RELEASED

by Rod Marining

I WAS SHOCKED AND ELATED when a major establishment paper hired a longhaired, counterculture, anti-establishment reporter to be their new columnist to discuss current issues. It was 1968, and Bob Hunter would be the youngest reporter of a major newspaper, the *Vancouver Sun*, to reach the status of columnist, with his own platform and his own untethered voice.

Bob Hunter had jumped on to my radar with his new job. I was now stalking him. I found him getting a coffee at the Pacific Press lunchroom, on the fourth floor. I was nervous. I was just a lowly copy boy, but I gathered the courage to zero in and congratulate him on his new job. A connection was established.

A copy boy in 1968 looked after the Teletype and photo-fax machines, which were the source of all incoming news. These stories and paper photos were then assigned to reporters by the news desk editor. Back then, many big stories, such as stories about the horrors of war, were being deposited directly into wastebaskets. "We are a family newspaper," said the chief editor. I was horrified and seemed to be one of the few who knew about the travesty of the deception that was happening. I was looking for an ally to share my awareness of this deceit with. Bob was the man – he gave voice to all societal grievances.

My next meeting with Bob stood out for what I learned from him. We both attended a book award event, sponsored by the Cold Mountain Institute. *Erebus,* Bob's first book, had been nominated for the Governor General's Award for fiction. I grabbed a beer and made my way over to Bob, and he greeted me as a fellow friend.

I started our conversation with "Congratulations again, Bob, on your nomination."

He thanked me, and then our conversation evolved into one of those serious moments, when I asked Bob, "What is the secret of communication?"

He told me a strange story. "You remember the story of the Martian who lands on a farm?"

"Oh yes," I said, "I remember the story."

Bob continued. "The Martian is able to be whatever the person who sees him wants him to be. At the farm, the mother and father saw their lost son who had been killed in the war. They were overjoyed to see their son had finally come home."

Bob was saying that we all have a brain with a conditioned lens. We all want to hear what our heart and emotions desire. The role of the media was to expose the Martian among us.

Bob was rising in respect and popularity. He was blowing readers' minds. In my circle, he was the talk of the town. I started to notice young people buying the newspaper and going right to his column. They had found an advocate in the *Vancouver Sun* newspaper, and the *Sun's* circulation was increasing because of it.

Early in 1970, I gave Bob the news that I was now an assistant reporter. I told him how I felt like I was dying in the job and needed to do something more exciting, so I'd joined with several friends and formed a group called Rent a Demo. We would protest almost anything for two gallons of red wine. He laughed. "Sounds like fun." He then said, "You know that life is about having fun, the more fun you have in life, the more life you are living."

Wow, light bulbs went off in my head! I lived by mottos.

I set a date for my notice of departure as an assistant reporter. At the same time, I told Bob that I was so aware of how to manipulate the news that I could be on the front page of the *Vancouver Sun* or *Province* newspaper four times in one month – and I accomplished just that.

Actions included: signing a brief at Vancouver City Hall; protesting a six-lane waterfront highway; pushing a proposal for Jericho Park; and participating in a riot at UBC led by Yippies Jerry Rubin and Abbie Hoffman. All one needed to do was to be where the action was and call Bob. He would be there making each protest a triumph.

In early spring 1971, I teamed up with the notorious rabble-rouser Paul Watson. Paul announced that he was going to tear down the fence surrounding the two city blocks at the entrance of Stanley Park. Paul went over to the fence with a crowbar and removed one cedar plank from the fence. He was immediately arrested for mischief by the Vancouver Police. After the police carted Paul away, I moved in with my hidden Rent a Demo crowd. We snuck through the opening Paul had made and started planting flowers and trees inside the fenced area. We issued a press release: *A new park has been created at the entrance to Stanley Park. It's called "All Seasons Park."*

Bob, with his reports in the *Vancouver Sun* on our positive actions and behaviour, became the main media champion for this mass peaceful takeover of the park entrance. Within two weeks, over 200 Yippies were in control of the construction site. As stated in his column, we were surrounded by "glass castles," with the people on our side. This was a stand for nature. Enough towers and more flowers.

On the weekends, the young crowd grew into the thousands. A large stage was constructed, and rock music bounced off the surrounding glass castles. Through positive protest by the people, the entrance to Stanley Park was saved and made into a part of Stanley Park.

Bob Hunter, Paul Watson and I knew each other through a mutual friend called Irving Stowe. We were invited to meetings in the basement of the United Church at Oak and 41st streets. The purpose was to stop the US nuclear testing on the island of Amchitka in Alaska. We walked into a group of about a dozen people. After some brainstorming, the group came up with the name "Don't Make a Wave Committee." This lightly attended meeting changed our lives forever.

Little did we know it, but a destiny was now beginning to rise. Bob Hunter the Columnist, Paul Watson the Radical, and yours truly, Rod Marining, the Non-Leader of the Northern Yippie Lunatic Fringe, would go on to meddle in the affairs of the establishment and push political non-violent action forward for various causes whose focus was protecting the environment. We become Warriors of the Rainbow for Mother Earth. This early bond would last a lifetime.

THE SEA CHANGE

by Bobbi Hunter

THE VOYAGE TO AMCHITKA was life changing for Bob. He set out on a mission, expecting an ending; he had no idea that the mission would last his lifetime.

Late in the 1960s, the US was preparing to perform an underground nuclear weapons test on the island of Amchitka in Alaska. This raised serious concerns that the test might trigger earthquakes, causing a tsunami. In 1969, Bob was the keynote speaker at a demonstration at a major US–Canada border crossing in British Columbia. Seven thousand people blocked the border, carrying signs reading *Don't Make A Wave* and *It's Your Fault If Our Fault Goes*. But the protests did not stop the US from detonating the bomb. No tsunami or earthquake resulted from that early test, and, undeterred by the concerns of the people, the US announced that, in 1971, it would detonate a bomb five times more powerful than the first one beneath the island of Amchitka.

In response to the announcement of the new testing, the newly formed Don't Make a Wave Committee hired the *Phyllis Cormack*, with its skipper, my step-grandfather, John C. Cormack, to take them to the testing zone off Amchitka, where protestors would put their bodies in harm's way. In the fall of 1971, the ship sailed toward Amchitka. On board was Bob Hunter.

On that initial voyage, Bob's life changed forever. At the beginning of the expedition, he was in fearful awe of the destructive power of the bomb. Along the way, during the voyage, he came to feel an immense depth of anxiety and veneration for the power of the ocean.

I had always believed the raw fear he felt of the ocean and for the bomb is what led to the huge shift in Bob's life trajectory, but as I reviewed his writing, I began to understand that Bob found his grounding. That his awakening was the most powerful positive event in his life. During the voyage, Bob discovered his foundational mother and father.

During a meditative episode on the voyage, Bob experienced a primal and visceral connection to the planet and ultimately to the universe:

> I am kneeling on the slope by the stream, arms thrown toward the sky, and offering a prayer to Mother Earth. Down beneath my wet knees the grass and the moss and the scrub willows sink toward a mushy embrace with the rocks of the island to the seabeds and the seabeds spreading like a palpitating tissue around the whole globe and there is no point where anything on Earth is finally divided or sundered from anything else..."I am the Earth!!!"

Bob found his grounding as he faced down a man-made demon – the bomb. He also connected strongly to one mighty man, Skipper John C. Cormack. In John, Bob found his father figure, his role model for strength. A man who would never give up. A loyal man of immense will power and resolve.

Bob had found his archetypal father figure and his true and genuine Mother, who would protect him and whom he needed to protect. He took this message of Planet Love, of love for Mother Gaia, with him for the rest of his life's journey, always trying his best to make people understand that we are not *on the earth, but of the earth.*

Unfortunately, well into the voyage, the Amchitka activists were forced to turn back by orders of the US Navy, and because of increasingly bad weather. When the boat retreated, Bob was devastated, defeated by weather, internal politics and political interference. On October 13, 1971, his 30th birthday, Bob's life turned around at the same time the boat changed course and headed home.

A second, larger ship had been dispatched by Greenpeace, and they met on the ocean, one coming, one going. Neither boat got to the test site in time to stop the bomb's detonation. It took 17 days for the *Phyllis Cormack* to arrive back in Vancouver to cheering crowds and horns honking in celebration.

What Bob had initially perceived as a failure turned out to be quite the opposite, as the media blast was so much larger than the bomb blast. He went from his initial thoughts of fear and negativity to a final new strong sense of grounding and to an awakening of the power that he held as an individual. Bob and fellow journalists Ben Metcalfe and Bob Cummings created an enormous blast of their own. They had generated a storm of media that carried to the halls of power, not just locally but globally, and had a direct effect on the ultimate outcome of the campaign. As a result, all future Amchitka underground testing was stopped.

He had set out as an angry soul, expecting disaster, and he came home slowly becoming aware that, in life, if you expect the best outcome, then that is what will be. He realized the value of bringing the world into the situation, putting them in shock so they could no longer ignore it, so that they too would add their voices to the outrage. That is the message of Amchitka.

On Bob's return from Amchitka, he had to work behind the scenes with Greenpeace for the next few years because his job as a reporter meant he had to appear neutral. Greenpeace's main focus at the time was on the French underground nuclear testing at Mururoa Atoll in the South Pacific. Ben Metcalfe was now the leader, and together with a handful of people they raised the funds and hired a ship with a captain willing to sail into harm's way at Mururoa Atoll. That captain was David McTaggart. Ben Metcalfe joined McTaggart on his ship the *Vega* for the campaign, but Ben soon left in disgust. These two alpha males were in constant dispute, and decisions were being undermined. Later, the apex of the campaign occurred when French commandos boarded McTaggart's ship and clubbed him. This beating was captured on film by David's girlfriend, Ann-Marie Horne, who was able to escape with the brutal image. She passed the film on to Bob. While hospitalized, David fought with Bob over control of the photos that showed this brutal encounter. David wanted the release of the photos to wait for his release from the hospital. Bob prevailed, and the news of the campaign went global instantly, thus making the campaign an international success. Bob understood that old news is never news. David threatened to sue Bob.

These years were high profile, dramatic and successful, but internally the group was in disarray. Infighting and financial decline were tearing Greenpeace apart. The fledgling organization was in complete shambles, when a new path appeared to Bob. The whales called him! It was time for Bob to step out of the shadows, it was time for Greenpeace to be more than a one-issue group, it was time to care for more than just the welfare of mankind.

Mother Earth called, and his surrogate father, John C. Cormack, was by his side to sail with him in this new direction. And thus the first Greenpeace Save the Whales expedition was born.

Many years later, when we were living in Toronto, we got a call from one of Bob's Amchitka voyage shipmates, Dr. Lyle Thurston. Lyle told Bob that John Cormack was dying of cancer and had only hours to live. Travel arrangements were difficult, and all we could afford was one ticket for Bob to get there in two days. I wanted to go as well. I loved my step-grandfather too. But we both knew it was a call Bob needed to answer. We asked Lyle to tell John that Bob was coming, and to ask John to hold on. Lyle thought Bob would never make it on time, but two days later, an emaciated John was still waiting when Bob walked in to embrace him. A man like no other, who had shown Bob the power and strength of positive actions.

The last moments these two bonded souls spent together are best expressed by Bob in his novel *Long Way to the Horizon*. In that novel, the fictional daughter emotionally bonds with her father at the time of his death, a scene that was inspired by the last moments together between Bob and his guide, the rudder of his destiny, his surrogate father, John C. Cormack. In the passage from the novel reproduced below, the names of John and Bob have replaced those of the fictional characters.

I pressed against John, clutching his hand, and forcing myself to breathe exactly the way John was breathing, matching his jagged, convulsive rhythm. John writhed for several minutes, but sure enough, the rasping broke a bit, and relaxed slightly. That was better. I adjusted my own breathing to match this new pace. And then, after several minutes had passed, and John grew calmer, I deliberately slowed his breathing down. Slowly. Slowly. In. Out. Slower. Good. It felt right. I was so awash in emotions there really wasn't any part of me staying objective or thinking things through. What I was doing felt like an instinct, like the contractions Bobbi felt when giving birth to our children, only this was the opposite. I pushed inward against John's body, melding with his heartbeat, the rising and falling of John's lungs, until it seemed we were almost one body. Breathe. In. Out. Slower. Slower. He shuddered once and started to cough, but I soothed him, and the fit past. Soon he was back to breathing alongside me, not resisting, as though he was driven by some instinct too. Perfectly matched, as though we were gliding through water, just as we had experienced the Orca whale family swim in unison years ago in Hecate Strait, so, so many years before. Now, slow it down again. Down further. A long, long slow breath in. A long, slow breath out. No hurry to return. A rocking motion almost. A deeper breath, the deepest yet. An exhaling that went out and out like a peaceful tide, came back, out, back, the interlude between each intake getting longer, and as this happened, his grip loosened, a notch at a time, until John's hand simply lay in mine. I by now was letting my breath go out longer than I'd had ever done. It felt like being on a pendulum. I was swinging back and forth, and he was simply riding it out, out, out into nothingness, and then ever so slowly, the breath creeping back into his lungs as they filled and at the same moment, taking forever to fill up, and then beginning the journey through the darkness back through and out, out, out – out. John's eyes closed. Softer breathing. Gentler. So gentle.

Until, like a leaf finally finding its way to the ground, John C. Cormack died in my arms, in the arms of the man he had treated like the son he never had.

TWO
ERUPTING

A LOVE STORY

by Bobbi Hunter

I FIRST MET BOB when I was married to Dr. Myron MacDonald. We were introduced by a mutual friend, Dr. Lyle Thurston. Bob and Lyle had been crew mates on the first anti-nuclear campaign to Amchitka in 1971. It was soon after they returned from that pivotal campaign that we met.

Lyle and I accompanied Bob to a large "Be-In" gathering at a small town outside of Vancouver. Bob was a keynote speaker, promoting his newly formed Whole Earth Church, a funding vehicle for Greenpeace. Bob, a bearded, Messiah-like figure, enthralled the audience with his talk of universal love for the planet. He ordained the audience, including a monkey, as newly minted ministers. Once ordained, I glided through the crowd handing out flowers, ordaining converts, proclaiming, "A flower is your brother." Heady stuff, that.

Early in 1974, Myron and I invited Bob and his then-wife Zoe to our penthouse apartment for cocktails. Both our marriages were faltering, although it was not yet public knowledge. When I opened the door to them, I gave the customary greeting of a peck on the cheek, and I smiled broadly at Bob. There seemed to be a jolt, a spark as he and I looked at each other intently. That was the "aha" moment – that "love at first sight" feeling.

Bob held the floor that evening with rapid-fire stories and engaging jokes. Zoe sat glaring at Bob while Myron tried hard to keep up. I was laughing uproariously, finding myself delighted in a way I had not been in years. It was a cathartic release. Later, after Zoe left by taxi, and Myron left for bed, Bob and I went late into the night drinking, laughing and getting to know each other as unexpected equals.

A few months later, Myron and I ended our short-lived marriage. We had married on impulse with one promise between us: if the marriage failed, we would split and stay friends. We have kept that promise.

With a heavy heart at the failure of my marriage, I packed my bags and went to stay in my friends Davey and Carolyn Gibbons's spare room. Davey was a good friend and a great lawyer who later volunteered his services to Greenpeace. Three friendship-filled weeks later, just as I was ready to rejoin the world, the phone rang. It was Bob. He asked me out on a date.

"I don't date married men."

He quickly answered, "Well, consider me 'Not Married.'"

Just as quickly, I asked, "What time?"

A few hours later, his old, grey, well-worn Volks van arrived. We were a perfect match. I was dressed in my hippie finery of jeans, tie-dyed T-shirt, sandals. He wore his second-hand-store pants, a T-shirt and beads. He took my hand, smiled and, with a familiar ease, led me to his van. We headed off to Spanish Banks just as the sun was setting. As the magic of the Georgia Strait sunset unfolded before us, we shared our histories, careers and personal situations. The hours passed by in a flash. Our conversation was deep but natural, and we meshed immediately. When the sky darkened, and the lights came out on the opposite expanse of Burrard Inlet, revealing the North Shore skyline in a twinkling magic show of hearth and home, we felt a strange compulsion to be enfolded in that scintillating display. It was as if we were tethered and drawn in by the lights. Setting off in the van, and following our instincts, we found ourselves on the opposite side of the waters and high on the hill where the light display originated. We were juxtaposed in time and place, and our dialogue naturally altered. We went from speaking of history to speaking of the present and the future. It was a new and exciting level of connectedness emerging between our souls. There was an instantly wonderful feeling of contentment and belonging.

After some passionate front seat caresses and kisses, we travelled down the mountain. As we were about to head over Lions Gate Bridge, we noticed a lodge near the Capilano River. We veered off and giddily booked a room. That night, in that simple room, we were joined body and soul.

From that first date forward, we became a couple. We joined forces with our friends who were pushing Greenpeace to the front of environmental consciousness. We opened the first and then the second (much larger) Greenpeace offices. Our small band of friends, with Bob as the leader, orchestrated international incidents with our Save the Whale and Save the Seal campaigns. We felt the power of our connectedness, grounded and whole.

Two intense years later, Bob had taught me much about how to keep our relationship strong. We lived by two rules that were cast in stone: first, never go to bed angry; and second, the person with the most passion in an argument is the winner. Live with it! We had withstood a number of challenges externally, internally and organizationally, and now we were about to enter the challenge of matrimony.

The word *love* was spoken continuously, and when he tried to explain his deep feelings for me, he would simply say, "I am you."

The morning we were to be married, we awoke bare, warm and full of expectations. Lying on our bunk in our old diesel engine police boat, aptly named the *Astral*, we turned face to face, looking deeply into the wonder of each other.

It was a typical cloudy, heavy, rainy Vancouver day. Not what I had imagined on our wedding day. I looked at Bob with sadness. He jumped up and held me in his arms, saying knowingly, "Don't worry, it's the perfect day, it's our day and the sun will shine, O ye of little faith." By the time we were ready to leave the boat, the universe was unfolding as Bob had predicted; the rain had stopped.

We were meeting our friends and family at the Buddhist temple at 4th and Macdonald, located above a hippie art shoppe. We would be married in front of a Tibetan Buddhist monk. Our marriage had been personally sanctioned by the Gyalwa Karmapa the 16th, who had requested a meeting with Bob, honouring him as a saviour of the non-humans of our planet. The statue that we knelt before looked like a purple Dr. Spock with pointed ears. The saffron-robed monk who performed the ceremony spoke no English. We were joined in matrimony in his native Tibetan tongue. The fact that we had no idea what we had promised one another was a source of laughter for years. When the monk seemed to have finished his ceremony, we held hands and stared deeply into each other's eyes once again on this day. We said a wordless "I do," feeling a depth and strength in our silent but heartfelt vows. We would be there for each other always. We knew the best and the worst about each other. We understood and respected our complexities. We were the best of friends. The one thing we did say out loud was, "It will never be dull."

We drove to our reception in the town of Ioco, where I had grown up. The sun was in full shine, just as Bob had prophesized. It was a true hippie wedding where people drank, smoked pot, laughed, danced, played guitar and made fools of themselves. At the end of that momentous day, Bob and I left with a "Just Married" sign and tin cans rattling behind our car. We were off to our first love nest, that lodge near the Capilano River under the twinkling lights of North Vancouver.

Bob was a man of high intelligence mixed with captivating relatability. People just loved him, period. And I am forever grateful that I was so truly blessed to be his soul mate. Bob embodied deep passion, combined with an infectious wit. Through his joy, his actions and his unending storytelling, he taught me some of the simplest but most profound lessons in life. I have found that, just as you cannot unlearn lessons learned, you cannot lose genuine love. He was and always is with me, and my being is strengthened by being him.

I am you, Bob.

THE GREAT WHALE CONSPIRACY

by Paul Spong

WHEN BOB AND I FIRST STARTED TALKING about whales, we were on his boat the *Zoe Too*, drifting around English Bay, chatting and drinking beer on a sunny spring afternoon in 1973. Farley Mowat had given me the "save the whales" bug the previous year when he was in Vancouver promoting *A Whale for the Killing*. Farley told me about the desperate situation facing whales, and I told him about my experiences with whales. We formed a natural alliance, campaigning as Project Jonah, gathering signatures on a petition, and by December 1972 had succeeded in convincing Canada's federal government to end Canadian whaling. Since we'd succeeded so easily with Canada, the idea to take on the world came naturally.

My purpose in talking to Bob was to enlist him and Greenpeace into the whales' cause. He got it immediately, in much the same way he got the climate issue in Kyoto years later. Our conversation shifted to practicalities. How to confront the whalers? Greenpeace was perfect: experienced in non-violent direct action, but laser focused on the nuclear weapons issue – and it was broke. Stepping around hard-core resistance to a new idea, Bob and a few others formed the Stop Ahab Committee. It was an arm of, but not controlled by, Greenpeace. We met around the pool table at the back of the Cecil Hotel pub, drank 25-cent beers, and plotted. Thus, what Bob came to call The Great Whale Conspiracy was born.

The list of essential elements was short: money, boat, crew, where to find whalers. We decided to have a go at convincing Japan to stop whaling first. It was a long shot, but we felt it important to make the gesture; if it succeeded, the whales would win big time. We decided to fill the Queen Elizabeth Theatre in Vancouver to plead the whales' cause, and in turn make sorely needed money. Greenpeace objected to the risk, so I personally promised to cover any loss. The Greenpeace Christmas Whale Show on December 28, 1973, proved to be a resounding success. We began to relax as the theatre filled, then totally relaxed when Gordon Lightfoot called to say he was sending us $5,000. Bob's easy manner was instantly convincing and perfectly complemented the wonders and horrors of the slideshow and film. The next day, when the headline in the *Vancouver Sun* proclaimed, "Had Whale of a Time, Hope Whales Will Too," we knew we were off and running.

By late 1974, our plan was making serious media headway. *TIME* magazine sent a reporter out to Vancouver, and the Vancouver Public Aquarium agreed to let us hold a press conference announcing our anti-whaling campaign, so long as we did not get into the captivity issue. It meant that Bob and I would be able to see Skana, the orca who had set me on my journey. For me it was like no time had passed; for Bob it was a life-changing experience. He knelt on a little training platform to greet Skana, tentatively at first and then enthusiastically, rubbing his hands and then his head over Skana's head. Suddenly, Skana opened her mouth and Bob's head was half inside. Entranced by what was happening, Bob did not react. Skana slipped back below the water, returning moments later with her jaws wide open and seized Bob's head in her mouth. He could do nothing; she was in total control. Skana could have snapped Bob's head off like a twig but did not. After few seconds, Skana released him. Bob was unharmed. In the brief moments inside Skana's mouth, Bob's life flashed before him; he was left reeling, stunned by what he had experienced, and what he had learned about whales and about himself. Later, he wandered off and sat under a tree blubbering helplessly.

With the funds from the Christmas Whale Show, my family and I set out to make an impact in Japan. Unsurprisingly, our attempt to persuade

Japan to change course failed. We did, however, convince many Japanese people about the whaling issue during 19 presentations of the Whale Show at venues ranging from theatres in shopping malls to schools. We made many friends in Japan. A CBC film crew followed us, sending stories back to Canada that kept our efforts alive locally. When we returned to Vancouver, Greenpeace was abuzz with energy. Bob had convinced John Cormack to take the *Phyllis Cormack* out again; the campaign was happening.

The biggest gap remained finding the whalers. Vaguely knowing where we were headed, we put together a cross-country tour of Canada with the Greenpeace Whale Show in early 1975. It was still winter when my wife Linda, our 7-year-old son Yasha and I drove out of Vancouver laden with slide projectors, tapes and brochures. It was 40 below in Saskatoon. In Ottawa, Iceland's embassy gave us introductions to Icelandic scientists and the Bishop of Iceland. In Iceland we got an introduction to a leading Norwegian whale scientist. After a lecture at his university, he introduced us to Einar Vangstein, the head of the Bureau of International Whaling Statistics in Sandefjord. There, Linda and Yasha charmed Mr. Vangstein and his secretary while I had free rein to comb through stacks of records that spanned decades. We struck gold. Bob was ecstatic at the thought that he knew where to head with the *Phyllis Cormack*, and when. Wisely, he kept the information to himself.

As things turned out, the outcome of our plotting could not have been better. Bob and crew met Russian whalers off the coast of Mendocino, California; Fred Easton's camera came to life just in time to film a harpoon flying over Bob's head; Walter Cronkite told the world about it on his nightly broadcast; and the news arrived in London just in time to shake up the last day of the 1975 meeting of the International Whaling Commission. Nine more years would pass before the IWC imposed the moratorium on commercial whaling that we were seeking.

Years later, after Bob returned from Kyoto, prescient as ever, he was inspired to take on the climate crisis. He convinced me as quickly as I had convinced him about the whales.

MYTHOLOGIST AND IMAGE WARRIOR

by Rex Weyler

BY APRIL 27, 1975, the first Greenpeace whale campaign had been a year and a half in the making: raising money, securing inflatable Zodiacs for harassing whaling ships, organizing a crew and helping Captain John Cormack prepare his boat, the *Phyllis Cormack*, for the voyage.

Now, at last, we stood on the deck of the boat, waving to the crowd on Jericho Beach on Vancouver's west side. Captain John Cormack stood on the flying bridge of the *Phyllis Cormack* and surveyed his unconventional deckhands with a fatherly tolerance.

Hunter gripped the gunwale with one hand and clutched his notebook to his chest with the other. His reedy, 34-year-old frame stretched as he held his notebook aloft in a clenched-fist salute to the crowd on the pier. This voyage represented the manifestation of Hunter's vision, forged five years earlier when he wrote his first non-fiction book, *The Enemies of Anarchy*, about a "consciousness revolution" that would include the rise of ecology activism.

Sailing into nuclear test zones had been a statement for world peace, but we had contemplated a campaign that would put the "green" in Greenpeace and awaken a global ecology movement.

Our Japanese translator, Taeko Miwa, stood beside Hunter. Over Taeko's head rose the triangular white mainsail with an orca painted at the peak, the ecology and peace symbols, and the Kwakwaka'wakw emblem of an orca below, a symbol given to Greenpeace by the Kwakwaka'wakw community in Alert Bay.

The *Vega*, which had sailed into the French nuclear test sites, bobbed in the waves upwind of us. At the bow of the *Phyllis Cormack*, massive Czechoslovakian George Korotva stood at the anchor winch. Hamish Bruce braced himself at the stern, feet apart, hands clasped behind his back. Zodiac technician Carlie Trueman busied herself with stowing equipment. Paul Watson coiled rope and barked orders. "Whose gear is this?" He smiled as if it were a theatrical production and he'd landed the role of first mate. The Warriors of the Rainbow were at last putting to sea, not simply on behalf of human concerns, but for all sentient beings.

Hunter appeared to glow in quiet satisfaction. As he raised his fist, the crowd roared on the pier, and he twisted to find the skipper on the bridge. "Okay, John."

"Hoist anchor," Cormack said, and Korotva started the winch. Cormack sounded the horn, and the crowd on the beach cheered again. The *Vega*, with peace and ecology symbols on the mainsail, flew past us through the whitecaps, west out of English Bay. The *Phyllis Cormack* followed, surrounded by a flotilla of pleasure boats. After months of work, thousands of phone calls, many a pint around the pub tables, and late-night meetings, we were moving at last.

The *Vega* tacked northward and would sail the inside channel, 300 nautical miles around Cape Scott to Winter Harbour. The *Phyllis Cormack* would take the shorter route to Winter Harbour, along the Pacific coastline of Vancouver Island.

We were three hours across the Georgia Strait in a following sea, the winds gusting to 30 knots and kicking up whitecaps atop the swells. Half the crew was feeling seasick. Hunter climbed the ladder to where Captain Cormack stood in the wheelhouse at attention. The skipper nodded silently. Hunter nodded and gazed out to sea. Hunter's own father had left the family when Hunter was 6. He appeared to look up to the captain as a surrogate, a father figure. Likewise, Cormack clearly cared about Hunter and treated him with the tough love of a father.

As evening fell, Hunter performed a casual head count. To his horror, he realized we had left the film crew behind. They had been filming the departure from the pier at Jericho and missed the shuttle. "Great," said Hunter, "we just spent a year plotting the greatest ecological media event in the history of the planet, and we leave the film crew on the dock." On the marine radio he made arrangements for them to meet us in Tofino, on the west coast of Vancouver Island.

During the evening, tucked into a cove near Salt Spring Island, we sat around the galley table, and musician Mel Gregory played guitar. The Great Whale Conspiracy was at sea. Sort of at sea. Hunter rolled out a large chart of the Pacific on the galley table. The scale of what we contemplated sank in. We had crossed the Georgia Strait, a thin white line on the large chart. The vast Pacific lay before us. The task of finding the whalers felt daunting, but Hunter appeared calm. Whale scientist Paul Spong, who had first conceived of this campaign, had already found his way into the Whaling Commission files in Norway and discovered the routes of the whalers in previous years. Bob had shared this news with the skipper, with me, and others on the media team, but to keep the story alive in the newspapers that we were "hunting" for the whalers, Hunter had not told the rest of the crew.

We departed Salt Spring Island at first light and made our way south through Juan de Fuca Strait to the raging Pacific Ocean. Hunter gathered the crew on the quarterdeck, behind the wheelhouse. Will Jackson dragged himself up the ladder with determination in his eyes. Carlie was bright-eyed and eager. Al Hewitt slouched against the railing. Hunter wore a gaily dyed Peruvian wool cap with flaps turned up, forming pastel rainbows above his ears. He set out a bottle of rum and nailed a whalebone to the mast.

Hunter was a master at creating mythology to enliven the work. Here, he recreated Captain Ahab's performance on the quarterdeck of the *Pequod* before Ishmael, Starbuck and the other sailors. Ahab had served rum and nailed a gold Spanish doubloon to the mast. Reversing Ahab's vow – *"Whosoever of ye raises me a white-headed whale with a wrinkled brow and a crooked jaw, he shall have this gold ounce"* – Hunter declared that whoever saw the whalers first would have the whalebone as a prize. Whereas the sailors of the *Pequod* drank to the death of Moby Dick from the sockets of their harpoons, we sipped rum from cups as Hunter thrust his sinewy fist to the sky and shouted, "Let them live!"

"Let them live," we chanted back.

"Greenhawks," Hunter shouted, echoing an earlier version of "Greenpeace," and he added the classic comic book salvo, "Hawkaaaa!"

"For the protection of all sentient beings," David "Walrus" Garrick whispered.

Al Hewitt leaned against the wheelhouse wall, drinking from a cup but not joining the chant. He looked as if he might be contemplating Starbuck's *"God keep me! – keep us all!"*

After the ceremony, Hunter set out his Underwood typewriter, the one his mother had given him on his 15th birthday, and he pecked away in his speedy two-finger style.

We arrived at the fishing town of Tofino in Clayoquot Sound at five in the evening. The camera crew stood on the dock, filming our approach. Nuu-cha-nulth children climbed onto the boat. Mel told them his name was "Captain Melo," gave tours and played his new song, "The Whale Anthem," for the children.

Hunter grabbed the *Vancouver Sun* newspaper from the dockside marine shop. The April 28 edition front page showed us departing English Bay, but the five-column headline across the top was from another story: "Cong pierce Saigon defense." It turned out that we had launched our crusade on the last day of the bloody Vietnam War. Hunter, always mindful of our media presence, shook his head. "Tough competition," he said.

For Hunter, we were engaged in a global media battle, "a war of images." His stated intention was to flip the old "Moby Dick" image of the whale on its head. Instead of brave men in tiny boats facing the fierce Leviathan, modern whaling was the opposite. Giant factory ships and steel-hulled killer ships, equipped with 500-pound exploding harpoons and sophisticated sonar, hunted the vulnerable whales nearly to extinction.

Hunter phoned in the first news story from the voyage: "Project Ahab is at sea. We are heading for Winter Harbour. From there we will begin our search for the whalers."

At first light on the morning of May 1, we headed north for Winter Harbour. By the time we reached Brooks Peninsula above the 50th parallel, the wind had turned directly into us from the north, and the *Phyllis Cormack* beat against the waves.

We entered Quatsino Sound, and Hunter pointed out the gap at Kains Island. He had seen two grey whales there a year earlier. He said, "We'll start right there."

We got a phone call from Rod Marining that a journalist from *The New York Times*, Charles Flowers, was on his way by floatplane. We drank wine that night and toasted our good fortune. When the journalist arrived, he told us that stories of our planned confrontation with the whalers had reached Japanese newspapers, and the whaling company officials had attacked Greenpeace for "regrettable" and "foolish" actions. This played right into our efforts to wage a media war.

Hunter responded with information about the decline of whale populations. The Japanese whaling companies retaliated with, "They're fanatics, their movement is like a religion. It's not normal."

We cheered at hearing this. "*Like* a religion?" scoffed Hunter. "Wait 'til they find out we *are* a religion."

The kafuffle escalated when Canadian Minister of Fisheries Roméo LeBlanc came out in support of the whalers. The United Fishermen & Allied Workers' Union challenged the minister and pledged support for Greenpeace. "We deplore Canada's failure to speak out against whaling," barked union leader Jack Nichol. "The UFAW lends its full support to the actions by the Greenpeace Foundation to interfere with the Pacific whaling expeditions of both Japan and the Soviet Union. The wasteful slaughter of these magnificent animals must stop and the efforts of the Greenpeace crews to harass whale killers deserve nothing but praise and solid support from everyone."

"This is historical," Hunter declared to journalist Flowers. When the unions came out against nuclear bombs, he recalled, it signalled an important shift of public awareness. "But this? It's epic. A workers' union speaking out for whales over an issue that will impact the livelihoods of workers on whaling boats. The campaign is already working." To Flowers, Hunter proclaimed, "We are completely dismayed by the decision of the Canadian government to hand the surviving whales over on a platter to a handful of nations now bent on destroying them."

Flowers diligently scribbled notes in his notebook. "Roughly speaking," said Hunter, "it looks like China, the US, the Fishermen's Union, and Greenpeace are aligned against Russia, Japan, the whalers, and the

Canadian government. I'd call that a new political gestalt." Many months had passed since I had seen Bob Hunter look so calm and confident.

Flowers gleefully scribbled this down. "The irony," he said, "is that American whalers were once as ruthless and guilty as anyone for decimating the whales. Now they are the champions of the whales. And you know why, don't you?"

We sat in silence.

"The 200-mile limit," said Flowers. "The Law of the Sea Conference is going on in Geneva right now, as we speak. The US," Flowers said, "wants to increase their territorial fishing limit from 12 miles to 200 miles. The small countries like Sri Lanka and so forth don't want the superpowers to unilaterally take over large coastal regions, but the US wants control of the continental shelf. And it's not just about fish or whales." He paused for dramatic effect.

We waited.

"It's about oil. They want the mineral rights."

"Sounds about right," said Hunter. "The Americans are supporting the whales to get the deep-sea oil rights."

"Yeah," said Flowers, "and you guys are right in the middle of it. Welcome to global politics."

I CHING ON THE SHIP OF FOOLS

by Carlie Trueman

IT WAS JUNE 1974. The crew of the *Phyllis Cormack*, also known as the *Greenpeace V*, had been sailing up and down the coast of British Columbia for about three months, talking to people, filing media stories and generally raising awareness about the plight of the world's great whales. Now, thanks to the undercover work of Paul Spong, who had infiltrated the International Whaling Commission, we finally knew where to find our ultimate target – the Russian whaling fleet. We set a course straight for the Mendocino Ridge, 250 miles off the coast of California.

The idea was to photograph the Greenpeace crew in inflatable Zodiac boats as they positioned themselves between the Russian whalers and the pods of sperm whales they were hunting. We hoped that such photographs would bring the world's attention to an ecological slaughter sanctioned by the International Whaling Commission.

The Russians were in the *Dalniy Vostok*, a 600-foot steel factory ship, and they had 17 kill boats armed with explosive harpoons. Our ship was a 60-foot wooden fishing boat that had seen better days.

The Mendocino Ridge covers a lot of ocean. It's huge. It was frustrating, because we could hear the Russians on our old radio, but we couldn't find them, and we were running out of time. The Russians only hunted the Ridge for about five days every year, and if we didn't find them immediately, we would miss them. We ran search patterns for two days, and we debated what else we might do.

And then John Cormack, our skipper, told Bob Hunter, our expedition leader and the head of Greenpeace, that he had dipped the fuel tanks and estimated that we had two days of fuel left. From where we were, we could probably make it to San Francisco, but only just.

The question Bob had to answer was this: Do we stay and keep looking for Russian whalers, which we might or might not find, and end up adrift at sea, or do we run for San Francisco, now, empty-handed?

It was one hell of a choice.

I was sitting at the galley table when Bob Hunter and Pat Moore sat down with a book and three coins. Bob started shaking the coins in his hand and throwing them down on the table, as one might throw dice. Each time he did so, he counted the heads and tails, came up with a number and recorded it on a piece of paper, with a series of solid and broken lines.

"What are you doing?" I asked.

"Throwing the I Ching."

"What's the I Ching?"

"It is a book of divination."

"What?" I asked, startled. "A book that tells the future? What do you want to know?"

"If we should stay and keep looking for the Russians."

I was certain that I was on board a ship of fools, and I made my feelings known.

"This is bullshit!" I said.

Bob ignored me and, checking the six lines (called a hexagram) on the paper in front of him, looked up what he had thrown. It contained the phrase "It furthers one to cross the great waters." Of the 64 possible hexagrams, only four contain this particular phrase, and it means supreme good fortune. Bob grinned and handed the coins to Pat.

When Pat Moore threw the coins, he got a second one of the four hexagrams that contained the phrase "It furthers one to cross the great waters." The men were becoming excited.

Rex Wyler then threw the coins and got a third hexagram with the same phrase. They were now ecstatic, and I was even more vocal in my derision.

And so, the three of them turned to me, and laughingly told me how to consult this ancient Book of Changes. I listened carefully and then, to humour them, I did. And I got the fourth hexagram. They were jubilant and the issue was decided: we were staying.

But I kept protesting. I said, "Look, you can throw these coins again and again and the book will tell you anything you want!"

Rex replied, "No. Asking questions of the I Ching is like asking questions of a venerable elder. You don't ask a question, get an answer, and then ask the same question again. It is not a polite thing to do."

"Right," I said, as I threw the coins again.

Out of the 64 hexagrams, there is only one hexagram that tells you, in no uncertain terms, that you are an idiot. It is called "Youthful Folly." That's the one I got. The three men laughed with delight. It seemed as if the book wanted us to go and find the Russian whalers.

That night, there was a beautiful full moon. Mel Gregory had the wheel watch. For some reason known only to himself, he decided to disregard John Cormack's orders and ignored the compass. Instead, he followed the path the moonlight made on the water. The *Phyllis Cormack* followed the moon as it transected the sky and carved an arc across the face of the Pacific. When Cormack discovered what Mel had done, he was livid because we could not figure out where we had actually searched.

In the morning we found the Russians.

As planned, we deployed the Zodiacs. Bob Hunter and George Korotva got between a kill boat and a pod of sperm whales, the Russians fired their harpoon, and Fred Easton got it all on film. Rex Weyler says that image is what started the modern environmental movement. It was a pretty exciting time.

Forty years later, images from that voyage to save the whales stand out clearly in my mind, and one of them is the first experience I had with the I Ching. Never mind statistical probability. That series of improbable coincidences still seems somehow – well – completely improbable.

And then, of course, there were the rainbows. We who called ourselves the Warriors of the Rainbow saw rainbows where no self-respecting rainbow had any right to be. We all saw them, and we all talked about how they simply shouldn't be there, in a variety of bright, clear, blue skies.

There is an old Sioux legend that says that the world will be saved by the Warriors of the Rainbow, and that is what we hoped to do.

There was, and still is, a real magic to Greenpeace because, in Greenpeace, these kinds of things just keep happening. I worked in Greenpeace for four years, and only left when I finished law school and headed north to practise criminal law.

Without my realizing it, when I focused my mind on practising law, these kinds of strange happenings disappeared from my life. Except, they didn't. It just took me a very long time to get in touch with them again. When I started judging, they came back into my life, big time.

Not that they had much to do with the law or courts or witnesses or anything else. Odd things just started to happen, like being absolutely certain that a Greyhound bus had left the highway I was driving on and, several minutes later, driving around a corner and seeing people climbing out the windows of a Greyhound bus that had obviously just crashed into a ditch.

I saw a raven sitting on a dead tree on a gravel bar in the middle of the Stikine River, and I knew it was the harbinger of death. I was certain of it, even though I had seen countless other ravens on our trip. When we paddled our canoe around the next corner, we saw men dragging the river for someone who had drowned shortly before. They were trying to find the body before it washed too far downstream.

But the most powerful experience occurred when I was meditating on my dying friend and felt something enter my chest. I opened my eyes in surprise and watched a dirty grey ball move through my chest wall and disappear inside me. I felt it surround my heart with an amazing feeling of love.

Events like these are hard to dismiss as odd coincidences. After a while, I started to write them down. Yet again I became a student, this time of consciousness. I attended the Monroe Institute and eventually became an outreach trainer.

I wondered how often I had dismissed experiences like this as patently absurd. David Hume, the Scottish philosopher, once said that when we first encounter an idea that is foreign to us, we usually ridicule it. I tracked backwards through my life and found the memory of Bob Hunter throwing the I Ching on the *Phyllis Cormack*.

These events are based in actual, lived experiences. They are not issues of belief, and they are not issues of faith. I have stopped trying to figure out how it all works, I just know it does. To me, it is the difference between trying to run the world, as determined by the human mind, and trying to live within it, as determined by nature herself.

I have no problem if you conclude, as the I Ching did so long ago, that I am an idiot. To me, that just means you haven't had similar experiences, and, like me on board the *Phyllis Cormack*, you are choosing ridicule as your first human reaction.

It is just a different way of knowing, and I highly recommend it. Thank you, Bob.

FOG RAINBOW

by Ron Precious

AFTER THE *PHYLLIS CORMACK* DEPARTED San Francisco on July 6, 1975, following the first confrontation with the Soviet whaling fleet, Greenpeace was looking for one more encounter to hammer home the message "Stop killing the whales." Bob was prepared to sit naked on a dead whale if we could locate the fleet again.

Heading north this time, Captain Cormack and George Korotva listened intently to the single sideband radio for Russian voices. Most of the crew were scattered around the ship – a few on the bridge, others hanging out in the galley or in their bunks, when we heard, "Guys, come check this out!" It was David "Walrus" Garrick calling from the bridge.

The *Phyllis Cormack* had motored into a misty blanket of fog. The skipper slowed the engine, and the ship drifted in eerie stillness on a dead calm ocean with absolutely no wind. What made this relatively common occurrence so unusual was the rainbow that appeared to embrace our entire boat from bow to stern.

"That's just a fog rainbow," barked old Cormack. "I've seen plenty of them but never as close as this."

I was awestruck and immediately thought that Bob needed to witness this phenomenon. How would he interpret it? Was it some sort of cosmic omen or blessing? I shouted his name a few times, checked the wheelhouse, crew's quarters and "the head," but couldn't find him anywhere.

Someone suggested the engine room, where he often went for solitude to write his press releases, wearing headphones to muffle the sound from the Cummins diesel engine. I opened the hatch cover and looked in. Sure enough, there he was, pounding out another story for the insatiable media. I screamed his name over and over, but he couldn't hear me over the drone from the engine. Out of desperation, I descended into Bob's sanctuary and tapped him on the shoulder.

When he looked up from the keyboard of his Underwood typewriter, he could see from the expression on my face that something serious was happening. Now that I had his attention, I tried shouting, "Rainbow!" and pointed upwards.

Unable to decipher my meaning, Bob followed me up the ladder to the deck, where the entire crew was assembled. Everyone directed their attention to our "fearless leader," waiting to see his reaction to what appeared to be "a miracle."

Captain Cormack cut the engine, but we were still carried along by the ocean current. By this time, the rainbow had shifted, with one end on the *Cormack*'s bow and the other now 20 metres away. Standing beside Bob, I noticed his facial expression transform. His eyes welled up, and a smile formed on his lips. Without uttering a single word, he proceeded to strip naked in front of us and, in two short steps, plunged over the gunwale into the frigid waters. He swam furiously toward the end of the illusive rainbow. The entire crew was transfixed by the scene unfolding in front of us. It was a totally mystical moment for us all.

When Hunter reached the point where the rainbow appeared to enter the water, he submerged, leaving only a trail of bubbles on the surface. He was underwater for what seemed an eternity. He was a heavy smoker, though, so I knew he couldn't hold his breath for long, but Bob surprised all of us with the extent of his lung capacity.

When he finally surfaced, he looked like a drowned muskrat with his long hair and beard matted together. By the time we convinced him to climb back on board, Bob was trembling from hypothermia. He seemed to be in a state of bliss, as if he had undergone a spiritual transformation. After a long, hot shower in the engine room, Bob took some time to reflect on what had just occurred.

As the sun descended into the Pacific that magical day, Bob announced to all of us that he was calling off the search for the whalers. We would be returning to Vancouver. It has always been my belief that Bob Hunter received a message that day when he swam to the end of that fog rainbow. That message: "Mission accomplished, Uncle Bob. It's time to come home."

On May 10, 2005, a West Coast Celebration of Life was held for Robert Lorne Hunter at his favourite drinking establishment, the Bimini Pub. Located in Vancouver's trendy Kitsilano neighbourhood, it was across the street from the first Greenpeace office. Some might say that more Greenpeace business was conducted at the Bimini Pub than at its home base. So it was fitting that our final farewell to "Uncle Bob" would be held there.

With the addition of alcohol, what might have been a solemn, tearful occasion became more of an Irish wake with much laughter and a few tears shed. There was a stage and a microphone where anyone could say a few words, or just sing a song to honour Bob's life. Perhaps the most surprising of guests to attend that evening were Patrick Moore and Paul Watson. They checked their egos at the door, put aside their philosophical differences and spoke from the heart about their love and respect for Bob.

Feeling overcome with emotion from the heartfelt messages told by so many of Bob's closest friends, I shared the rainbow story because it had such a profound impact on me and my relationship with Bob Hunter, the mystic. Rest in Peace, you Warrior of the Rainbow.

Bob has left the world with his words in so many formats: his books, his erudite press releases, editorials and newspaper columns, his screenplays, his hours of interviews and speeches. But actions speak louder than words, and in that department Bob exceeded all expectations. His ability to create a symbolic gesture that could capture the moment was his genius. These "mindbombs" will live forever in the global media landscape. I feel privileged to have been under his aura during the Greenpeace years, and to have recorded some of his most iconic moments. Bob said it best in his book *Warriors of the Rainbow* (1979): "We have brought the great glass eyes of the mass communications system to bear with more intensity than ever before."

SKID ROW STARTUP

by Will Jackson

[Excerpt from Will's book *Once Upon a Greenpeace: An Eco Memoir*, quoted with permission from his son, Captain Ryan Jackson.]

GREENPEACE'S REALM had expanded; engaging America was inevitable. So, where else for a provincial gang to start but in the counterculture mecca of San Francisco? And who else to get it started but an artist who disdains fame and fortune? Who better to trust with donations?

The first momentous call, in 1975, came from Bob Hunter, inviting me to join the Greenpeace anti-whaling campaign, the second most important call came later that year, from Bobbi. It came as a surprise, and even more so why. Bob and Bobbi wanted to open a US branch of Greenpeace in San Francisco, and they needed me.

The Hunters knew I was no business head, but I came cheap. All artists are cheap – unless they get famous. But as Iron B would say, fame, like business, demands moral compromise. So, I was hooked back in, for $75 a week, to fund everything. "Make it happen. We started on a shoestring too," Bobbi said.

To give the Rent God the slip, I got a friend to let me move into an abandoned hotel where he and other artists lived rent free as building caretakers, some in lush multi-floor studios. I carved out a space, literally, down a dark, dust-thick hallway; busted out a few lead and asbestos filled walls, swept up, made a bed and desk out of old doors, and my digs were set. When Bob and Bobbi first came to inspect my digs, they were enthralled and even found a vacant room to lay down their sleeping bags for a free night's stay. They hung out with me a few times to try to help me get things off the ground. I ordered one of those fancy phones with six pushbuttons, and when the phone man plugged it in, Greenpeace was in business. Its first office: Reno Hotel, Clara Alley. The whales had landed in the heart of skid row.

WHO'S FLYING MY PLANE?

I was assigned a co-worker, an airline pilot named Al Johnson, nicknamed "Jet" by the Vancouverites. He was a pushy guy, like a jet engine; always chattering away on something urgent, hyping, rushing and fretting. He was vaguely distrusting, but his saving grace was his almost erotically desperate bleeding heart for helpless animals. His hide-away bachelor pad in Sausalito across the Bay featured black satin sheets and would become Bob and Bobbi's honeymoon destination. He offered his time and energy most eagerly to Greenpeace "because the stewardesses want to save baby seals."

The Greenpeace folks used everybody who came through their door, so he was in. We were all from some weird place or other, so why not weird Al? As Hunter put it, "The longer you go with the weirdos, odds demand that you come back around to perfectly normal. Except nothing is ever perfect. Or normal." In this case he was certainly right. Despite a jovial wit, Al's nervous urgency began to drive the Vancouver people nuts. Bobbi realized he needed a short leash, lest his steamrolling enthusiasm runs over everyone. But she also knew I needed help...and he was in the right spot at the right time. So, she made him a co-worker over whom I had no authority, gave him carte blanche to do whatever he could to develop the US base.

Al would find me amid heaps of papers and tapes, organizing shows and laying plans for a larger office somewhere. Or he'd find me just arising after a late-night jam session. These for me were as inevitable as him flying a plane. In fact, we joked about the different highs. He appreciated my angle on things, although he thought I was a borderline bum. By some standards, I was; but this was Frisco, where the artist was still respected no matter what his state of funk.

FRINGE BENEFITS

Greenpeace's sudden high-profile appearance in the Bay Area eco-community was met with harsh skepticism, jealousy, fear and resentment from the established groups. San Francisco had grown up as a maritime society, a fishing and union-based culture; by nature, it saw Vancouver as a rival West Coast city. Bob could never forget meeting Joan McIntyre, an icon in whale-saving history, because her reaction to him was one of disdain. Instead of congratulations, she said to him, "Well, I don't want to save whales that way." Bob was confused and upset until I explained the long tension between the two cities.

January 1, 1976: our chapter was three months old. The next campaigns were coming fast...and landing right in our lap. It was only six months until the next whale expedition, and only three until the first ever seal campaign. We needed support from this community. But the feedback gathered the previous summer on the image of Greenpeace in California was that it's a domineering, macho bunch, with a singular, selfish ambition. It was obvious to me, although not to Vancouver, that a more collaborative posture was necessary.

Go with what you know, they say, so I chose to work through the art community; it seemed the collaborative world of artists would be the best startup model, on a low budget.

With this approach, several benefits coalesced quickly, sometimes even despite themselves. The curtain rose on our first show at the fabled Grace Cathedral downtown, where many a counterculture and multi-ethnic movement had begun. Though funky and amateurish, the show introduced a more inclusive Greenpeace to the eco-community, while on the art side the show provided a venue for community. To connect with the eco-conscious health food market, I hustled counterculture greengrocers, organic co-ops, and local producers to set up booths and donate their goods, services or profits.

Hunter and I discussed it over the phone. "Nice politics," he said, somewhat cynically. "Theater and lettuce have their place."

"Lettuce is green," I said hopefully.

"We didn't make a profit?" he asked for the fourth time.

"No," I repeated, "but the bills are paid, and we've incurred no debt. We drew a lot of new members and created a solid coalition."

"Yeah...uh, beware of that coalition thing. It can get sticky with Vancouver when the money starts coming in."

I assured him I was making no contracts written or verbal that offered the sharing of anything. "We have good relations," I said. "But to build any kind of community structure using the volunteer counterculture model that Greenpeace still uses is a tough proposition. People are just into the money now."

With the tireless efforts of a small but undaunted cadre of volunteers and professionals our campaign met its goals. Radio interviews, personal appearances, meetings and local actions like the Canadian consulate's protest over harp seals kept the media on the story.

I surmised that a rising tide lifts all boats, and our presence boosted that tide. Sharing the power made it stronger, but Vancouver disagreed. They thought otherwise. The Vancouver harpies were demanding full control over every dollar and decision.

It took special effort on my part to get Bob to see, understand, accept and support my approach. He had to stand firm when Vancouver wanted profits that were not forthcoming from our seminal efforts. Factions developed and flanking manoeuvres began. I didn't realize until much later that, even at this early stage, my position was already foredoomed. Nothing mattered except getting Greenpeace established.

I quickly found myself in the same fight Hunter had experienced. Power corrupts. Bob was battling a lot of factions and all he wanted was for us to all work together. It would be years before a workable formula was settled upon. Close to the same time, Bob, Bobbi and I exited Greenpeace with the same disheartened sense of futility. Thus was the way of the expansion of the whale and seal saving business. Turns out hippies and business expansion are not a natural fit.

A GREENPEACE TOEHOLD

by Joyce McLean

AS THE HIPPIE ERA was dying out, the Left's traditional communication forms were evolving. But Bob Hunter, using only the written word and compelling imagery, raised awareness and got people to make the big leap – no matter the issue – without having to bring down capitalism and force a revolution! "Mindbombs" were born. The hippie days were done.

By the mid-1970s, as the images and goals of Greenpeace began to take shape in the Canadian consciousness, fundraisers and events were staged in cities and towns across Canada. In Toronto, the gospel of Greenpeace began to have a firm toehold.

In 1975, John Bennett attended a Save the Whale lecture by Bob Hunter at the Ontario Institute for Studies in Education in Toronto, a forward-thinking University of Toronto institute. "The more Bob talked, the more I realized I wanted to be in Greenpeace," John says, and so he offered up his U of T office as support. Their first event was with environmental activists Dan and Patti McDermott. A few months later, Rex Weyler showed up with a fax machine to distribute news releases for Greenpeace's campaign to save the Newfoundland baby harp seals. The Toronto "office" was born.

"Auntie Nuke Wants You" was the start of Greenpeace's anti-nuclear campaign in Ontario. John and Dan set out to prove just how terrible the security was at the Bruce nuclear power plant by canoeing directly into the plant from Lake Huron. From a local phone booth, John reported their success to a delighted Bob in Vancouver. The Bruce nuclear officials almost lost their minds.

While on vacation on Vancouver Island in 1975, I was introduced to Greenpeace by a friend who implored me to take a photo of the *Vega* in Victoria Harbour, insisting that it would hold great meaning for me in the future. He told me all about Greenpeace, and their heroic efforts against whaling and nuclear weapons testing in the South Pacific. The *Vega*, captained by David McTaggart, was the vessel that had entered and globally exposed the French government's horrific nuclear testing program near Mururoa in French Polynesia. I obligingly took the image and then did not think about it again for years.

While I was living in Vancouver, I was invited to write a Greenpeace fundraising letter. I quickly entered the Greenpeace Vancouver world, and what a time I had! As executive assistant, I helped manage communications and started a mail-order merchandising operation.

My first impression of Bob was of a tall, skinny guy whose eyes held the biggest twinkles I have ever seen – ironic, sardonic and funny. He was an icon. He held enormous sway over any room he was in. This was especially true at crazy drinking, dancing and joint-smoking parties where the giggles came easily. Bob was a splendid storyteller and was capable of holding us all spellbound while the story – sometimes highly suspect, but entertaining nonetheless – inevitably took many twists and turns. There was always some sort of campaign angle at play, and we were able to really connect on issues. There were many Greenpeace parties where the social and ideological bonds among us were cemented. Talking Heads, anyone?

By 1982, I was appointed to the board of Greenpeace Canada, and soon after became the board chair. My appointment as the first female board chair was in part to change the impression that Greenpeace was male-dominated. It was not easy trying to channel the big personalities of big guys with big egos. By then, Bob had taken a break from Greenpeace, so I did not see Bob and Bobbi very often. I remained in that role when Greenpeace moved Maury and me and our young daughter, Lilly, to Toronto. We helped reshape and expand the office on Bloor Street West, with the assistance of Dan McDermott, Karen Pierce and John Willis.

John Willis was just a kid when he signed on to Greenpeace. Bob didn't expect deference or celebrity status. He was honest, humble and constantly on the hunt for wisdom. As John says, "It was striking that Bob was a famous celebrity; he was always just Bob to us." Bob's respect for mysticism in a genuine, down-to-earth way always impressed John.

Conversation and camaraderie came easy to Bob. Karen Pierce remembers when Bob came looking for Dan just after Bob Cummings had died in 1987. Karen was the only one in the office that day. Being the egalitarian sort that he was, Bob took Karen to the Brunswick House, where they proceeded to drink a lot of beer, reminisce, laugh and cry about Bob Cummings.

Bob had a great nose for a story. He was a dream reporter for environmental organizations because he just got it. The big push to eliminate elemental chlorine from the industry-wide pulp bleaching process was embedded in the Great Lakes campaign I ran from 1985 to 1990. To show how much harm organochlorines were inflicting on the environment, we had documents, reputable science, and even video showing the open-air toxic waste stream flowing from the Kimberly-Clark pulp mill in Terrace Bay. At the Toronto press conference, over 50 news organizations attended. We were excited to see the coverage. But there was only one story with our video that surfaced – it was Bob's, and it was brilliant.

I left Greenpeace in 1990 to become senior policy advisor to the Ontario minister of the environment. Bob was a frequent visitor to our office. He honoured our embargoes, worked effectively on the sly, followed up on our leads, broke some great stories and was respected and appreciated by NDP ministers Ruth Grier and Bud Wildman. He was the first reporter to thank us for the 2003 regulation that eliminated elemental chlorine from the bleaching process at Ontario pulp mills.

By the time Bob had written the prophetic *2030: Thermageddon*, I was Toronto Hydro's green energy manager. He asked me if I would accompany him to a BOOK TV interview as a climate change expert and comment on the warnings in his book. After the interview, we went for the customary beverage at the nearby rooftop tavern. The sunset was particularly spectacular, with colours shifting from coral, pink, orange, tangerine, to red, even purple, and the ominous clouds were moving rapidly. We were consumed by talk of dark climate change scenarios, corporate corruption, political indifference and the end of the world. We complained about how humans are the authors of their own demise. Bob put his unique stamp on that night – one of the last I spent with him. Even after writing *2030* and knowing all things "Thermageddon," he turned to look skyward, characteristically seeing the humour and optimism in everything, and said, "The apocalypse is beautiful isn't it, Joyce?"

LISTEN TO THE MUSIC

by Sandra Maskell

WHEN I WAS YOUNG, my brother Tommy told me about the school walkouts all over BC, in support of the protest at the US–Canada border at Peace Arch Park. These protests were directed at stopping the US nuclear testing at Amchitka Island.

Little did I know that Bob Hunter, one the main people behind that protest, and one of the founders of Greenpeace, would later become a big part of my life. Bob and his friends had plans to take a boat to Amchitka to sit near the test site in a seagoing protest to stop the nuclear blast. They hired my grandmother Laura's ex-husband, Johnny Cormack, to take them up to the Amchitka Islands on his boat, the *Phyllis Cormack*.

Soon after that, my older sister Bobbi and Bob got together, and then the magic happened.

I remember when Bobbi and Bob picked me up to visit their friends in South Delta. These friends lived by Mud Bay, a stretch of water that was warm and shallow. We swam out there for hours. We laughed and played as if we were imagining going back to the time of the dinosaurs as we swam in the warm waters of Mud Bay. So much fun!

That's the first time I remember Bob asking me something he often asked people, young and old: "Sandy, what is the meaning of life?" Of course, I had no answer, but he asked in a way that indicated that he hoped someday I would come back with a profound answer.

Much later I worked for Greenpeace doing anything I could to help, but mainly I worked on fundraising and as a receptionist in the office. Bobbi and Bob were always at the office. Bob was the president of Greenpeace, and Bobbi was the treasurer and office manager. It was exciting to be there and see everyone working so hard. Bob was always so positive and inspiring. The positive vibe he projected spread out. People wanted to be involved – including musicians.

I used to go to the benefit concerts that raised money for the Save the Whale campaigns. Many musicians donated their time to Greenpeace, often playing at the Commodore Ballroom on Granville Street in Vancouver. Greenpeace not only had purpose, it also had fun.

As Bob returned from the first Save the Whale campaign, a concert was organized at the Old Roller Rink, a local concert venue. I had been to fundraising events before and after each of the whale campaigns and danced to music of the Cement City Cowboys, Pied Pumpkin, Bruce Miller and Greenpeace's own Iron Buffalo. Even in the campaigns there was music: Paul Horn playing his flute, and Will Jackson reaching out with his Moog synthesizer to commune with the whales.

In 1976, the Habitat Conference was held in Vancouver, and representatives from 140 countries came to discuss global housing issues. At the same time, Greenpeace organizers held a non-governmental conference at Jericho Park. Jericho used to be an air force base during the 1940s. It had several huge aircraft hangars, perfect for the venue's seminars and workshop spaces, and there was also a main stage and a massive bar.

In a matter of months, a core group of about 30 people had organized a major outdoor music festival, prepared our huge anti-whaling ship, the *James Bay*, fundraised, and kept the office and financing afloat. When June 12, 1976, the day of the festival arrived, the park was all set with display tables. I was there to help sell Greenpeace merchandise. As the day unfolded, this huge multi-acre site kept filling up until it was finally packed with over 20,000 people from all strata of society. It was like the Old Roller Rink on steroids.

It was a spectacular launch of the second Greenpeace whale campaign, and the highlight and main draw was a well-advertised outdoor concert. Country Joe McDonald, Ronee Blakley, Paul Winter and Daniel O'Keefe performed alongside Greenpeace's own band, the Migrating

Whale Medicine Band, made up of Mel Gregory, Rex Weyler, Bill Gannon and Tusi Spong. When the band belted out one of their signature songs, "The Whale Anthem," the crowd joined in triumphantly, singing the chorus: "We are whales…swimming in the sea, come on now, why can't we live in harmony." It was so powerful it sent chills through your soul.

Bob stood on stage to huge cheers and promised to do his best for the whales. He bowed and thanked everyone for their love.

If Bob were here today, and he were to ask me one more time, "What is the meaning of life?" I think I would say to him, "It's all in the harmony."

WHALE COMMUNICATION

by Paul Spong

WITH THE SUCCESS of the first whale campaign came the knowledge that we were, of course, not finished. The next year, in 1976, Bob and I were together aboard the old minesweeper *James Bay* when it left Vancouver, heading for another round with whalers. This time, we knew much more about where we were going, thanks to covert sources who told us the whereabouts of the two Russian fleets on an almost daily basis. We headed for Mendocino, California, expecting the Russians to stick to their decades-old habits. There was no sign of them. I'd built a small shelter beside the chimney stack, where I slept and where Bob and I could talk privately. Though we felt a bit like pawns in the Cold War, it was a relief knowing that our actions the previous year had radically affected the whalers' plans and effectively protected a vast swath of ocean off North America's west coast We decided to head for Hawaii, hoping to intercept the Russian fleet along the way and improve our chances of meeting up with the Japanese fleet.

About 1,100 miles out from San Francisco we received word that the *Dalniy Vostok* was within range. A day later there were dots on the horizon and Russian voices on the radio. As we closed the gap, puffs of smoke emerged from one of the killer boats, and it started to charge toward us. Spouts from fleeing sperm whales were ahead of it. We leapt into action. Bob had insisted on taking the kamikaze role in the Zodiac, and

I had insisted on driving it. Bob's wife Bobbi leapt into the Zodiac first. The camera crew's Zodiac got hung up, so we sped away first and were soon positioned in front of the killer boat, weaving back and forth as the harpooner aimed. After a couple of minutes, the harpooner stepped away from his gun, and the speeding vessel slowed to a stop. By the time the camera crew arrived, we were drifting below the high rusty bow with the Russian crew peering down at us. As Bob reached his hand out to touch the bow, the NK-2007 put its engines into reverse and slowly started to back away. It looked like Bob had pushed the giant killing machine away by himself. We felt victorious. A few days later, running low on fuel, we turned back and headed for Honolulu, coming across a pod of five sperm whales. They cruised quietly along with us for an hour, lifting their giant heads out of the water to peer at us, and then they disappeared. I was convinced they were the ones we'd saved.

In Honolulu, our sources were coy about telling us the whereabouts of the Japanese fleet, so we spent huge energy and time following up on hints and scouring the ocean from the air as far as Midway. In the end, we failed to get any leads on the whereabouts of the Japanese fleet and decided to go after the Russians again. On August 12, our final encounter with their fleet became a tense drama when two of our tiny rubber boats were in hot pursuit and fog closed in. We lost contact with each other, and the *James Bay*. Needless to say, there was huge relief all round when we finally heard the *James Bay*'s foghorn and she appeared out of the fog. We took it as a sign and decided to head for home.

LATRINE OFFICER

by Rex Weyler

IN 1976, the second year of the whale campaign, Greenpeace secured a bigger and faster vessel, the Canadian minesweeper *James Bay*. In mid-July, after a brief stop in San Francisco for fuel, we headed southwest toward the last known location of the Russian whaling fleet, the seamounts near Hawaii.

Compared to Captain Cormack's fishing boat from the previous year, this ship extended our range and allowed us to keep pace with the whaling fleets. We could see farther out to sea from the elevated upper bridge, five miles to the horizon and perhaps ten miles to the mast of a ship beyond the horizon. Bob Hunter and I often stood together on the upper bridge, silently gazing out to sea, learning how to pick out the tiniest discrepancy in the boiling grey patterns of water and atmosphere – a whale blow or a strange vessel.

On the second day out, I surveyed for whales and ships as the *James Bay* rolled incessantly over eight-foot swells. The wind felt chilly, few of the crew were up, and some remained in their bunks with seasickness.

On the forward deck, Bob Hunter walked alone to the bow as the sea mist swirled around him. He wore a white wool sweater and sandals. A brush dangled from his belt. He held onto the cable that served as a railing and stared out into the grey void of the sea. The pressure of leading this expanding ecology movement had rattled him. A year ago, the pressure had been to find the whalers. This year, we received daily reports of the Soviet fleet position, and we had a much faster ship. We knew exactly where to go, and when. Yet the worldwide acclaim and notoriety had changed everything, attracting thousands of new people to Greenpeace. Managing campaign logistics now felt simple compared to the complexity of managing all the competing egos. Hunter often quoted his media mentor Ben Metcalfe: "Fear success."

Hunter looked weary, from my perspective on the bridge, head bent, taking a quiet moment with the solace of the sea, clinging to a halyard as a child might cling to his mother. By 1976, administration had become the new Achilles heel of our movement. Our own organization had grown into a bigger mystery than finding the whalers. Twenty Greenpeace offices, big and small, now operated around the world.

Yet, even with supply lines and communication lines intact, which ours were not, the forward motion of a social movement can founder on the delicacies of administering these relationships. Hunter's natural style was to include and encourage everyone. "Let a thousand flowers blossom," he proclaimed, paraphrasing Mao Tse-Tung, fully aware of the irony that Mao's revolution had long since adopted iron-fisted tyranny. Hunter, at the hub of an expanding movement, and not prone to authoritarian rule, suffered exhaustion and private anguish.

Some of Hunter's antics, possibly a way to dissipate the pressure, appeared wacky to some of the crew. Musician Mel Gregory had brought his pet iguana, Fido, aboard the Greenpeace ship, and since this was the Year of the Dragon, Hunter had declared Fido "commander-in-chief" of the campaign. He regularly posted written communiqués, allegedly from our reptilian leader, headed *Secret Memo from Fido*, in which he outlined strategies for the summer.

Several crew members wore metal dragon pins we'd picked up in Vancouver's Chinatown for the Year of the Dragon, and Fido had free run of the ship. Hunter built a nesting platform for the iguana under a skylight near his berth. The final crew member, according to Hunter, was "Otto." The *James Bay* had been fitted with an electronic autopilot to steer the ship on a set course. Hunter concluded that if we were in the hands of a machine, we should afford the device full crew status. His daily *Memo from Fido* quoted *sources close to Otto* revealing items such as "a rainbow

Bob Hunter at his typewriter during the very first Greenpeace voyage, which departed Vancouver on September 15, 1971. The aim of the trip was to halt nuclear tests at Amchitka Island by sailing into the restricted area. Crew aboard the ship were the pioneers of the green movement who formed the original group that became Greenpeace. © GREENPEACE / ROBERT KEZIERE

Bob Hunter at the helm of the *Phyllis Cormack* together with Ben Metcalfe en route to Amchitka, September 1971. © GREENPEACE / ROBERT KEZIERE

Bob Hunter, official chronicler, aboard the *Phyllis Cormack* (also called the *Greenpeace*) on October 11, 1971. © GREENPEACE / ROBERT KEZIERE

(*top*) Greenpeace president Bob Hunter and Japanese translator Taeko Miwa during a meeting at Greenpeace's first public office, on 4th Avenue in Vancouver, BC, Canada, January 1975. © GREENPEACE / REX WEYLER

(*bottom*) Bob Hunter in 1975. © GREENPEACE / REX WEYLER

(*top*) Greenpeace president Bob Hunter with David McTaggart, who sailed into the French nuclear test zone at Mururoa Atoll during the second Greenpeace campaign, at the Greenpeace office in Vancouver, January 1975.
© GREENPEACE / REX WEYLER

(*bottom*) Greenpeace activist Bob Hunter in a boat ahead of the *Phyllis Cormack* in the north Pacific on the first Greenpeace anti-whaling campaign, June 1975.
© GREENPEACE / REX WEYLER

(*top*) Rex Weyler, John Cormack, and Bob Hunter aboard the *Phyllis Cormack*, June 1975.
© GREENPEACE / RON PRECIOUS

(*bottom*) Bob Hunter returning the Greenpeace flag to the Kwakiutl Indigenous nation
in Alert Bay, British Columbia, Canada, July 1975. © GREENPEACE / REX WEYLER

(*top*) Greenpeace activists Paul Watson and Bob Hunter kneel down in front of a sealing ship to stop it from moving through the ice. Resting on the ice between them is a "whitecoat" harp seal pup. Labrador coast, Canada, March 1976. © GREENPEACE / REX WEYLER

(*bottom*) Greenpeace seal campaign activists Paul Watson and Bob Hunter sit down with a harp seal pup to block a Norwegian vessel on the Labrador ice floes during the spring Canadian seal hunt, March 1976. © GREENPEACE / PATRICK MOORE

(*top*) Bob Hunter on the ship's radio with George Korotva as the *Phyllis Cormack* approaches San Francisco after the 1975 whale campaign, July 1975. © GREENPEACE / REX WEYLER

(*bottom*) Bob Hunter on the radio phone in the wheelhouse of the *Phyllis Cormack* with Captain John Cormack at the Dellwood Knolls Seamounts off the coast of Canada, June 1975. © GREENPEACE / REX WEYLER

(*top*) Cree Elder Fred Mosquito stands with Bob Hunter at the launch of the second Greenpeace whale campaign, May 1976. Mosquito told the Greenpeace crew: "You are the Warriors of the Rainbow." Greenpeace had adapted the Cree legend of the "Warriors of the Rainbow" from the book by William Willoya and Vinson Brown in 1971. Mosquito's presence and pronouncement confirmed for the Greenpeace crew that they were living up to their commitment to this legend. © GREENPEACE / REX WEYLER

(*bottom*) Paul Spong and Bob Hunter during the Pacific Ocean Russian whaling campaign, May 1976. © GREENPEACE / REX WEYLER

Bob Hunter with Greenpeace's pet iguana, Fido, during the June 1976 whale campaign.
© GREENPEACE

Bob and Bobbi Hunter aboard the *James Bay* during the June 1976 whale campaign.
© GREENPEACE / REX WEYLER

(*top*) Bob Hunter with Walrus and other Greenpeace crew in the Tofino pub, June 1976.
© GREENPEACE / REX WEYLER

(*bottom*) Bob Hunter talks with the *James Bay* crew at the beginning of the 1976 Soviet Whaling Tour to the North Pacific. Wickaninnish Bay, Canada, July 1976. © GREENPEACE / REX WEYLER

(*top*) Bob Hunter on the radio as the *James Bay* crew tracks the Soviet whalers. North Pacific, between Mexico and Hawaii, July 1976. © GREENPEACE / REX WEYLER

(*bottom*) Bob Hunter on the deck of the *James Bay*, with Rod Marining in the background, during the 1976 whale campaign. North Pacific, between Mexico and Hawaii, July 1976.
© GREENPEACE / REX WEYLER

(*top*) *James Bay* crew tracking the Soviet whalers, with Bob Hunter pointing out ship movements on the chart. From left: Michael Manoloson, David Garrick (Walrus), Michael Bailey, Bob Hunter, Susi Leger, Paul Spong, Lance Cowan. North Pacific, between Mexico and Hawaii, August 1976. © GREENPEACE / REX WEYLER

(*bottom*) The first global (international) Greenpeace meeting, October 1, 1977. First row, from left: David Garrick (Walrus), Hal Ward (CIA), Dexter Cate (US), Rod Marining, unknown, Carlie Trueman, Cindy Baker, Margaret Tillbury, Nancy Jack, Don White; second row, from left: David McTaggart (France), unknown, unknown, Michael Bailey, unknown, Campbell Plowden (US), Bob Hunter, unknown; standing, from left: Al Johnston, John Frizell, unknown, Bill Gannon, Patty and Dan McDermott, Dino Pignataro, David Tussman, Linda Spong, Eileen Moore, unknown, John Cormack, Patrick Moore. Also in attendance were Gary Zimmerman, Elaine Tilbury (US), Susi Newborn (UK), Paul Spong, Rex Weyler and Bobbi Hunter. © GREENPEACE / REX WEYLER

(*top*) Greenpeace Foundation accountant Bill Gannon, with Bob Hunter and Patrick Moore on the deck of the *Rainbow Warrior*. Amsterdam Harbour, November 1979. © GREENPEACE / REX WEYLER

(*bottom*) At the founding of Greenpeace International. Portrait of Bob Hunter, June 1979. © GREENPEACE / REX WEYLER

Premiere of the movie *How to Change the World* at Kant-Kino in Berlin. From left:
Bobbi Hunter, widow of Bob Hunter; Jerry Rothwell, director of the film; and Emily Hunter,
daughter of Bob Hunter. September 10, 2015. © ANDREAS SCHOELZEL / GREENPEACE

was reported landing on Saint Melville...it might have been a dream... we don't know, it could all be a dream."

However, now, as I watched him at the bow, Hunter's acclaimed sense of humour appeared to have been bruised. He had been called "crazy" by more than one observer, but most of his antics – naming Fido "Commander," inducting volunteers into the Whole Earth Church with a "zap" to the forehead, screeching as a "Greenhawk" – were all in fun. Even though Hunter was completely serious about honouring the sacred qualities of nature, practising compassion for all beings, expecting miracles or consulting the I Ching, he was not fanatical about any of this. Hunter would freely mock himself to take the edge off his spiritual passions. The mystical wing of Greenpeace was not a cult or collection of psychotics. We understood the importance of having a political strategy, a clear message and a skilled team, while also inspiring myths and having a good laugh. The debate between the mystics and mechanics in Greenpeace felt like a modern adaptation of classical mythos and logos, magic and science, the perennial play of novelty and tradition. Nevertheless, ecology was our mission, and in spite of a vast spectrum of styles, we remained resolute about delivering this message.

His now-famous "mindbomb" theory of social change suggested that the fastest way to change society involved launching images and stories – "mindbombs" – that would "explode in people's heads all over the planet." Greenpeace would let others sort out the details; our goal was to infect the entire human family with an idea: we are all children of our Mother Earth, and we have a responsibility to care for her.

Hunter's instinct to take the crusade lightly contributed a great deal to the success of Greenpeace in the 1970s. There were plenty of strident, serious personalities, but Hunter infused the campaigns with humour and irony, inspiring others to exhibit some humility in the face of our ambitious mission.

I watched Hunter fondly as he stared out to sea, with the long brush hanging from his waist. I felt his vulnerability and his disappointment at the bickering among some of the crew. "Our own egos are our weakest link," he had said to me only a few days earlier. The unique blend that had become Greenpeace – ecology, media awareness, spirituality, humour and seagoing direct action – grew from a blend of bold creativity and modest humour. Hunter embodied these qualities more than anyone. However, our president was burning out like a meteor racing through the thick political atmosphere within the organization. His apparent madness on board the ship, however, concealed Hamletic method. As the burgeoning corps of volunteers proliferated, the competition for power had intensified. Hunter had been influenced by Buddhist and Taoist notions of eschewing power. "Power corrupts" was a message that he understood, so he asked one of his mentors, Beat poet Allen Ginsberg, "What do we do with this power that is coming our way?"

"Let it go," Ginsberg had replied bluntly, "before it freezes in your hand."

Hunter took this admonition seriously. As a theatrical retort to the crush for power on the ship, and within Greenpeace in general, Hunter had assigned himself the role of ship's "latrine officer" and took to wearing the latrine brush, which now dangled from his belt as he shuffled about the ship. He could be found each morning in the latrine, cheerfully scrubbing away at the sinks and toilet bowls. To some, this was pure delirium, but his latrine officer act was not madness, it was a little internal mindbomb. "Don't take yourself too seriously," was the message.

THE HUNTER SAVIOUR

compiled for George Korotva by Bobbi Hunter

Bobbi Hunter: George Korotva is unable to write a personal piece at this time, so this chapter is unique in that it's Bob's recollections of his times spent with George on the epic first Whale Campaign and the tension-filled second Whale Campaign, which Bob humorously called "Bob and Bobbi's honeymoon cruise to Hawaii."

"I felt Bob was a visionary and very determined. He would never give up. I felt my job was to keep him alive and as close as possible to reality," said George when recently asked about his friend Bob.

First Whale Campaign (1975), from Bob Hunter's book *Warriors of the Rainbow*:

At the outset, George Korotva's role was simply that of an experienced sea dog who happened to speak some Russian. Thirty-three years old, he had skippered ships along the west coast. A Czechoslovakian, he had been imprisoned by the Russians during the 1965 student uprisings in Prague and shipped off to a camp in Siberia, where he learned what he knew of the Russian language the hard way. After 18 months of imprisonment, he escaped, later finding his way to Canada. His English was delightfully atrocious. He never had a "hangover," instead he would be "hanging over." He had difficulty distinguishing between nouns and proper nouns, so that Will Jackson became "The Will," Cormack became "The John," I was "The Bob," and George himself, of course, became "The George."

Whatever he was, The George was not at heart a sentimentalist. It was he who grabbed me one night shortly after we took off. He pushed me up against the wall and said, "Look, brudder, it matters for nothing that you get falling down pissed and stoopid, aye? I like it. But to deese people you the guru, and if you turn into a cabbage, the whole trip turns into cabbage, no shit. Get it together, brudder! These people counting on you. So dem whales."

It was evident to Korotva, from our first night on the *Phyllis Cormack*, that I was having a lot of trouble with my role as "expedition leader." The George, from that point onward, became virtually my personal psychiatric advisor. He also became my bodyguard. I don't know, during that voyage and the ones that were to come, how many times he saved my life, but a rough guess suggests at least a dozen.

When the *Phyllis Cormack* eventually met up with the Russian whale killing fleet, we all saw the white puffs of vapour in the water directly ahead of the *Vlastny*, maybe a dozen of them. Cormack roared: "Zodiac launching crew!"

The months of preparation paid off. Within less than three minutes, three Zodiacs were in the water, Watson and I in one, Moore and Easton in the second, Weyler and Korotva in the third. But something was wrong with the third one – the propeller wasn't working! Up on the mast Walrus yelled, "They're turning, they're turning! Hurry up!"

Watson immediately opened up our engine full blast, and without a backward glance we screamed away from the *Phyllis Cormack*. Moore's engine roared as he came out directly.

The problem with the third Zodiac was quickly overcome. Will Jackson flung himself into the hold and hurled a spare 50-horse-power outboard at least six feet straight up in the air. Cormack's tree-like arms shot out to grasp it and threw it over the side to Korotva, who somehow caught it in his arms and jammed it into place.

Meanwhile, Watson and I started having engine trouble. "Oh-oh," Paul said.

The *Vlastny* was coming down on us like an express train. Our outboard engine coughed briefly, but we were lifted and swept lightly aside – the *Vlastny* passing so close at full speed I could have reached out and touched it. The feeling was that guardian angels had swooped down at the last second and given the Zodiac a gentle nudge.

We were bobbing in the harpoon boat's wake when Korotva suddenly appeared, yelling, "Get in! Get in!" Rex and I changed places without a single comment. Korotva and I, powered now by the big 50-horsepower engine, surged after the *Vlastny*.

We'd just manoeuvred ourselves to be a shield for the fleeing whales, when we heard the sound of the harpoon gun going off. Instinctively, we both ducked, while Korotva moved the Zodiac with intuitive grace. The cable lashed down less than five feet from the port side of the Zodiac, like a massive sword cleaving.

[Bobbi Hunter: That was the sound that reverberated on TV –
the sound that truly heralded in the Whale Saving Movement.]

**Second Whale Campaign (1976). George is promoted to captain of
the *James Bay* –from Bob Hunter's book, *Warriors of the Rainbow*.**

It was George's job to pull the boat together. That meant countless parts for the engines and electronic gear, countless trips through marine-supply shops and warehouses. It meant getting engineers, and no professional engineer comes free. It meant hiring welders and shipwrights and marine-radio specialists, but he pulled it off. The *James Bay* was launched.

Eventually, the crew of 35 were off on the long trek to the mid Pacific.

Then we encountered the Russian fleet again. The water was choppy, and the dark bulk of the factory ship lay silhouetted on the horizon while the killer boats worked zigzag patterns in the water all around.

Once again, the whales were running directly to our side, bringing the whalers along in their wake. Many had heard us describe from the campaign of 1975 how the whales would come to us for help but had dismissed it as exaggeration. Paul Spong, who years before had insisted, "You can count on the whales to help."

Within minutes, the *James Bay* was slicing to a halt, and the Zodiacs were being lowered swiftly over the side. Bobbi was first down into the Zodiac, followed by myself.

Bobbi had a white scarf wrapped around her head to keep her long hair out of her eyes and hung on against the fierce pounding of the Zodiac against the waves. As we finally came parallel to the racing whaler, it was evident that the men on deck and the bridge could tell there was a woman in the rubber craft. The gunner stepped back from the harpoon. "He's moving away from the gun!" I yelled, daring for the first time to hope that they might not shoot after all.

Minutes later, three more of our Zodiacs arrived and pulled in on either side of us. It had worked! We had blockaded them! The crew exulted. We had stopped a killer boat in its tracks.

Later, as the *Vostok* and the *James Bay* raced side by side across the ocean, Korotva rumbled, "Dat captain," jabbing a big finger in the direction of the *Vostok*, "he's no dummy. He's taking us in exact da goddamn opposite direction from Honolulu. He knows dat's where we gotta go for fuel. He don't give a shit. He's got tankers come out and feed him. Pretty soon we gotta turn back. Simple like dat. He knows it."

Then we arrived in Hawaii, and all hell broke loose! The *James Bay* was designed for cold, northern ventilation. The fierce, steady sunlight turned the ship into an oven – the decks so hot no one could walk barefoot on them. Most of the crew were impatient to plunge after the Japanese and could not endure the tension of waiting. Between the heat and the restlessness, the frustration of not knowing which way to go, and a certain degree of simply being tired of each other's company, the crew quickly broke down into a half dozen dissenting factions. Fights erupted and crew left.

Without the strength of George by my side, the campaign surely would have ended.

BLOOD ON THE ICE

by Ron Precious

TWO SOLITARY FIGURES in bright orange survival suits stood on a massive, undulating ice pan in the North Atlantic Ocean off the coast of Labrador. Robert Hunter and his comrade in solidarity, Paul Watson, stood side by side with their backs turned against an advancing ice breaker. It was March 19, 1976, and I knew that this moment on the frozen ice would be forever etched into the zeitgeist of ecological activism. However, it would take a Herculean effort, with a minefield of obstacles and regulations to overcome, before we would find ourselves poised to record another historic moment.

Underfinanced and highly contentious, this first seal campaign would test the very foundation of the organization and push Bob to the limits of his sanity. Little did I realize our fearless leader was suffering from huge bouts of anxiety and self-doubt in his role as leader of this neophyte organization he had helped found back in 1971. Bob Hunter, while president of Greenpeace, had reluctantly agreed to join the seal expedition as media coordinator and general flack deflector. Paul Watson was our de facto expedition leader by virtue of the fact that he and David "Walrus" Garrick had proposed the idea to Greenpeace. Just getting the crew to one of the most isolated regions of Canada was a logistical nightmare. It involved travel by transcontinental railway, icebreaking ferry, rented passenger vans and helicopters.

Our first test came when we attempted to enter the town of St. Anthony, Newfoundland, our centre of operations. A mob in excess of 100 angry citizens set up a human blockade. This could have been game over had Bob Hunter not sprung into action. He surreptitiously blended into the crowd and, using his reporter's instinct, managed to locate Roy Pilgrim, head of Concerned Citizens Committee of St. Anthony Against Greenpeace. While the angry mob focused their anger on the leaders of the group, I jumped into the fray with my fully loaded Eclair ACL camera, hoping I could record the chaos without invoking the wrath of the mob.

In a matter of minutes, Bob managed to defuse the ugly situation. The Greenpeace contingent would be allowed to enter the town provided they attended a town hall meeting at the local elementary school auditorium that evening to present their case for permission "to observe the hunt." I was impressed and relieved, as this could have turned into the shortest GP campaign ever mounted, and I would have nothing to film.

That evening, the auditorium was filled to capacity. Standing room only for spectators eager to see and hear what these "tree-huggers" from Lotusland had to say. I was the only person with a camera prepared to record what would be a pivotal moment in the arc of this campaign. I had no idea that Bob had met privately with Pilgrim and other members of the sealing community to hammer out an agreement that would allow the campaign to carry on.

So, when Hunter announced that Greenpeace would drop its plan to spray green dye on the fur of the whitecoat pups, the audience and many Greenpeacers were stunned. Bob used a classic "bait and switch" strategy to enable Greenpeace to carry out its plan to get out on the ice and document the atrocity that masqueraded as a "hunt."

Space was limited on the Greenpeace helicopters. Only a select few would get a chance to witness and protest the ugly slaughter of innocent harp seal pups. The demand for seats from the international media was intense. Some had their own helicopters, while others insisted that Greenpeace provide them with free transportation to and from the ice pans.

Hunter was the final authority in determining who went and who stayed behind. The situation became more complicated when David McTaggart arrived with a French television crew and a photographer.

Bob was torn between McTaggart, the veteran of two campaigns against the French nuclear testing in the South Pacific, and his in-house film crew – Michael Chechik and me.

Now politics entered into it. Hunter was under immense pressure to allow McTaggart's crew first access because of his pending legal case against the French government for a brutal attack on him by French commandos in 1973. International publicity would be crucial to winning the "hearts and minds" of Europeans who ultimately would be needed to put pressure on Canada to end its involvement with the seal hunt. McTaggart's crew would get first crack at the confrontation on the ice.

I recall the moment when the decision went down and my feeling of righteous indignation. What eased the pain was the offer of access to any footage that the French crew managed to obtain for their own documentary. In hindsight, it was a logical and prudent decision – Bob's inner wisdom prevailed because he saw the entire picture. It wasn't about hurting somebody's feelings, it was for the good of the mission – and he was right, goddamn it!

When tensions had subsided, and the McTaggart crew had the footage they came for, I was on the first helicopter to our base camp on Belle Isle. Soon after my arrival, a major storm struck with gale force winds that stranded our crew for three long days and nights. Forced to adopt survival tactics, we had to resort to using our helicopter JP-1 fuel in our small cooking stoves as we had run out of naphtha gas. This unorthodox solution provided extraordinary heat for our tents, but the by-product was excess carbon soot that coated the interior of my tent and, most unfortunately, my lungs. After our rescue and return to St. Anthony, I developed a raspy cough and black-tinged phlegm that earned me the nickname "Black Lung Precious." The weather had improved enough for another attempt to get to "the Front." This time, Michael and I would have unfettered access to the events that would unfold before our camera lenses.

It was a long hike across the constantly shifting ice to where the sealers were clubbing and skinning seal pups. In the still air, all we could hear were the cries of the whitecoats as they called out for their mothers. A cloudless sky made everything blindingly bright on the ice. Even though it must have been minus 20 degrees, we were warm in our survival outfits and thermal-insulated boots. Bob was easily recognizable because he was wearing the very same Peruvian alpaca wool cap he'd worn when we found the Soviet whaling fleet the previous summer. I was hoping that this was perhaps Bob's personal talisman and thus an auspicious sign.

We encountered our first group of "swilers" (seal hunters) amid the carnage of their handiwork. Heated words were exchanged, but the killing went on in spite of the intervention. Moments later, Bob stopped, dropping to his knees in front of a harp seal pup. He seemed to be staring right into its almond-shaped eyes and mumbling something. Bob seemed mesmerized. Perhaps he saw his own reflection in the vastness of these all-encompassing eyes. Like a camera's "fish-eye" lens, they seemed to distort perspective – but then our whole perspective was being distorted by the events that were unfolding around us.

Bob was finally jarred from his near trance-like state by Eileen Moore bellowing, "Bob, quit your praying, we've got some seals to save!"

This command seemed to break the spell Bob was under. He immediately stood up, removed his cap, bowed to the whitecoat pup he had just bonded with, and broke into a slow jog to catch up to the rest of the crew.

I barely had time to record the images of the harp seals before and after they were met with the skull-crushing blow from a hak-a-pik when I noticed that Bob and Paul were running toward the ship that was advancing in our direction. It was a Canadian-registered vessel, the *Arctic Endeavour*.

As Hunter and Watson positioned themselves directly in the path of the enormous icebreaker, Michael and I took our position about 20 metres in front of the eco-commandos. I used a chunk of ice as a platform to stabilize my camera for the telephoto view of the standoff between man and ship. This was a monumental moment that could end in tragedy or victory.

The ship wasn't slowing down, and I wondered if the captain knew there were people in front of his vessel. I tilted up and zoomed into the forecastle, where I saw a deckhand looking down and yelling at Hunter and Watson to move or get run down. Neither man was going to budge an inch. Both stood with their backs to the oncoming ship with arms folded across their chests. It was a powerful image of defiance in a totally hostile environment.

The ship had stopped about ten metres behind our boys when we heard the engines reverse – the ship was backing up the same distance it had just travelled. Soundman Chechik yelled out to our reluctant heroes, "What are you guys doing?"

It seemed like a stupid question at the time, but we needed to get either Bob or Paul to say something during this tense standoff.

"We're blockin' the ship!" shouted Hunter.

"We're not moving," added Paul.

Would these be the last words uttered by Hunter and Watson before entering the bone-chilling waters of the North Atlantic? At least we had something on tape besides the dramatic images of these two solitary figures in orange jumpsuits silhouetted against the blood-red hull of the ship.

Moments later, the ship was again advancing with speed toward them. It was like a classic Mexican standoff – who would blink first, captain or protestors? The ship closed menacingly upon our protagonists, but just as suddenly creaked to a halt with a shudder that had ice piling up on either side of Bob and Paul. Bob seemed to be in a trance again, as he never flinched when the masses of jagged ice mounted up all around them.

There they were, frozen in time – having brought a 300-ton vessel to a complete standstill less than three metres behind them. We had our "harpoon shot" on the ice, and it would be seen around the world.

Much has been made of Jerry Rothwell's award-winning documentary *How to Change the World* (2015), which claims that the first seal campaign took a heavy toll on Bob Hunter and ultimately led to his departure from the Greenpeace organization. While any campaign can produce significant tension and turmoil, the friction between Bob and Paul was insignificant when you examine the net results. I believe that an unbreakable bond was formed when they stood their ground before the icebreaker. Bob maintained a long and collaborative relationship with Paul Watson, even after Paul's departure from Greenpeace in 1977.

So how has Robert Hunter impacted my life? Deeply and profoundly.

I was left with an undying admiration for the man who many of us called "Uncle Bob." When we first met, Bob immediately picked up on my unique surname. To Bob, I was "Rinpoche," which comes from Tibetan Buddhism and translates as "precious one."

I have literally worn this honorific very proudly over the intervening years. On my back – between my shoulder blades – the Tibetan characters for *Rinpoche* are tattooed. My three adult children all have the same tattoo on different parts of their bodies. If this wasn't enough homage to my beloved friend, my first-born son is named Robert.

I will admit that I still have intense and vivid recollections about my Greenpeace days. These memories weren't all captured on film and tape but are indelibly burned into my psyche in Technicolor – waiting for any excuse to tell my story.

THE THREE SHAMANS

by David "Walrus" Garrick

WHEN BOBBI ASKED ME to write about Bob Hunter alongside many of Canada's best-known and influential talents, I immediately felt warm and fuzzy. Bob had inspired and "enabled" me to put my normally unused and unappreciated abilities as a shaman to the test: telepathy and "seeing" unleashed, mind reading put to daily use.

Looking back to 1976 and 1977, Bob Hunter, Paul Watson and I had some powerful experiences where life, death, injury and mindfucks conspired to interfere – hurled on by enemies, friends, partners, governments, and perhaps even aliens. We three quite different shamans learned from these negatives.

On the first Save the Seal campaign, Paul Watson planned to spray a harmless but permanent green dye on each seal pup, just enough dye to ruin the pelt's value as a commercial commodity. The day before the hunt, with the local seal hunters threatening to stop us from taking helicopters to the ice, Bob Hunter was on stage telling the angry crowd opposing our action that we would abandon the plan to use dye on the seals. It appeased the crowd, who cheered wildly, and pissed off our seal campaign brothers, yet it meant that we could go to the killing fields.

It was sickening. Blood trails stretched across the ice – Norway's carnage. I physically blocked sealers and barely escaped being clubbed on the head.

On the second Save the Seal campaign, Brigitte Bardot, France's famous "sex kitten," joined us to prevent the slaughter and send her message to the fashion-minded that wearing seal fur was wrong. The camp on Belle Isle had twice the crew and many more media – but no Bob Hunter.

In Bob's words: "The first act of the new Seal Steering Committee for the second Greenpeace Seal Campaign was to make sure that I was excluded from the crew. They were determined to run a, pure, campaign, which meant that there would be no further talk of negotiations or compromises with the Newfoundlanders." (from *Warriors of the Rainbow*)

Before heading to Newfoundland, in mid-March 1977, I had felt it essential to address the spiritual dimension. Three ceremonies took place after I offered a pouch of tobacco to a Medicine Man. In the final Sweat Lodge, I was told the campaign would be difficult, the objectives not met, and Norway would continue to slaughter the seal pups at their nursery, with the Canadian government's connivance. It wouldn't matter. The message was strong on one thing. We had to try anyway.

My friend Laurent Trudell from Quebec City was on my team alongside a San Francisco photographer, two Norwegian Viking warriors and a Norwegian woman who considered herself a witch (Wiccan). The sealers didn't stand a chance.

Having been transported by helicopter to the killing fields, the team chased the bewildered sealers back to one ship. Laurent and I accessed ice pans to reach the ship. Upon our approach, the ship backed up and headed elsewhere. We chased after the swilers. I caught up with the vessel and tried to block it. The captain couldn't see me from the bridge and eventually halted. The crew caught up, but we had to return to the helicopters and go back to Belle Isle. We were told a bad storm was fast approaching, so the *Beaver* arrived, and everyone was evacuated.

Our anti-sealing group set out again to confront the main sealing vessel, the Norwegian-owned *Martin Karlsen*. My friend, Paul Watson, along with our Greenpeace lawyer-turned-activist Peter Ballem, were in the lead. As they approached the seal factory ship, a blood-smeared sealer was busy slaughtering and removing the pelt from a baby seal. Paul spotted the sealer's knife and threw it into the ocean. The sealer snarled and retrieved his knife. Paul in turn picked up the pelt and threw it in the Atlantic waters. This incited the sealers. Nearby was a bale of pelts attached to a cable that had been readied to be hauled on board. Paul pulled out a set of handcuffs and attached himself to the pile of pelts. He had planned to stage a protest by staying attached to the pile until he could talk to a Fisheries officer and make the case for not killing the seals. Shouts ensued by the swilers to *"Haul ta bye in."* Unexpectedly, Paul was hoisted in the air, slammed against the side of the steel-hulled vessel and repeatedly dunked in the frigid ocean and slammed again. Peter was screaming, "For Christ's sake, haul him up the rest of the way!" Peter jumped in to pull Paul to safety and was dangerously dunked as well. Peter was finally able to capture and haul Paul back to the ice. At this point, Paul was suffering from fractures and hypothermia. Paul was then left out in the cold for a half-hour while the Fisheries officials determined what was to be done. Peter Ballem took charge and pushed to have Paul placed on board to recover from the extreme cold before he passed out.

Later in the day, when Peter Ballem appeared at a press conference that was set up by Greenpeace to introduce Brigitte Bardot, the huge crowd of fawning media were not the least bit interested in the real action of the day; their eyes had been set exclusively on the French icon.

Bardot, who was a dedicated animal rights activist and anti-fur fashion advocate, said the following: "The pilots decided that we can't afford the risk of going back to Blanc Sablon, we leave the encampment in an atmosphere of warmth. They are fabulous people. Vivent Greenpeace!"

By March 20, the second Greenpeace Save the Seal campaign was over. They had taken the message to the world's media, but, sadly, out on the ice fields, over 24,000 seals had been slaughtered.

Thinking back, I remember now that Bob, the leader who was banished from the second seal campaign for the crime of trying to negotiate with the local fisheries and sealers the year before, was now forced, as the sitting president, to face national Canadian media, the CBC. He had to speak about the horrifying experience of his friend Paul Watson. Bob was vehemently attacked for his stand on the seal hunt by the media, who defended the Newfoundlanders. The media attack must have been a repugnant situation for Bob. However, having to stay back – and not be involved with the second seal campaign – was harder on him.

Fielding complaints from self-entitled new activists, having friends turn on friends, plus the sheer exhaustion of being Greenpeace's leader through their most impactful campaigns – it all finally caught up to him. Bob abhorred conflict, and here he was surrounded by it daily. These tensions in part led to his decision to leave Greenpeace in April 1977.

In Bob's words: "After years of feeling so passionately about the Greenpeace fantasy, I suddenly felt nothing but apathy."

Paul led the charge to save the seals for several more years. Bob joined him on later campaigns independent of Greenpeace. Finally, in 1987, a moratorium on the baby seal kill was enacted. It was a ten-year brave battle for we three shamans: Paul, the healer of wrongs, Bob the communicator of spirituality, and me, the telepathic guide for the departed, along with Greenpeace, the Sea Shepherd Conservation Society and several other animal rights organizations – and in the end, it was a bloody but successful campaign.

MONEY EXPANDS

by Bill Gannon

"MONEY EXPANDS TO FILL THE NEED." When I said that to Bob in 1985, he asked me to write it down and to explain what I meant. I tried to, but I told him, "I can't prove it, but I know it's true."

I served as Greenpeace's financial officer from 1975 to 1979, a time when, as "Warriors of the Rainbow," we saw Bob as our guiding light.

I met Bob at the end of the 1975 *Greenpeace V* Save the Whale campaign, when I was asked to help with the organization's finances. I had followed Bob's adventures since the 1971 Don't Make a Wave protest. When I was introduced to the group, it had been renamed Greenpeace, and it was $40,000 in debt but had huge fundraising potential and a movie deal in the works. What they did have was credibility, having evolved from a one-room office, donated by Gary Gallon at the Society Promoting Environmental Conservation (SPEC), to an emerging eco-force with a large office, multiple campaigns, benefit concerts and fundraising schemes. But they needed organizational professionalism.

Bob was the visionary and now president. With help from his soon-to-be wife, Bobbi, we created cash-flow forecasts and designed an accounting system that produced monthly budget-versus-actual financial reports for each of our fundraising activities, which in turn served to secure the line of credit that allowed the office and the campaigns to function. Fundraising activities at that time were all generated from private monies and included the GoAnywhere lottery; a computer mail-out, with news and a donation request; door-to-door donations; merchandise; and the *Greenpeace Chronicles* newspaper, which had blossomed into a profitable venture with paid advertising. Bob and Bobbi had already learned the lesson of not trusting public or corporate donations. Many of these fundraising approaches are still used today in Greenpeace offices. The reports we hammered out guided us financially from the first whale and seal campaigns on through to the establishment of Greenpeace International in 1979 in Amsterdam. I signed off at that point, but the Greenpeace energy continued to expand over the next 40 years, to annual gross revenue of more than €90-million (over C$133-million), as stated in its 2019 annual report.

My day job as the chief accountant at a local firm was the foundation of my experience that I offered Greenpeace. However, it was Bob and his vision that led me up to the top floor of the Royal Bank in Vancouver, where our biggest financial miracle was realized.

In 1976, we met the Royal Bank officials with $150,000 owing to them on the line of credit. We had to prove our worth. We had a letter from the executor of an estate, in which Greenpeace was the beneficiary of an estimated $150,000! That helped, but more importantly it turned out the head of the bank was a fan of Bob's, and quickly we had a reprieve. Money expands to fill the need!

Later, at the send-off for the second Save the Whale campaign, a concert for *Greenpeace VI* at Jericho Park was organized. Bob said there could be 25,000 attending. Realizing that, with a $5 entrance fee, there could be more than $100,000 raised, I organized a system of preprinted tickets, and the money was securely collected hourly by Brinks trucks. Police estimated the crowd to be over 20,000, but some of the crowd pushed over the fence and thousands got in free! At the end of the day, the Brinks deposits totalled $27,500. I didn't know the actual costs because our bookkeeper, Starlet, explained that in the rush to get everything ready for the launch, there had been many blank cheques signed to suppliers. On Monday, the bank informed me, "Your account is $27,000 overdrawn." But they had not yet received the $27,500 in Brinks deposits! Once more, the money expanded to fill the need!

At the end of the first Save the Seal and the beginning of the second Save the Whale campaign, I got a call from Bobbi, who informed me that Lorene, our loans officer at the bank, had been replaced. Bobbi had asked the new loans officer for a $15,000 temporary bulge in our $150,000 line of credit, but he'd refused. She knew the bank balance would exceed the line of credit limit by $5,000 when outstanding cheques came in. Plus, the *James Bay* needed $5,000 for fuel in Seattle, and the post office needed $5,000 cash for our mail-out. I made an appointment to see the new loans officer to take him through our projected mail-out income of $96,000. Meanwhile, our senior volunteer receptionist, Julie McMaster, mysteriously received a paper bag of cash in the mail slot from a man dying of cancer. His unsigned note read, "Felt you guys could use the money." The cash amounted to about $15,000! When I walked into the loan officer's office, he said, "I have no idea how you qualified for this line of credit, but as I told Bobbi, the answer is no!" I raised the bag and poured the bills onto his desk.

"We have other sources," I said. The overdraft was covered, we fuelled the *James Bay*, and a request for donations was mailed to about 80,000 supporters. Once again, money expanded to fill the need.

But to my mind, the financial miracles surrounding Bob were surpassed by the opportunity he created when he announced in April 1977 that office workers like me could be included in the crew of future campaigns. This allowed me to become a real "Greenpeacer."

The next campaign was the Ambush at Douglas Channel, a protest against efforts to promote Kitimat, BC, as a port for crude oil supertankers. The Kitimat Pipeline Company was hosting the conference of municipal mayors aboard the *Princess Patricia*, a 350-foot cruise ship. Greenpeace had discovered that the oilmen had set up a tour for the mayors.

Our plan was to blockade the *Princess Patricia*. I was ready for it. Veteran crew member Mel Gregory, guitarist and leader of the Greenpeace Migrating Whale Medicine Band, insisted that I bring my bass and amplifier, and Linda Spong, her violin. Other crew members were Rod Marining and David "Walrus" Garrick. The *Greenpeace IX* vessel was the MV *Meander*, a beautiful, classic, 65-foot yacht, built in 1934, owned by our captain, Dennis Feroce.

Our first stop was at Bella Bella, a small community en route to Douglas Channel. At the dock, Linda, Mel and I began playing an eclectic selection of well-known fiddle tunes mixed with some of our own compositions. During that time, the *Princess Patricia* passed by us in the middle of their Captain's Dinner. We politely waved to them and began a new song.

We arrived at the entrance to Douglas Channel early in the morning of May 10, 1977. Bob had flown to Prince Rupert with Pat Moore, our new Greenpeace president, to catch a ride on the 90-foot *Thomas Crosby V,* a United Church missionary boat joining the blockade. When they joined us at Hartley Bay, they were pleased to point out that this was the most successful campaign so far, in that the oilmen provided most of the media coverage, and the campaign was showing a positive cash flow of more than $3,000, after fuel and grocery supplies.

With a fleet of fishing boats, we left Hartley Bay and positioned ourselves in the middle of the channel. When the *Princess Patricia* entered the channel, the *Thomas Crosby* radioed the cruise ship, asking it to stop and allow the village Chief and delegates to board and deliver their statement in opposition to the oil supertanker port.

The cruise ship's captain refused to stop and increased its speed to about 15 knots as it moved through the fishing boats. Captain Feroce moved the *Meander* directly into the path of the *Princess Patricia* and blew its horn four times, indicating it was dead in the water. In nautical terms, this put the onus on the *Patricia* to avoid collision.

The *Patricia* moved on regardless. Mel and Rod jumped into a Zodiac and were crossing the bow of the *Patricia* when something caused the Zodiac to flip them into the water and under the ship. Luckily, another protester wheeled his skiff around and hauled them out. By then, RCMP officers had come aboard the *Meander* to make a report.

"Is the Zodiac licensed?" they asked. "Yes," said Linda. "What is the licence number?" was their comeback. Linda rattled off the first numbers that came to her mind, the licence number of the CB radio of the Orcalab on Hanson Island, where she used to live. That satisfied them. Mel and Rod were shivering and throwing up sea water, but they were otherwise okay and quite pleased, as they knew that Bob would turn our trip into a media success.

I am most grateful to Bob for putting Linda, a.k.a. Tusi, and me on the *Meander* for that one-week voyage. Although we did not commit to each other until November 1977, I know my love affair with Tusi began on the

Meander that May. A love affair that lasted over 43 years until Tusi passed into the next dimension.

Thank you, Bob! My life would have been a lot different if it weren't for you. Your pursuit of your vision brought various forms of energy together in an extraordinary way: financial energy and love energy are the ones that affected me.

ECO-JUDAS

by Bobbi Hunter

HISTORY HAS IT that Bob Hunter stepped away from his role as president of Greenpeace because he was burned out and could not handle the internal conflicts of that time. That's a pretty loose description, and it makes him sound weak. Bob was far from weak, and he agonized over the decision to step aside. Bob's book *Warriors of the Rainbow* is his journalistic view of the history of those formative Greenpeace days. He did not write about his personal sense of events. The book was not about him, which is why I want to tell this story.

Bob's erratic behaviour on the second Save the Whale campaign was largely due to his dependence on Valium, which had been prescribed to calm his anxiety. This negative energy was a product of not looking after his health and of being at the centre of all the decision making at Greenpeace during its formative years. Much later we learned that a side effect of that drug is rage. And rage he did.

In 1976, in order to recover from that downward and destructive period in his life, he took a break and went to Wales to write David McTaggart's book *Journey into the Bomb* with him. David was not a writer, so Bob took over and produced a remarkable book for him in a very short period of time. The deal was that David would share his royalties with Bob. Unfortunately, this did not happen.

But, thankfully, the time away and focus on writing healed Bob. Feeling rejuvenated and prepared to get on with the battles ahead, we returned to Vancouver only to find the boat we had been living on, our *Astral*, had sunk, due to human incompetence. Without us knowing, our hero John Cormack had raised the boat. It was unlivable for some months, so we were now early couch surfers. We had no money to fix our boat. Bob had given up his establishment newspaper reporting job to work for, and lead, Greenpeace into the future, all on a pittance of a wage.

At this point in his life, he'd suffered the side effects of prescribed drugs, been excluded from the second seal campaign and been exploited as a writer. Our boat had sunk, and we were living as vagabonds on less than minimum wage. We also learned on our return from Wales that Pat Moore and his lady Eileen, who had been our best friends, had convinced anyone who would listen that Bob was unfit to run Greenpeace. Pat had been at Bob's side from the first campaign to Amchitka. He was younger than Bob but was university educated in ecology. This was a draw for Bob; having barely completed high school and been self-educated, he appreciated the prestige of academia. Pat was vice-president of policy at Greenpeace, and Eileen was the secretary of our board of directors. We campaigned, laughed and lived as close friends for three years. While Bob and I were away in Wales, we'd left them in control. The annual general meeting for Greenpeace occurred soon after we returned, and the fracture became public. At the meeting there was a vote on the leadership between Bob and Pat. Bob retained his position, but only by one vote.

Soon after that we took a long walk on a beach, where all the pent-up anger, tears, internal turmoil and exhaustion erupted. In the end, we decided that Bob could not go on. His power came from his relationships. If those who had turned on him wanted the power so badly, then he should not let the power freeze in his hands. It seemed the gods were clearly speaking to us, and they were saying it is time to move on.

Bob may have stepped aside in April 1977, but the war to save the whales was not over. The seal campaign featuring Brigitte Bardot had just ended, and rumblings, emanating from the various Greenpeace offices and media outlets, were demanding more Greenpeace action. They needed to send a ship out, once again, to focus attention on the still-endangered whales. By this time Pat Moore was the new president, and he now had the pleasure of assuaging all the varied interested factions with all their demands and opinions.

Bob and I were still on the board of directors, and through the Vancouver office it was decided to enlist George Korotva and Paul Spong to locate and ready a larger, faster ship from Hawaii. After months of money being directed to that cause, the ship was found and was being prepared. This larger ship, the *Ohana Kai*, should have been named "the hole in the water you dump money into." There were endless problems and delays, and as whale slaughter season approached, the problems with the ship just never seemed to be righted.

Pat Moore needed a backup plan. The trouble was, Pat had never organized a campaign on his own, and he didn't have Bob's persuasive powers. It was decided the *James Bay* would be sent out once again. Bob was ready to retire and wanted little to do with the day-to-day organization. He'd been undermined and lost power; he owed Greenpeace nothing. But, for the sake of the whales, he made a deal with Moore. Bob would get the *James Bay*, Captain John C. Cormack, the other essential officers, and take care of the media. I would get the money, the supplies and the secured contracts. Pat would get the ship ready just as he had in the past. Bob and I agreed to get this campaign launched on one condition: that Pat and Eileen would take the ship for the first part of the campaign, and Bob and I would take over in San Francisco and lead the second half of the campaign. We shook hands on the deal. Being in the fray of the action was addictive.

The *James Bay* was launched to great fanfare and much media attention in Vancouver. The *Ohana Kai* tried to do a simultaneous launch to make the campaign feel twice as large, but mechanical issues had them turn back to port again in Hawaii.

The *James Bay* did encounter the Russian fleet, and Zodiacs were launched to move in to protect the whales. Captain John Cormack was in his glory, being aggressive with the killer boats. John had become more than a captain; he was a true Greenpeacer now.

The *James Bay* successfully found and harassed the fleet, but in the end they did not save the whales. The Russians called in their full fleet and slaughtered the whole pod. This was witnessed on film by media and by the crew, and the footage was brought to San Francisco to be released to waiting TV stations.

In the meantime, the *Ohana Kai* continued to be plagued with issues. The worst of it was they had signed a contract and received a good sum of money from ABC for exclusive rights to the whale slaughter footage. ABC was furious when the ship they were on proved to be a lemon, and they demanded the rights to the footage from the *James Bay*. Legal issues abounded and, in the end, as a media event it was a nonstarter. Only two stories were to come out of the entire 8,500-mile voyage, and they received little notice.

When the ship arrived in San Francisco, the media jurisdictional dispute overwhelmed everything. However, another more personal dispute awaited Bob and me. We found out that Pat and Eileen were not going to hand over control of the ship to Bob and me, as promised. They were reneging on our deal. Power corrupts.

Then we got a call from Jean Paul Fortom-Gouin – he needed us in Australia for his Australian Whale Campaign. The gods were on our side all along. It had been the right decision to listen to the signs and step aside months before.

That afternoon, over beers with Pat and Eileen, we asked them one more time if they would let us take over the ship. Once again, they gave us a list of excuses as to why they needed to lead the show. We laughed and said, "That's okay, we're off to Australia."

The gods were still guiding us. An important new – and less onerous – chapter was beginning for Bob, that of being a freelance advocacy activist. He was following his instinct to move on. A beneficent hand was guiding his way.

The Australia campaign was the most immediately successful whale campaign to date. A great group of people awaited us in Oz: Jean Paul Fortom-Gouin, Tom Barber, Jon Lewis, Aline Charney, Pat Farrington and several others, including Chris Pash, who later wrote a book about this incredible expedition called *The Last Whale*.

From the high of the success of this Australia campaign, we flew to Amsterdam, where Bob was featured on a three-day telethon that raised $150,000 for Greenpeace. This sum was exactly what was needed to cover the Greenpeace debt in Vancouver, or it could be used to purchase a ship. Because Greenpeace was now so well known as the wild and crazy protesters taking hair-raising chances at sea, we would never get insurance for a ship again. We knew our days of leasing ships were over. Bob made that agonizing decision and wisely agreed to purchase the ship that Greenpeace London had located, the *Sir William Hardy*, later named the *Rainbow Warrior*. That decision turned into a whole new, intriguing chapter in the life of Greenpeace.

A WHALE OF A MAN

by Chris Pash, with additional material from
Aline Charney Barber and Jean Paul Fortom-Gouin

IT WAS SEPTEMBER 1977, and I was a pimply and unsophisticated journalist from Albany, in Western Australia, having a drink at a long bar, a long way from nowhere, in a small town at the bottom of the world. Bob Hunter was there with Jean Paul Fortom-Gouin, the Frenchman who'd paid Bob and Bobbi's way to Australia to take on that country's last whaling station. Jean Paul, nicknamed "The Phantom" for his ability to appear out of nowhere to fight the bad guys, couldn't believe that at the bar with them was Kase Van Der Gaag, a Dutch-born Australian, and master of the *Cheynes II*, one of three harpoon ships hunting sperm whales in the Southern Ocean off Albany. Kase had just led them a merry dance across the sea, trying to lure the Zodiacs away from the hunt and away from the journalists on board looking for a confrontation story.

The cold, weary activists had dragged themselves into the Esplanade Hotel, only to find the whaler waiting for them. The whaler had the faster ship and had reached port before them.

They put aside the day's confrontation to talk. The activists talked about how the sperm whale had the biggest brain on the Earth; the way the whales talk to each other; and the way they catch those big squid. You need speed, and the sperm whale is a slow-moving animal – they must work the hunt together. And then they pointed to the cruelty of using harpoons to kill. Kase knew they were right. He'd once used 11 harpoons to kill a single whale.

"Bob Hunter was a nice guy," Kase told me. "We made a pact: I would stop whaling if he would stop the seal kill in Canada. That was the thing, Albany was a small place where they could easily get press coverage, yet tuna fishermen kill 250,000 dolphins a year in purse nets well out at sea and out of sight. Nothing was said in America about that atrocity because it was big money. It's easy to attack a small whaling company, get coverage, and get the reporters. But I did like Bob Hunter. He meant well."

Jean Paul: "Kase was pissed off because we called them 'sons of bitches' on our radio, which he was monitoring. He said it was a job, just another fishery. It was not a hostile talk; he explained his position and we explained ours. No one convinced the other."

The three men continued to meet during the campaign, discarding their daytime battles to drink and talk. One night, Kase took them to his house. The drinking was heavy, and he woke the next day to find a cheque on the table. He remembered the protesters had talked of buying him a ship so he could sail the world and stamp out whaling. They argued that he had the skills as a seaman, the knowledge of a whaler, and he would be perfect. He jumped into his car and took the cheque back. He couldn't do it. This was his community after all, but internally he was in conflict; his mind was quickly changing on the morality of the hunt.

The campaign had started a month before when Bob and Bobbi Hunter arrived in Australia. The plan was to replicate Greenpeace's action in the North Pacific against the Soviet whaling fleet, using Zodiac inflatables to place people between the whales and the harpoons – human shields. The goal was to win newspaper headlines and lead broadcast bulletins to place further community pressure on politicians, adding to the growing wave of public opinion against whaling. Jean Paul saw Australia as a weak link in the world of whaling; flipping Australia to a pro-whale nation could turn the tide worldwide.

Bob and Bobbi were greeted by a diverse group of people, many of them inspired by Greenpeace. Among them was Jonny Lewis, a photographer who became the Australian spokesman; American, Pat Farrington; Australian architect, Tom Barber; and American, Aline Charney, who had arrived in Australia via a yacht trip across the Pacific.

Aline: "Bob and Bobbi had jet lag, and they really had no idea what they were coming into."

There was also talk at the time about a film on Greenpeace, with Robert Redford to play Bob Hunter. Bob told Jonny Lewis, "I'd prefer Woody Allen."

They found themselves in a road convoy driving across Australia. Close to 4000 km of seemingly endless road, some of it a treeless plane, carrying equipment including outboard motors and two Zodiacs. Bob and Bobbi gave the campaign a huge kick along. "They connected our campaign to the rest of the world, giving it more credibility," said Aline. "Without them, it would have been just home-grown Aussie stuff. It gave us a form of legitimacy, and it also helped start Greenpeace in Australia."

Arriving in Albany, Bob attracted the press who had gathered in the small coastal town on the promise of confrontation with the whalers.

When asked about the prospect of violence, Bob replied, "We're peace-crazed."

Bob used his knowledge and his way with people to manage the media. He talked their language, and he was always one step ahead of them. As Bobbi says, he was a great manipulator.

We staged a land protest at the whaling station. Bob, Bobbi and some press were arriving at the station by Zodiac. The locals thought they were nuts – the waters of that bay were known for huge white pointer sharks. The land protest suddenly looked dangerous when local workers, backed by a bikie group, arrived to counterprotest. The answer to that was to get everyone holding hands, singing, chanting and hugging. In the end, the protest broke up without major incident.

The direct action followed over the next two weeks with early morning launches of the Zodiacs from Middleton Beach. Lying in wait for the whaling ships to depart, they then followed in their wake. It was more seat-of-the-pants than a slick operation. They picked up skills and tactics as they went along. Bob had experience, but that had been in a different ocean, launching Zodiacs from ships not from the shore in Australia. If anything went wrong, they were alone.

Albany resident Keith Ford: "They've either got guts and conviction, or they were stupid...probably all three."

Jean Paul: "I am a yacht captain from way back, and I knew what we were doing was risky. The area is close to the Roaring Forties, with big winds and waves. I was preoccupied all the time that no one got in trouble. Bob Hunter went out, Tom, Jonny Lewis, me, and others. We could not see land, but I wasn't worried about getting lost. I was worried about the engine breaking down and drifting away into the open seas. We were pretty lucky. There were big, long swells, but not really rough."

Bob and Jean Paul's main outboard did break down during one trip. They had to motor back using a tiny 15-horsepower engine. It took hours, crawling up and down the huge troughs of waves. They got used to drinking rum and eating chocolate at sea. But they kept going out.

Aline: "It was so spontaneous, and that's what made it even more altruistic. It came from the heart."

Aline kept a diary at that time: *Bob and Bobbi are in a motel down the way, soon we'll be up and out the door for another round of the whaling boats. The weather's making it possible. This is what we've been working for, taking the Zodiacs out, interfering non-violently with the chaser boats, getting in the way of the harpoons, making our presence felt. The elements are against us. One thing I've learned, to deal with Mother Nature, to deal with the ocean and sea, is to confront it, to relate with it, which must be done from a position of respect.*

Harpoons flew close as the 16-foot Zodiacs zigzagged to put the harpooner off his aim. Tom Barber, an Australian voice, went on national radio, the ABC. Prompted and schooled by Bob, Tom talked up the incident, creating dialogue and media coverage.

Aline's diary: *Telephone going, media reporters, TV station interviews, amazing press coverage, front pages. This as a result of the experience Greenpeace brought to us via Bob and Bobbi Hunter.*

She remembers being in a pub in Albany with Bob when one of the workers from the whaling station smashed a beer bottle under our noses. The incident made it clear what some of the locals thought about those trying to shut down the whaling operations.

Bob laughed when he heard that the whaling company's public relations manager, thinking it was a good idea, allowed journalists to view Greenpeace at work from the decks of the whale ships.

"All that happened was they were horrified by the poor whales being slaughtered," Bobbi said. "That got out onto the wire services, and everybody thought – you're doing that? They did our job for us. It was great. Bob bought the PR guy a couple of beers. We'd already received a huge amount of attention all over the world. The Russian campaign was the first. Then Australia second."

Aline: "I feel very proud. I think it made a little bit of a difference. And with Bob, he was wonderful, a good guy. He made a big difference in the world."

Jean Paul: "Bob was a prince, and his wife Bobbi a princess. I had a lot of respect for them."

The brief campaign had a significant impact along with work by other groups, including Project Jonah, which managed to secure a federal government inquiry into whales and whaling. Headed by a judge, Sir Sydney Frost, the inquiry recommended that whaling be stopped.

At the start of that inquiry, a year after the direct action in Albany, the whaling company announced it would close. The market for its sperm whale oil, the most valuable bit of the catch, had collapsed, influenced by the international anti-whaling campaign. Australia became a strong pro-whale country by joining the call for a global stop to whaling.

At the 30th anniversary of Greenpeace Australia, most of the original crew reconnected in Sydney, and it was as if time had stood still. Rainbow Warriors share a common heart. Bobbi and a few others flew to Albany, and she raised a glass with Kase Van Der Gaag, the former whaler turned whale crusader, and talked of the interesting juncture in their lives three decades earlier.

MY BROTHER TOO

by Teri Innes

1969 WAS A STRANGE YEAR at the end of a strange decade. We had gone from the *Leave it to Beaver* mentality to Woodstock. How things had changed in ten years. 1969 was also the year that I first heard the name Bob Hunter.

The world was chaotic at the time, as anyone who lived during the '60s knows. It was hard to make sense of anything, but Bob Hunter had taken on the monumental task of trying to do just that.

I remember sitting at the dining room table when my brother Tom came rushing in, newspaper in hand, saying excitedly, "You have to read this guy...he's amazing!" The guy he was referring to was Bob Hunter.

Bob was writing for the *Vancouver Sun*, trying to make sense of the confusion. His column reflected the philosophies of the Left, the hippies: possessions did not rule; being happy wasn't based on what you owned but on who you were. Tom found a kindred spirit in Bob. My brother had a profound mind. He loved history and was extremely interested in what was happening all around us at that time. He was four years older than me, but we had always been close. We spent countless hours discussing current events and pondering the state of the world. I always considered Tom to be a genius in his own right. In discovering Bob Hunter, he felt he had found someone who thought the same way he did.

On August 29, 1972, my sister Bobbi showed up at my door at about 6 a.m., and I remember how happy I was to see her. Then she told me that our brother, my best friend, was gone. Tom was just 23 years old. He had died instantly in a motorcycle accident. We collapsed into each other's arms. I remember being in a state of shock.

He was the only son in a family of six offspring. Arriving at the family home, we found the whole family in the same state of shock. Bobbi arranged the funeral, as my parents weren't capable of making any decisions.

By 1974, Bobbi had left her husband, Myron, and was living in a houseboat in False Creek, directly down the hill from my place. She wasn't alone in this funky new home; she was living with Bob Hunter. This was the first time I had met him, and I found Bob fascinating. He had a great smile, a ceaseless sense of humour, and an acute understanding of the world around us.

Fast forward to early 1975. I had just returned from Ontario and decided to go to Jericho Beach, along with throngs of others, to greet the Greenpeace boat on its return from its first whale protest. When the boat pulled up to the dock, it unloaded a ragtag group of hippies. Bob was the journalist on board who had been sending out stories of their anti-whaling adventures. Now he was on a stage giving messages to the crowd as Bobbi was telling me the great news that Bob was soon to become my brother-in-law.

Bobbi and Bob's wedding took place in 1976 in a field in Ioco and in the Ioco town hall. We had lived in the house beside the hall many years before and spent countless hours playing in the field when we were children.

I worked at Greenpeace when Bob was president and was always introduced as Bob Hunter's sister-in-law, never as Teri. My first day turned out to be the day Bob returned from Newfoundland after the seal hunt protest. Bobbi had hired me to run the Greenpeace lottery.

I also ended up moving into the basement suite of Bobbi and Bob's rented home. Bob brought some happiness back into my life and the life of our grieving family. We often took their boat the *Astral* up Indian Arm, marvelling at the beauty of the landscape we had seen many times before, but it always seemed new and more breathtaking when seeing it with Bob.

I stayed on at Greenpeace for a while after Bobbi and Bob's departure in 1977. The Greenpeace president was now Patrick Moore. Greenpeace moved out of the original office, out of the hippie zone, down the hill to a newer, bigger and more expensive office.

The atmosphere of the office changed noticeably once Bob was gone. The positivity was replaced by resentment. The office staff was still working for minimum wage, as they had always been. Pat Moore brought in the corporate mentality. He was an executive and felt he should be paid as such. He was the boss, and we were the minions. Rumours flew that he was making $35,000 to $40,000 a year. In today's dollars that would be about $150,000 a year, but there was no way to verify that the office gossip was true. Nevertheless, gossip can be destructive to morale and is often based on some form of truth.

Greenpeace was losing its appeal, and I left in 1979.

Bob and Bobbi started their company called Sunnyside Communications, aptly named for the road they now lived on in the village of Anmore. Bob was now freelancing from his little cabin at the back of the property. He had his phone, computer, modem, files and desk set up back there. He could write and send his work over the modem. He had a great setup. Bob's routine was to rise about 11 a.m, grab some food, get dressed, grab a beer, grab a joint and head off to the cabin to write. I worked as his assistant from about 1982 until 1985. I did the bookkeeping, scoured the newspapers for articles of interest and did the filing and typing.

We did our fair share of drinking in those days. Bob was always a lover of a good brew. I remember one heart-to-heart conversation when I told Bob how much my brother had marvelled at Bob's writing and how he had told me that I had to read Bob Hunter. This conversation brought out some deep emotions. It was cathartic. We both cried and felt much closer. I realized the loss of my brother had affected Bob deeply as well. As it turned out, Bob regretted the fact that he never had a chance to have Tom in his life.

So there it is, life gone full circle. From my brother introducing me to Bob's work to me telling Bob about my brother's admiration for him.

Bob and Bobbi moved to Toronto in 1988, but they kept in close contact with the family. In the fall of 2004, Bob and Bobbi came to Vancouver for a Greenpeace event. My sister Pat had a party at her beautiful home for Bob to allow him to mingle with his closest friends. Bob had been sick for quite a while. He had been trying every cure out there to battle his cancer, but nothing worked. He felt lousy, but he soldiered through.

I remember him smiling and making everyone feel as comfortable around him as they could.

The next day, Bob emerged from his bedroom around noon, looking weary. He gave me a copy of his new book and inscribed it to me. When he waved goodbye to us, I realized that might be the last time I would ever see him. I drove away with tears running down my face.

I was right. I never did see Bob again. He died May 2, 2005, and I lost my other brother.

THE *ANMORE TIMES*

by Linda Weinberg

I MET BOB AND BOBBI in the summer of 1980. They had just moved with their children to Anmore – down a country way from us. It was a warm August day at the annual Ioco picnic on the lawn of the company town's former bowling green. I knew he was Bob Hunter, the former president of Greenpeace and, more relevant for me, a columnist for the *Vancouver Sun*. He looked to be the most interesting person at the picnic, so I gathered my courage and walked up and introduced myself.

Not long after that first picnic meeting, as I was making my run up Anmore hill from Ioco, I saw Bob and Bobbi, along with their baby, Willy, and Bob's young daughter, Justine, sitting on the sundeck of their first home in Anmore. The house had been the Innes family home until Bobbi's parents had built and moved into a new home two doors up the hill.

I hadn't seen Bob and Bobbi since the picnic, and I thought to myself, "Oh hell, no time better than the present." So I turned and marched with purpose down the driveway and yelled, "Helllooo!" No one noticed at first. "HELLOOO!!"

Bob and Bobbi's slightly bewildered faces appeared above me. I laughed and said, "Hi, I'm Linda, your neighbour, and I'm going to be your new best friend."

Over 40 years have passed, and those words still stand the test of time. The four of us really hit it off! Bobbi was smart and funny, and also loved to laugh and to drink wine, and we became good friends as well as neighbours. We knew each other's children, we often ate dinners together, and we talked and talked.

It wasn't long before our shared interests led to a successful protest in our neck of the woods. My husband, Hal, read a 1982 planning report on the expansion of an LNG transfer terminal just around the corner from our pristine area. The report made a case for an expansion project. Something had to be done; there was potential for a catastrophic explosion that could kill thousands and destroy property for miles around.

After much wine, and much more conniving, we came up with a protest plan. We talked late into the night. We concluded that the big fear for locals would be that new people would not want to move to the area with the plant being built, and therefore property values would go down. We knew it was cynical, but we also knew it was true.

So Bob wrote an alarming insert piece for our newly formed local paper, the *Anmore Times*, inciting fear about lost property values, and I made sure that this notice got to every doorstep in the area. The *Anmore Times* was a Weinberg/Hunter creation, put together to highlight this local potential ecological catastrophe. Justine, a budding journalist, had her first published newspaper article in the *Anmore Times*.

A meeting had been arranged to have local politicians and representatives from the LNG terminal come to defend the expansion project at a local school. To our surprise, hundreds of people attended. The plant expansion was never built. This astonishing success with the LNG plant protest led us to other community initiatives.

We talked in our newly renovated bedroom, in their basement, on our back lawn, on their side deck. We ate and drank and hammered out a philosophical concept of what we wanted to create for those who lived in Anmore. It was called "The Anmore Concept," and it was an attempt to create a semi-rural environment for folks who wanted a country life.

There was a lot of joy in our shared times, but as you get closer to someone you start to see the cracks. Bob had begun writing what he thought would be his breakthrough book, a blockbuster Canadian novel, only to have the editor die and the next editor fail him. That book was going nowhere. He was making little as a writer at a local North Shore community paper, which must have felt like a huge step down in stature and a blow to his writer's ego. He was still viewed as an icon, yet he was living from paycheque to paycheque.

One night when we'd all had too much wine, he confessed that he'd once tried to have himself admitted to the psychiatric ward. The trouble was that once he got in the door, someone asked him, "Hey, aren't you Bob Hunter from Greenpeace?" After admitting he was, he turned around and walked out the door.

He spent all his days thinking about, and writing about, the ills of the world – how to get people to focus on solutions and not on problems. That was Bob – one of those people we could all count on to see the "big picture."

I have a picture of the last time we saw Bob. He is standing on a street corner in downtown Vancouver. He had just been honoured by a Green-peace group. He was already in the midst of the cancer that would soon end his life – and yet we are all still smiling.

BOB'S YOUR UNCLE

by Darren Hunter

I WILL ALWAYS REMEMBER Uncle Bob saying to me, "There are two kinds of people in this world, the Hunters and the Hunted," and then he would laugh and say, "We already know which one you are!" My version of that is, "Would you rather be the hammer or the nail?"

I was adopted by Bob's younger brother, Donald, and his first wife, Shirley. Their son Conrad was 2 years old at the time of my adoption, and we lived in a nice neighbourhood in a comfortable house in Winnipeg. We had all the perks of life – two cars, a boat and snowmobiles – but it didn't feel all that nice. I was just a little kid, and my memories aren't clear, but I was told later that the marriage and family life was full of fighting and unhappiness.

By the time I was 8 years old my parents' marriage had ended. Dad moved away, and my brother and I stayed in the family home with our mother. I'm told I was a rambunctious, difficult boy, and my adopted mother tended to take her anger out on me. The fights became more common, and so I became even more rebellious. It was a vicious circle. By 13, I'd left home to live in friends' basements. The streets of Winnipeg became too much to tolerate, so I decided to head west to try to stay with my dad. At 15, I flew to Vancouver.

On arriving in Vancouver, I discovered that my dad's new wife did not want me. So I was sent to visit Uncle Bob and Aunt Bobbi in the village of Anmore. It didn't take them long to figure out my predicament and without hesitation they welcomed me in. I was so thankful for a place to belong.

I had known Uncle Bob and Aunt Bobbi from an early age because they had come for a few family visits to Winnipeg. After my parents split up, my dad had brought my brother and me out to Vancouver on holidays. I had good memories of my times in Vancouver. We had a great trip out on Uncle Bob's boat, the *Astral*.

In Anmore, I had my own room and was enrolled in the local junior high school. On the first day, there was a bit of difficulty, and I was kicked out of school. Aunt Bobbi finally found a place for me at Como Lake Junior High School, where my cousin had been sent a few years earlier for similar bad behaviour. I guess getting kicked out of school ran in the Hunter family.

Life with Uncle Bob and Aunt Bobbi was very different for me. I felt accepted. I felt someone had my back. I felt like I belonged in the Hunter family. Emily was 1½ and Will was about 7 years old when I moved in. Having more kids in the home didn't really change anything; it was the same constant feeling of being loved.

Having wheels is the biggest thing for a 16-year-old. Bob and Bobbi bought me an old beater to fix up, and then they took turns teaching me how to prepare for my driver's exam. I had been driving since I was 13, but they helped me figure out how to parallel park and how to act during the driver's exam.

I often worked on boat maintenance. By this time, they had a boat called *Venator*, an ancient name for *Hunter*. I helped scrape and paint the hull. But it wasn't all work. Once, Uncle Bob took me out on the boat with a couple of his friends. We headed under the bridges to the open waters of Georgia Strait. Just for thrills, we motored between two huge tankers that were heading for the harbour. The bow waves of the two ships formed a huge pyramid-shaped mountain of water directly in front of us. Bob yelled at me to take the wheel, and to head straight into it. It was mighty rough going up that peak, and the downward motion was even scarier, but we managed it, and we laughed like hell.

It all seemed great, and Bob and Bobbi were great. But what they didn't know was that the call to the streets was inside me. I didn't like school, and I would skip classes and walk around all day before heading home. I remember walking by a Hells Angels' clubhouse near my school and thinking that it looked cool. I eventually got into trouble with the law. Because I was a minor, and there was no legal guardianship established with Bob and Bobbi, I wasn't allowed to stay in BC. I didn't want to disappoint or cause further trouble for Bob and Bobbi. I know now they would have been there for me, but I was a kid, and I was ashamed.

I returned to the streets of Winnipeg and ultimately found a family with the Los Brovos motorcycle club. I bought my first motorcycle in my late teens. I got into some serious trouble while I was a member of the club, and I paid my dues. By the time I was 30, our club had become the first Hells Angels charter in Manitoba.

And then I had a son. Cyrus was born in 1999, and he changed me. I wanted to give him a home, and I wanted him to grow up with a parent who was there for him. I worked so hard to secure custody of my son, and I have raised him on my own since he was a young boy. Cyrus and I live outside the city on a nice property.

I remember how I felt loved and accepted for who I am, and to this day I still think of my Aunt Bobbi as a surrogate mother, a loving person I still turn to for advice and conversation. I remained connected with my Uncle Bob, often going to him for advice.

When Uncle Bob died, I felt a very painful loss. I recall attending Uncle Bob's memorial. It was held at an impressive hall at the University of Toronto. There had to be a thousand people there. I had only known Bob as the centre of our family, but at this gathering I began to understand that he was the centre of a much larger community of people. I learned from the speeches that he had more to do with people caring about the environment than any other person in Canada. I thought to myself, if the premier of the province of Ontario delivers a eulogy at your funeral, you must a big deal.

A few years ago, I took my son to the home in Anmore where I had spent the best years of my young life. It's good to reflect on those times. I pass on to him stories of a great man I am proud to say was my Uncle Bob. As Bob would say, "Bob's Your Uncle."

NO GURUS

by Rex Weyler

IN JULY 1982, Bob Hunter and I travelled to Boulder, Colorado, for the Jack Kerouac Conference, celebrating his impact on American literature on the 25th anniversary of Kerouac's classic *On the Road*. The guest list of Beat-era luminaries included Allen Ginsberg, William Burroughs and scores of other writers. Pundits were calling the event "The Woodstock of the Beats."

Bob and I were covering the event for our respective magazines, but this journey was primarily a pilgrimage. These writers – "the gods and demi-gods of the counterculture," Bob swooned – had inspired us in our own careers. We shared Ginsberg's commitment to subversive literature and to Buddhism. Bob wanted to reconnect with his mentor.

I had met Ginsberg in Colorado while campaigning to close the Rocky Flats nuclear trigger factory. Subsequently, Ginsberg had invited me to the Kerouac event, I extended the invitation to Bob, and we set off from the Vancouver airport, vowing to write our magazine pieces in Kerouac-style spontaneous prose.

At the University of Colorado convention hall in Boulder, Ginsberg – in white shirt and slacks, with an orange tie – greeted us warmly and introduced us to Kerouac's daughter, Jan, under a giant portrait of her father, whose piercing eyes seemed to ponder the milling crowd.

Bob and I sat in the front row as Ginsberg opened the proceedings with Tibetan chants and an appeal to "trust your mind." LSD pioneer Timothy Leary paced the stage, recounting psychedelic adventures and smiling at his recent bride, filmmaker Barbara Blum. Bob rolled his eyes. "Hmm," he whispered, "Leary leers."

Poet Diane di Prima insisted that the microphones be opened "to the people," drawing applause. William Burroughs – the enigmatic author of *Junkie* and *Naked Lunch* – mumbled almost inaudibly, "Political revolutions don't change anything, but art can exert profound change."

Buddhist teacher Chögyam Trungpa, whose Naropa Institute hosted the event, showed up drunk and incomprehensible. Bob acknowledged, "I'm experiencing celebrity fatigue." Ginsberg, however, remained modest and loveable. He took us under his wing and made sure Bob and I got invited to private gatherings, which included a party on Friday night and backstage passes to the Grateful Dead concert at Red Rocks Amphitheater near Boulder.

At the party, Bob and I chatted with Carolyn Cassady, author and wife of the legendary Neal Cassady, and with Ken Kesey, the author of *One Flew over the Cuckoo's Nest* and *Sometimes a Great Notion*. Bob pressed Kesey about what he thought Kerouac contributed to culture and literature. "Jack was a saint," said Kesey. "He soaked up all the loneliness around him. He tried to eradicate sadness. In his books, he never puts anyone down. He only criticizes himself. What an effort of will and heart to do that for 30 years!"

On the way to the Grateful Dead show, Bob and I sat in the back seat with Carolyn Cassady, who shared stories about the night Neal revealed that "Allen was in love with him."

The concert was more than half over as we arrived and heard the closing chorus of the Dead's immortal song "Truckin'." Bob sang along, clearly in good spirits. A Dead roadie ushered us backstage to a place where we could watch the performance.

After the show, Jerry Garcia recognized Bob and me from a few years earlier when he had performed a benefit for Greenpeace in San Francisco. Bob seemed to be enjoying a moment of ecstasy, standing in the warm night, under the stars, trading stories with his literary peers. After the band departed, about two in the morning, we stood on the Red Rocks stage, shouting spontaneous verse to the audience of stars. For an impromptu rhyme with Kesey's "ain't it surprisin'," Bob spoke a line recalled from his father during his childhood: "It's a long way to the horizon!"

A few years earlier, in Vancouver, when we were embroiled in Greenpeace politics, Bob had interviewed Ginsberg and asked the poet how to deal with power. "Let it go," Ginsberg had advised, "before it freezes in your hand." Bob reminded Ginsberg of this advice, now that we had both stepped away from the crush for power within Greenpeace.

Ginsberg replied, "Did I say that? Well, either that or use the power judiciously."

Bob looked stunned, and later fumed, "We gave away the most effective environmental organization on Earth, based on Ginsberg's advice, which he now has altered!"

On the airplane journey home, Bob, still processing his disappointment in Ginsberg's revised advice, shrugged and said, "There are no gurus." He fell silent for a while and then recalled the Neal Cassady proclamation that "your life really is your art."

TACKING RIGHT

by Peter Speck

BOB LOVED BOATS OF ALL KINDS. We spent time on Bob's boat, the *Venator*, in the calm waters of Indian Arm, but in the main we sailed my "stone" sailboat out into what is now called the Salish Sea, where there was more wind. Sometimes.

Bob had famously been on many boats, from fish boats to frigates, in the Greenpeace "armada" of the time. But sailing silently with the wind was new to him, and he took to it.

The *North Shore News*, where we both worked, was a "free" newspaper, entirely supported by advertising. Relationships were very important, so we often sailed with a crew of newspaper advertisers, staff at the *News*, lawyers, accountants, businesspeople, media figures and friends. Captain Bob was very genuine and charming, and people liked his warmth – he was a great ambassador. He also took to keeping the logbook. It was a good fit.

From Bob's log: *A burst of light. Vancouver hit by a fat rainbow that glows fantastically for a long time, silencing even the skeptics, if any can be found – the most incredible view of Vancouver ever! Can't be put into words – the sea ends up as serene as a goddess after orgasm.*

Sometimes when Bob and I sailed alone we'd take a younger deckhand, but when there was just the two of us it was a new kind of fun for two old guys, as we saw ourselves then. We were a Heineken crew in those days, and the hatch in the saloon floor held 48 cans of beer. Sailing could be a thirsty business.

From Bob's log: *The sea has calmed. Jagged sky, spilling pure cosmic light on the blazing gold-flecked waves. A BC ferry goes by off the Sechelt peninsula so awash with light that it blinds the eye. We drink Heinies, break out the sunglasses, and toast poor deckhand Robert, who has been afflicted with a hangover/ seasickness medical event.*

My boat, the *Talofa Lee*, was a ferrocement cutter, 50 feet on deck, a well-built vessel, but very heavy by today's standards. She had the ballast to support a 60-foot mast and a press of sail. While I did most of the deck work, Captain Bob liked to sweat the main up by himself with the winch on the mast. He said the exercise could be marketed as a bust developer and went on to reveal Hunter's Law.

Hunter's Law states: *The secret of selling writing to (middle-aged female) editors is to be boyish and charming and wear tight pants.*

We sailed in the scenic majesty everywhere we went – a small boat in a vast landscape. When the wind gods made it possible, the motor was cut, and we sailed in blissful silence as long as we could. All quiet except for the flutter of the flags and the groans from the autopilot…and the hiss of a beer can opening.

From Bob's log: *Down sails. Crew working with awesome precision, having discussed advertising, war, pestilence, the sea, and – surprisingly! almost nothing about women, or for that matter, ants.*

We motored a lot, which is not an unusual experience on a sailboat, but we never wasted a favourable wind or ignored the crisp rattle of the burgees overhead telling us the wind was here. By the time the main and jibs were up, we would be sweating. Then it was time to tune up the sheets, open another beer, and yarn some more. Bob was a gold mine of conversation.

From Bob's log: *Set off in the kind of weather that God invented the biosphere for. Entire crew feeling smug about living on the West Coast. Flat calm. No wind. Point Grey feeding into diaphanous blueness. Snow a-glitter on the mountains. Sunlight stroking our flesh like the breath of a lovely woman in love.*

Bob and boats were pretty happy together. One night we were alone on my sailboat at a mooring on Pender Island. It was a gorgeous night, cool, clear and calm. The sea was like glass, reflecting the stars overhead. We drank a bottle of rum, smoked a few joints and had a very special talk. Now that I'm an old man, I realize just how meaningful that evening was. Very rare.

He was someone special to talk to on a one-to-one basis – nonjudgmental, kind, deeply spiritual and sensitive. Our evening was a heart-to-heart of deeply shared thoughts, but we also talked about the old radio shows we grew up listening to at night on our crystal sets. We pondered the jingles that we still remembered and laughed a lot. Bob had just finished a screenwriting job in Hollywood. He didn't like Hollywood much and regretted going to work there. He had also gone to Cuba to vacation with his family. He offered a joke: How can you tell the difference between a Canadian and a canoe? A canoe tips.

Later that night, he stated his unique take on reincarnation: "Maybe the reason we get recalled is because of some fuck-up at the design stage..."

We closed up the fusty cabin sometime around midnight, hung around on deck looking in wonder at the amazing star display, then gingerly loaded ourselves into the canoe to paddle the few yards to shore.

It was miraculously dark. Phosphorescence filled the sea as a thousand stars filled the sky. We were enthralled and stopped paddling. Dipping one's hand in the water made the luminescence glow, while the gentle motion of the paddles made arcs of light in the sea.

One minute we were spellbound, gawking, and the next minute the canoe had tipped, dropping us into the freezing salt water. It was a bit sobering and frightening, but we had drifted close to the beach. I was very pleased to feel sand under my feet. We started laughing again.

As we sloshed ashore, Bob said, "There's the design flaw. They could have given us the ability to walk on water."

NO TURNING BACK

by Bobbi Hunter

"GET OUT!" I SAID. "Get out now before we say anything we'll regret! I need some space from you."

He looked at me, confused.

I snarled at him. "You love it here so much in BC. It's raining, Bob. So what? That's BC. Love the rains too. Get out and give me a few moments!"

He slowly opened the door of our family van and stepped onto the bleak dirt road. He peered in at me with anger, confusion, helplessness and obedience. I turned my head away from his stare and started driving, looking into the rear-view mirror at a lonely figure standing in the middle of the road.

His mood swings, depression and inability to make decisions were at their worst point. He was driving both of us crazy. It had been ten years since he left Greenpeace, yet in his heart he'd never left. It was a soul-wrenching period of limbo for Bob. He disliked being a freelance writer. As he'd once described it, "There's no freedom, you aren't your own boss, you have a multitude of bosses."

Bob had left his job writing a high-level newspaper column at the *Vancouver Sun* to lead Greenpeace. Now he couldn't get any position in any major establishment paper because he was no longer considered unbiased. So he slaved on as a freelancer from one disappointing compromise in his writing to another. He was losing his self-respect as a writer and as an eco-warrior.

We had a rule in this hardscrabble new career of his: you must always have at least ten irons in the fire in order to keep working every day. So when Moses Znaimer, a friend and ally from CityTV in Toronto, suggested Bob submit his name for a place in Norman Jewison's Canadian Centre For Advanced Film Studies, the first film school in Canada, Bob and I had to have one more of our epic struggles. After much arguing, I held my ground, and he finally accepted the idea of putting in his application. Only because I told him it was unlikely that he would get accepted. I told him, "Just try, no harm in trying."

A month later, he opened the envelope with much hesitation; once it was opened, he looked extremely upset. His kids, Justine and Conan, although grown up now, lived here in Vancouver. He had left them before, how could he leave again? He loved BC. He loved our farm. Moving was difficult enough, let alone all the way to Toronto. And anyway, who would trade BC for Toronto? On and on this miasma of doubt swirled in his brain. He didn't know what to do – the Norman Jewison film school had accepted him.

For my part, I'd always wanted to move away from where I had been born and experience a new city. But the most important thing for me was that I wanted the old Bob back. He needed to be energized and appreciated but, most crucially, he needed to be having an effect again. He was dying inside. He had given up trying to get his novel *Long Way to the Horizon* published and was beginning what would eventually become his magnum opus, *2030: Thermageddon*. The drive to have an impact on the emerging horrors of climate change was strong in him. He was feeling tortured that he had no platform to effect change. He felt useless. I knew I was right about this. He desperately needed a reboot. I understood that Bob sometimes needed theatre to get the message. In leaving him on that lonely road, my statement to him was, *you stay in BC, and you will continue to stay in this dreary space you have created.*

A half-hour later, I drove back to find an extremely cold, totally soaked, but clear-eyed Bob. He jumped in, rubbed his hands in front of the heater fan, turned to me, smiling, and said, "So when do we leave?"

A few months later, in early February 1988, after renting out our home, packing 17 supersized suitcases, selling one car, shipping the other smaller car loaded with household effects by rail, and renting a new home near the Toronto office of my employer (who had kindly given me a transfer), we were all set to leave.

One Friday, just a few days before we were to depart for Toronto, I was driving home from work, looking forward to my weekend with my family. It was on the last three-kilometre drive up the hill to our home that I noticed a sign on the road. It said *The MWMB Festival Ahead* with an arrow. I wondered what that was. Then at the next turn there was another similar sign still leading in our direction. I was anxious to get home and ask Bob who would be putting on a festival in our village, and why in February? Then, at the last turn to the last hill before our house, I saw signs and balloons.

The signs spelled out, in huge letters, H A P P Y 40th B I R T H D A Y B O B B I.

My heart was pounding with joy. I steered around the last turn and there were cars parked all the way up the hill. They had left just enough room for me to park. Bob was there with his huge smile and his arms opened wide, and I rushed to his embrace in tears.

This was Bob's theatre. It was his celebration and his acceptance of the start of a new path and new campaign in our lives. Friends, family and loved ones, nearly 70 people in all, were there. They were there for the birthday, for the Migrating Whale Medicine Band Festival, and they were there to see us off. The next generation of our tribe, the young offspring of our friends, were all there, soaking in the fun of the party. We had all been through so much together; we had grown, matured, procreated and felt that we had done something special with our lives. It was a celebration. We had much to be thankful for. No one was upset at this gathering, as everyone had been told we would be back in a year after Bob finished film school.

Two weeks later, on a bone-chillingly cold February evening, Bob, Will, Emily and I emerged with our massive pile of personal effects at Pearson Airport and hailed three taxis to take us to our new destiny.

This was another major turning point in our lives, and we instinctually knew there was no turning back.

THREE
FLOWING

PHILOSOPHER OF DEPTH

by Moses Znaimer

THE CONTOURS OF BOB'S CAREER are pretty well known; in any case, others will lay out that chronology more fully than I can. What I can offer to better fill out his story is how a postwar Jewish refugee and displaced person, born in Tajikistan to parents on the run from Nazis and raised on St. Urbain Street and the Montreal Main, with a degree from Harvard, met a Catholic-raised, profoundly Canadian mix of Anglo and Franco bloodlines, from St. Boniface, Manitoba, bonded over a love of new media, and shared a talent for exploiting television to engage in and publicize Daring Deeds in a Noble Cause.

The first time I met Bob was in the Greenpeace offices on 4th Avenue in Vancouver's West End in 1975 or '76. I had come upon them by chance – a handwritten sign in the window – and decided to go in on a whim. Once there, I asked to see the guy in charge, and out came this shaggy, loose and lanky fellow whom I recognized from a few news stories as Hunter, Saviour of the Whales.

"Hello," I said, "I'm fascinated by what you are doing, and how you're doing it, and I think I have something that can help."

"Oh ya?" he said, "what's that?"

"A TV station," I said, "maybe two!"

Fifteen minutes later, we were halfway down the next block at a bar called the Bimini, beginning what turned out to be an unusual, unlikely and very productive friendship.

But first, you need to know two things about me: In 1972, I had managed, against all odds, to get a low-power, low-cost, locally focused and wildly underfinanced independent over-the-air UHF TV station on the air in Toronto: the first of its kind in Canada. We had opened to derision and laughter and were still struggling to keep our understaffed and unconventionally programmed little ship afloat. But already the public could discern something different in CityTV's look and feel and focus; all of it delivered by an odd gang of newcomers, who were beginning to gain attention for their street-level style and energy, and diverse multicultural and multiracial on-air talent. So when a couple of years later the broadcast regulator announced that it was going to open a similar new licence opportunity in Vancouver, I thought, "Why not give it a shot?" Never mind that I had no money and that my backers in Toronto had neither the vision nor the inclination to pony up for a second CityTV station so soon!

So that's how I found myself in Van that day, without contacts or connections, making cold calls in search of capital and community support, and hoping that one thing might lead to another.

Because CityTV's entertainment offering featured old movies, I had begun to go to Hollywood to meet the studios. There, in 1975, at a party whose purpose or host I can no longer recall, I picked up a book lying on a coffee table called *Mind in the Waters* by Joan McIntyre, and was enthralled. Instead of hustling business or dates, I found myself spending the evening in a corner, ignoring the crowd, engrossed in a natural world of water and wonder completely foreign to me.

I'm an urban jungle kid, who grew up without plants or pets. I understood and was comfortable with asphalt and concrete; grass, real grass, made me nervous. To be so taken by the plight of the world's largest animal was completely out of character for me, and so I sought to learn more, and that brought me to notice a madcap group of what seemed like anarchists and hippies challenging Russian whalers and their explosive harpoons on the high seas!

Now we flash forward – a day, a week, or a subsequent visit months later, I can't quite recall. I'm on Bob's boat, and he's got me out on the water. All the times we'd been meeting, Bob was always puffing away and putting it away – he liked his beer and smokes – while I drank ginger ale or coffee with Bailey's. But out on the boat he brought out some marijuana – which was still illegal then – and proceeded to toke up a storm, offering me some. I've never even smoked tobacco, so getting anything down wasn't, and still isn't, easy for me. In fact, I was actually super straight when it came to alcohol and tobacco and, on top of that, I was trying to get a warrant from the Crown in connection with that new TV licence, so I was also a little paranoid. But after coughing my little heart out, what with all those vapours wafting about, I did manage to get some of it down, and, suddenly, I was running with the porpoises in the dazzling light. It was all quite magical and memorable; and that was when we became pals.

At the CRTC hearing that ultimately led to the licensing of CKVU Vancouver, I, the son of a waitress and a clerk in a shoe store, was denounced as a member of the Eastern Establishment and lost the licence to a local group. So my fairly regular contact with Bob began to wane, even as his fame and impact began to grow. His brilliant stunts and strategic shift from bombs to whales to environmentalism had grown Greenpeace into the world's largest ecological organization almost overnight.

As all that was coming together, Bob and Bobbi began to visit Toronto quite often, and would stay at my place. That's when I began to float the idea of his joining CityTV as the world's first ecology reporter. His answer was *No*, and *No* again, because he was committed to The Cause. But then internal struggles fuelled by the organization's explosive growth saw him walk away from Greenpeace and retreat to a cabin in an obscure little company town on the North Shore called Ioco, ironically named after the Imperial Oil Company. There he mouldered for a while, a general without a horse, a man at low ebb, bereft of purpose and activity, until one day I went out there by bus with another great idea. Because he so effortlessly spilled out torrents of words that read like a screenplay, I suggested, "Why not come east and try your hand at the movies, because I think I can get you a spot in the new Canadian Film School that is just forming in Toronto." A year later, he gave that up because learning to make "cinema" on the old E.P. Taylor Estate on Bayview was just too damn slow and genteel. That's when he finally succumbed to the medium that had propelled him to stardom.

Growing up, most of my peers found their role models in sports, movies or pop music, but I found mine in poets, novelists, journalists and revolutionaries who didn't just describe history but engaged robustly in it. That he wrote such vivid reportage and had a flair for camera-friendly stunts has obscured the fact that Bob was also a philosopher of depth and foresight. And, like my heroes Malraux, Koestler and Camus, Bob got into the thick of things, demonstrating a crazy combination of recklessness and courage, a closet intellectual who (like me) read widely and quoted well, but who understood that it was Action (and Television!) that created awareness in society.

Getting in front of those harpoons, or standing fast in the face of icebreakers and angry sealers, was nuts. It would never have crossed my mind to do it, which is why I admired him so and determined to help in the unique way that I could.

After I was forced out of City/MUCH/BRAVO! etc., I reflected on the way that he and I both had been separated from our greatest creation and instrument. But I had no delusions that the many people who mourned my departure, including my fiercest loyalists, would walk the plank into exile with me. Indeed, I expected nothing of the kind. They had careers and families to protect, money that had to be earned. I thought it would be best to distance myself, and them, from the tension that would inevitably arise from rehashing old events and wounds while they had to continue to work with, and get along with, those who had done me and my channels and stations wrong.

And so it was with Bob, the passionate Guru Adventurer, who was also a devoted family man with a wife and partner he adored and depended on, two kids and a suburban home with a pool to maintain. Not to mention the many pleasures of local fame as the guy who did his daily *Paper Cuts* review of the morning press in his ratty bathrobe (one of my better ideas, since, at first, Bob had hated the thought of getting up early, and worried about looking too made-up and polished). So, once again, we lost touch, which is too bad, because had I learned of his prostate cancer sooner, I think I might have offered more assistance than the mere money I provided toward the end, so he could make his Hail Mary trips to Mexico, looking to alternative medicine for the salvation that never came.

For all his gregariousness, Bob was also a loner, a writer happy with his thoughts, like me a contrarian by reflex, wary of dogma and not easily given to toeing the line, any line. As much as it would have gratified him to see the rolling takeover of climate change consciousness in both the culture and the economy, I think the man I knew and admired would have resisted the conversion of environmentalism, as expressed in saving whales and seals and giving warnings about warming, into an inflexible religion, complete with punishment for blasphemy, enforced conformity and compelled speech, social media lynching and cancel culture. I don't think Bob would have gone along with all that. Bob Hunter didn't have to hector or browbeat or command, because he could persuade, and what he achieved is far greater than being the founder of a company, a channel or a style. He was the principal founder of a great movement that has galvanized millions in defence of the planet, and still does so to this very day.

NO WRITING IN SCRIPTWRITING

by Peter O'Brian

I FIRST MET BOB HUNTER in 1988 on the terrace of Windfields, the mansion that serves as the home of the Canadian Film Centre. It was the film centre's first year of operation. I was its executive director, and Bob had won one of its 12 annual positions or residencies, in his case to study screenwriting.

I first knew Bob as a folk hero of the environmental movement and had seen him on television, so I was a little nervous about meeting the Great Canadian. I didn't need to be.

His first words were a question: "Don't you just love management?"

Right away he recognized that I was taking time away from filmmaking to try to "herd cats" and manage an institution, and simultaneously he was sharing his own experiences of trying to do the same thing at Greenpeace. I was impressed and delighted.

He gave me an infectious smile and giggled as if we were co-conspirators in the human comedy who both knew that the world was a wonderful place, as long you overlooked that people, despite being infinitely interesting, were thoroughly untrustworthy.

He took me (and everyone he met) to be at his own level, which felt like a huge compliment and a great honour. I loved him instantly, and we were friends as if we always had been.

At the end of that first year, Norman Jewison, our fearless founder, came to a celebration lunch for the 12 resident filmmakers. Over coffee, Norman asked each one to speak about what they had learned in their year at CFC. This took at least half an hour as the directors, writers and producers gave their thoughtful answers. Finally, Norman arrived in front of Bob.

"Well, I've learned lots, Norman, and thanks for the opportunity. But the most important thing is that in screenwriting you can't write, 'The future doesn't look too bright,' you have to say, 'Tomorrow ain't worth shit.'"

Norman Jewison looked stunned. He was speechless. Then the shrieks of laughter began and went on for minutes, it seemed. When the hilarity started to die down, Bob's own chortles fuelled another round of it. It was a great scene and a vintage Bob Hunter moment: irreverent, brilliant and true.

ECO-MAN

by Stephen Hurlbut

IN SEPTEMBER 1971, as a 22-year-old Ryerson University student, I was part of a mass demonstration in downtown Toronto in front of the US consulate. We were protesting the American nuclear tests on Amchitka Island. I was on the street because Bob Hunter was at the epicentre of that event. He was on board the *Phyllis Cormack*, a fishing trawler steaming toward the heart of the detonation site. Bob, a master communicator, was crafting "mindbombs" on his typewriter, and the shock wave pushed my friends and me onto University Avenue.

Seventeen years later we would finally meet.

It was late fall 1988 when Hunter walked into CityTV. I was the vice-president of news at CityTV Toronto, and, at the time, my boss, Moses Znaimer, was the ubiquitous Wizard of Oz and executive producer of all things television for our owners, CHUM Ltd. Moses had just hired Bob Hunter, a co-founder of Greenpeace, to join my newsroom and report on the environment.

While the ecosystem was generating news in 1988, the dialogue was not then at the crisis level it is today, but I knew I was looking at a visionary, a man who had changed the world's narrative on the living world. This new hire was more than a little prescient.

Hunter had walked into a newsroom that was progressive, inclusive and set a dynamic creative bar. We were outliers in the news business, the cool, "street" news team. An impressive collection of misfits, renegades and rebels; Bob Hunter would fit in perfectly.

Bob was beginning his third act. He was 47, fresh out of Norman Jewison's Canadian Centre For Advanced Film Studies, and his resume brimmed with the accomplishments of two lifetimes. He was an original, his first act a world-renowned eco-warrior and the second, a very accomplished author. Neither of these past lives was small, and both required passion, vision and the courage to man up. A third act, on-air at CityTV, should be a snap for the man who had stood tall in the face of an atomic bomb and a Norwegian icebreaker.

Television news is a service industry, and the harsh reality is that you deliver or you're gone. Vulnerable, naked to the world's judgment, you either have what it takes to be on air or you don't. Credentials as an environmental icon will get you in the door, but the audience doesn't relate to credentials, they relate to the person. The business of holding an audience demands you have that elusive "it," the ability to connect, and Hunter overflowed with "it." In a very short time, he found his TV legs, and his presence resonated on screen. He communicated brilliantly, with the added values of depth, intelligence and integrity. A rarity, a man rich in both personality and character, here was someone who should be on television.

An enduring image I have of Bob is of the day he first walked into the newsroom. Uniformed in slacks, sports jacket and tie, clean shaven and clean cut – his long hair had been hacked off. Always future casting, he was lugging two large metal suitcases, one for his mobile phone and the other for a barely portable computer. He sat down, plugged in for Act III, Scene I, and was off. Bob wasn't looking for any major power move in his life, just a return to his working roots as a beat reporter covering the state of his passion – the relentless attack on the planet. Within a few short months Bob had found his comfort zone; the jacket and tie were long gone, the hair was back on its way to his shoulders and his newsroom friendships were many. In particular, the news camera folk loved Bob, and that's the highest bar set in any newsroom.

Hunter was now "camera meat," the apt cameraperson label for all on-air staff. His "daily beat" was recycling, air and water pollution, species under siege, green space degradation, global warming and the enduring stupidity of political short-sightedness, and on and on and on. A big beat requiring a big man. A few of our producers, with respect and affection, started calling him Eco-Man, and for the final chapter of his working life Hunter had found a home.

Bob did important work for us. He brought to the newsroom a well-honed and impressive skill set. He was a gifted writer, and an excellent public speaker with extensive journalism experience. Covering the environment every day is akin to constantly shouting "fire" in a theatre, but Hunter did not proselytize doom, he charmed us into awareness. A master of his message, Bob blended his newsman's chops with his heart's empathy as an eco-warrior, and into that mix he injected a sharp, intelligent mind. He decluttered, distilled and purified truly one of the most important stories of our age.

Hunter's gifts found another perfect stage when his editorial scope was expanded. The concept was called "Paper Cuts." Every morning Bob reviewed the national and local morning papers, cherry-picking items of interest and controversy and then adding his truly unique commentary. He did this for our 5:30 to 9 morning show, *Breakfast Television*. Five days a week at 5 a.m., dressed in his bathrobe and brandishing a yellow highlighter, Bob would scour the papers and showcase his take on the news of the day. These daily sardonic editorials were a hit. There was a playful wit at work here.

Once the editorial was in the can, Bob would grab a few more hours of sleep before hopping on transit for an hour, numbing his way to the newsroom for his day job. He would lament to me that the "number one rule in television is to get parking," which he never did. Hunter rode the TTC most mornings, and that mindless transit time was something he had to endure. However, his distaste for transit flipped once *Paper Cuts* was established. As he transferred from bus to subway to streetcar, he was affectionately hailed as "that TV guy in the bathrobe." Bob was energized by these random encounters with strangers. These were fresh fans, and he was released from the burden of Greenpeace. His fellow travellers didn't care about his past; this was their Hunter, their Bob in the bathrobe, who helped them both understand and laugh at the day ahead.

Hunter's TV life was a busy one. His daily coverage of the ecology beat and morning editorials were augmented by documentaries and the occasional seafaring campaign with Paul Watson and the Sea Shepherd Conservation Society.

And then there was his river work.

While Eco-Man had once chronicled the high seas, he now found himself landlocked in Toronto. I suggested Bob take to river paddling the wilderness to get into the heart of his work. Every summer for 15 years, a small news team would canoe a river that Bob had identified as having an environmental hot issue. We began small with the rivers of Algonquin, Temagami, and Algoma, then intuitively moved north with guided trips to the Arctic and the rivers that flowed into Hudson's Bay. Hunter began by exposing the sordid damage left by resource mismanagement, the tragic scars of logging and mining, and then, as he moved farther north, Bob's foreboding call to arms was "Thermageddon" – global warming and the looming climate crisis.

Hunter's last two rivers were the Thelon and the Bloodvein. On those trips, I took a camera to shoot and produce. Our storyboard unfolded in that day's discovery on the river and Bob's innate wired-in awareness of a planet under siege. The plan was simple: every day Bob would write what he felt, and I would shoot what I saw. At day's end we'd gather what we had, Eco-Man would compose his thoughts, and then we'd shoot the on-camera pieces linking the day, usually one take and always strong. Light follows power, and Bob had his share; he came to life on camera. His message was the prophetic truth, and he delivered it with passion and conviction.

On every river trip Hunter was in his church, celebrating nature's life with condemnation against all who would dare desecrate the fragile balance of our precious ecosystem. Indeed, not small work at all.

Hunter also communicated goodwill. He believed in signs and rainbows and a glass that is always half-full. TV is riddled with an ego distortion virus on both sides of the lens. The "camera meat" were understandably more susceptible, yet Hunter was never afflicted. While he was proud of who he was and what he had accomplished in his life, he always presented himself as Bob, not the Eco God, not the Author or TV Star, simply just Bob.

Robert Hunter worked hard. In the decade and a half as a TV journalist he produced over 3,000 stories for our newscasts. Admirable. Then add in the daily 5 a.m. bathrobe editorials for *Breakfast Television*. Also in that mix were the longer-format news series and his documentary work. Bob also hosted a weekly show called *Hunter's Gatherings* on our 24-hour news channel. A prolific résumé by any standard.

After over a decade of remarkable work and memorable stories, years rich in friendship, Bob told me he had prostate cancer. In the time that followed, we often talked about the cancer, his latest numbers or the next hopeful option for treatment, but he was never the walking wounded. He kept working and fighting his good fight until the cancer was serious and he just couldn't do it all anymore.

In 2004, Bob left the newsroom to deal with his days ahead with his family.

May 1, 2005, at Scarborough Centenary Hospital, was the last time I saw Bob. He was close to the end, and we spent the afternoon together. Exhausted by the valiant fight, Bob was drifting in and out of consciousness. We talked a bit, a few sweet moments of conversation, but mostly I filled the air with chatter or sat in silence whenever he would slip away. There was one moment when he had to have a chest X-ray. A sickly green machine was rolled into the room. I helped prop frail Mr. Hunter up so a board could be positioned behind his back, then stood behind the machine. I caught Bob's eye. To distract him, I raised my clenched right fist in a power salute and then flashed him a peace sign, and, I promise you, the Hunter stiffened and, rebel to the end, shot up his arm and flashed me back.

My friend died the next day.

It was a blessing when Bobbi offered me some of my friend's ashes. She'd asked a chosen few to scatter his remains into the world's oceans. The ceremony I had in mind was one final river trip. In August, my wife Janice and I paddled the Coppermine River in Nunavut, a wild tundra river that empties into the Arctic Ocean at Coronation Gulf. With the journey behind us, we stood at the ocean's shore. It was cold, windy and wet. Fittingly, all of nature's harsh elements were at play at that place on that day. We released Robert Hunter and watched the waves lap his dust out into the gulf.

This is what I remember about Robert Hunter, this is what endures. The best of us remains alive in that warm part of your heart's mind. For

17 years I bore witness to the grace of his humanity. Bob was the smartest and most accomplished man in every room, and he never let on. Many missed that about Bob; they couldn't fully comprehend the life force in front of them. Hunter ticked all the big boxes, courage and compassion, and he was loyal, honest and forgiving. Bob was strong and never cruel. His minor flaws were endearing, he aspired to the myths of heroes, his message was true, and he was a great fucking time.

RELATIONSHIPS AND RELEVANCE

by Janine Ferretti

IN FEBRUARY 1988, Bob and Bobbi appeared on our doorstep on a chilly Toronto evening with their children, Will and Emily. They were there to reconnect with an old friend and fellow environmental activist, my husband, Gary Gallon. The Hunters had just moved to Toronto from Vancouver, and there was both a rekindling of a lifelong friendship for Bob and Gary and the beginning of a wonderful friendship between our two families. Our girls, Kalifi and Jenika, bonded instantly with Emily. Sleepovers became play production opportunities, with Emily as scriptwriter.

Gary deeply admired Bob for what he accomplished, for his wit and amazing prose, and loved him for the good and caring man he was.

Bob and Gary shared a passion for environmental politics that went back to their days in the environmental movement in the late 1960s. On that evening in Toronto, they shared stories of "meetings" over pints of beer at the Bimini Pub; their touch-and-go efforts to secure the *Phyllis Cormack*, the ship that launched Greenpeace; the loaning of SPEC office space and administrative support to the fledgling Greenpeace Foundation; and the larger-than-life personalities of fellow activists. That evening not only introduced me to Bob and Bobbi but also gave me more colour and texture to Gary's past life as executive director of SPEC in

Vancouver. Amid the reminiscing of the old days, it didn't take long to see the deep bond between Bob and Gary that had been forged in the heyday of the environmental movement in Vancouver.

During our shared time in Toronto, Gary was the policy advisor to Ontario's minister of the environment, Jim Bradley. Bob had become the environment reporter for CityTV. Once again, Bob and Gary were able to work together, albeit mostly behind the scenes, as Gary would give Bob background on an important developing issue. Gary valued Bob's reactions and insights and was able to bring these into strategy sessions to introduce environmental policies in Ontario. Bob always managed to shine a light on the absurdity of a situation. And while there was often (much-needed) humour in the environmental stories, he wouldn't hesitate to reveal with a cold eye the environmental tragedies caused by the negligence and obfuscation of government regulators, or the greed and short-sightedness of companies.

Bob also covered a lot of stories on Pollution Probe while I was there in various roles. He always managed to come by Ecology House, where I worked, before noon to film interviews, and afterward we would head to the pub next door for lunch and a beer, of course. During a particularly difficult year of controversy at Pollution Probe, Bob decided to present me with CityTV's Environmentalist of the Year award, which was a much-welcomed encouragement at the time. I have always suspected he did that as a supportive gesture rather than for any particular achievement of mine, but I greatly appreciated it. To this day, when I find things tough at work, I look at that plaque on my wall for a wink and a nod from Bob.

It was no surprise to Gary and me when Bob announced he would be running in the provincial elections. Bob had a great following from his work with CityTV, and had been providing the good people of the Greater Toronto Area with news analysis. He was an outstanding communicator and knew the challenges facing Ontario. While it was not uncommon for environmentalists to attest that one party or another cared the most for the environment, Bob and Gary didn't believe that was the case for one minute. They were realists and understood the forces that drive power, as well as what drives society and change. They had seen political parties deliver environmental progress in some areas, but also come woefully short in other areas. Personal commitment makes a huge difference in environmental politics. Bob had this, and we were thrilled at the prospect of having him speak truth to power in Queens Park.

Later, when we were living in Montreal and Gary was battling cancer, Bob and Bobbi would be frequent and devoted visitors, bringing love and light to us.

After both Bob and Gary had passed away, Kalifi and Emily became shipmates for a while on the Sea Shepherd Conservation Society's vessel, the *Farley Mowat*, braving the rough seas of the Southern Ocean in pursuit of whalers. Bobbi and I travelled to the Galapagos to visit them while they were in port, marvelling at how our girls had grown up and not too surprised that they had followed in their fathers' activist footsteps.

Bob's reporting and writing has left a huge legacy. His work and insights showed he was thinking ahead of his time, and his writings are still relevant today, as I personally discovered last year. Months before Gary died in 2003, Bob's book *2030: Thermageddon* was published. I picked it up again in the summer of 2020 as I prepared for a class I was teaching at Boston University on climate and development. While books on climate change are numerous, I couldn't find one that presented the science and politics of climate change simply and clearly. Wondering whether *2030: Thermageddon* would offer that clarity and demystification, 17 years after it was first published, I opened the book and the words that spilled out removed any doubt. With ease (and anguish) Bob cut through the complexity of climate science and the noise of climate politics, providing an analysis that is on point for today. For my students, who were merely toddlers when Bob wrote of his outrage and distress for what lies ahead due to our society's carbon addiction, this was the right book. I was moved to hear my students reflect on his writing, and I witnessed that, years after his death, Bob is still communicating and inspiring. With his trademark of hard facts, flawless logic and effortless clarity, Bob Hunter asked a new generation to take a stand and to act. And with that, I had done my job as a teacher.

THE ELITE MEET THE STREET

by Douglas Gibson

AS THE PUBLISHER at McClelland & Stewart, I spent a lot of time travelling, getting to know authors right across the country. I was well aware of the long-haired troublemaker named Bob Hunter who had introduced blue jeans to the *Vancouver Sun* newsroom and, in the words of a clever *Sun* advertisement, "wrote every column as if your life depended on it." Oh, yes, he had also helped to found an environmental group named Greenpeace and had written books about sailing into harm's way to prevent nuclear tests. He had also written a novel, *Erebus*, in 1968, as a young man.

Naturally, on one of my regular trips to Vancouver, I'd made a point of meeting Bob Hunter. It went very well. So well that he took me to his home to meet Bobbi and the family. He had a traditional Sweat Lodge on the property, where the impact of the steam on his Scottish Hunter skin produced many jokes about "redskins" from his Indigenous friends.

I was determined to publish Bob Hunter's work, and, in 1988, his first book with M & S, *On the Sky: Zen and the Art of International Freeloading*, was published. The book, described as "the craziest travel book of all time," featured Hunter getting into trouble whenever he leaves his Vancouver home to stagger around in foreign parts doing disgraceful things. He gained many envious readers among middle-aged men stuck in their boring lives.

But now Bob was involved in something far from boring. He had spent many years working for friends in the Indigenous world. Among them was Bob Royer, also known as Robert Calihoo. His life story was too awful to be true. Not only had he suffered terrible abuse as a young guy, but he had ended up doing serious time in prison. In jail he had studied hard and got a degree. So far, so very good. But then, as he worked to advance Indigenous causes, he discovered that his own reserve in Alberta had been illegally sold by the Canadian government, leaving him (and many others) without a home.

Bob heard about this travesty, investigated it in outrage, and decided that he and Robert Calihoo/Bob Royer should write a book about it together. I was proud to publish that book, *Occupied Canada*, in 1990. It won the Governor General's Award for Non-Fiction in 1991.

That year, the great, formal Governor General's Award Dinner would be held, not at Rideau Hall in Ottawa, but in Toronto at the top of a big bank tower at King and Bay Street.

Bob knew the importance of winning the award, so made some changes to his travel plans so that he could be there. When he finally tracked down his co-author, Bob had to work hard to persuade Royer to come to the event, and even when he had agreed, he kept going off the radar.

As Bob recounts in his book, *Red Blood: One (Mostly) White Guy's Encounters with the Native World*:

It wasn't until ten minutes into the ceremony, when we were all back in our seats in front of the stage, and the house was full of buzzing literary types, and the Gov-Gen was seated above us on something looking suspiciously like a throne, and the full primitiveness of this ritual was impressing itself upon me, that I spotted Royer seated by himself off to the side. He had just materialized in the seat. The good news was that he was wearing a suit jacket. The bad news was that it looked like he might have slept in it, not, in this case, a figure of speech. I slipped over to sit beside him. He was a lot more stressed than I was. Whether it was from lack of sleep, let's say, or sheer stage fright, I couldn't tell. His hands were shaking. Trying not to appear petty and annoyed, I slipped him a feather I'd brought from a collection at home, hoping it would help me to focus when the moment came to deliver a brief acceptance speech. Royer needed it more than I did. And it did seem to steady him. He nodded. For an instant, we were Brothers again. Then we were climbing up on the stage to applause, the Queen's boyo was shaking hands, and we took turns at the microphone.

I had hoped to muster the guts to cry out "Vive l'Oka Libre," but common sense prevailed. Instead, I made a nice little speech about trying to rectify injustices, setting a good example of brevity, and turned the mike, with some trepidation, over to Royer. He held the feather in his hand and quoted from Chief Poundmaker, who had warned his people that the worst ordeal would not be defeat in battle, but the mocking and being spat upon that would come afterwards. Not bad. Short. Lots of applause. We were both off the stage and back in our seats, and the worst, most vulnerable moment had passed, and Bob had behaved. We had both behaved. We were good little prize winners, and we were both clutching our five-thousand dollar cheques, savouring the applause.

Bob then confesses his shame at "wimping out" and recalls that his wife, Bobbi, who was sitting next to him proudly holding his hand, said, understandingly, "Nice restraint, tiger."

Afterwards, a glitzy reception. Media superstars everywhere. Living literary and journalistic legends galore. Much subtle sniping. But it was nice, being feted. In the early afternoon, Royer did a fade back out to the streets.

We didn't encounter Royer again until evening, just as we were waiting for the elevator to take us to the top floor of a mighty downtown bank. He was ripped. But then who was I to throw stones, as it were? I was just slightly on the ripped side myself. Sixty stories up we emerged from the elevator into an enormous dining area, with a string quartet playing, looking out over the lights of the biggest concentration of wealth and power in Canada. Surrounded by the nation's economic, political, and literary elite, we were guided to a round table where we joined our publisher, the urbane, erudite and merry Doug Gibson, as well as, among others, one of the vice-presidents of the bank itself (presumably a human monster beneath the veneer of charm and breeding), and his delightful and attractive running-dog trophy bride. It was hard, for an old leftist like me, not to feel slightly squirmy in the company of the corporate plutocracy. Supping with the devil, any way you looked at it, really. Who, after all, has looked upon the bank towers of Toronto, where their mortgages are stored, and not felt a twinge of hatred in his heart? Yet they were our hosts, the VP and his wife, and Doug was our publisher, and we didn't want to embarrass anybody, did we? We were quickly out-Canadianing each other with politeness. I think it's called being co-opted. It was appalling how quickly I went for it, along with the excellent wine.

And we were actually making it through. I was beginning to have hope. And then the subject of Free Trade came up. The VP was 100% in favour, of course. He had all the numbers about why it was such a marvellous, brilliant thing. He just had to assume that we common folk understood the benefits, too. Wasn't it so obvious, really? The imperative was irrefutable. At which point, alas, my co-author decided he had had enough of being co-opted. Maybe all those years he'd spent behind bars dreaming of getting even with the bigwigs were kicking in. Here was his chance, for sure. He wasn't likely to be invited back here for din-dins anyway. The banker, being the worldly fellow that he was, tried his best to be gracious, to employ his persuasive skills, underlining his points deftly, trying to keep it light, wry, and clever. But my angry co-author, deploying all the debating techniques learned at Stony Mountain, would have none of it. Basically, his point came down to: "You banking bastards are pushing Free Trade so you can suck more blood from the People, and you should all be hung by the balls with piano wire. On top of that, you're lackeys of the American military-industrial complex, every last fucking one of you."

Despite the urgency of maintaining decorum, voices began to rise at our table. The banker lost some of his colour. He was now leaning across the table, hissing at Royer, who was snarling back at him. My wife finally couldn't take it any longer and yelled at Royer: "Will you just shut up!" That created quite a stir at surrounding tables. It also slowed my co-author down a minute or two. But he was soon back on the attack. "Banking bastards living off the backs of the poor...Free Trade Mulroney goons..." It was beginning to look like my now thoroughly aroused warrior-brother was close to leaping across the table and grabbing the poor banker by the throat, although it was a moot point whether the well-fed banker, quite a tall fellow, wasn't about to do some throttling of his own. He looked in a lot better shape than my co-author, although he didn't have the pent-up fury. My money would be on Royer if he got the initiative.

There was a ten-second pause at the end of which the banker's wife – a nice, north-Toronto, respectable lady, who hadn't expected this as part of the "for richer for poorer" deal, finally cracked, letting out a small scream. We all sat there, interested. Gibson, unable to resist a joke, said, "Well, I guess you had to be there." Which was met with chuckles or glares.

My own happy contact with Bob continued. I published not only *Red Blood* but also his final book for me, *2030: Confronting Thermageddon in Our Lifetime*. In 2002, the year it was published, Bob suggested that we only had till the pivotal year of 2030 to clean up our global act, before the damage becomes irreversible. In his presentation copy for me, Bob wrote:

Doug, I phoned you twice to say, "I can't do this." But I was afraid of your...silence. Cheers, Bob Hunter

Prostate cancer took Bob in 2005, after he had tried everything to preserve the life he loved. A park just east of Toronto is named after him, and he lives on in his wife and kids, and their kids, in his books, in Greenpeace, and in many memories.

Gail Stewart, my faithful assistant for 11 years before cancer took her, had such a protective attitude toward my excesses. Gail knew instinctively that Bob Hunter was precisely the wrong man when it came to influencing me to choose the careful path. She knew that we egged each other on. Every time we left the office together, her face told me that she was worried that after our lunch we would both end up in jail.

I remember that Bob and I were at a restaurant, laughing ourselves silly over something, when the waitress stopped by the table to ask, "Are you guys brothers?"

A wonderful compliment, all things considered.

TREE-HUGGER'S GRIT

by Lea Ann Mallett

I'M SITTING WITH BOB HUNTER in a beat-up 4x4 rental, parked in the middle of the Owain Lake Forest Defence Camp in the wilds of Temagami, Ontario. It doesn't seem at all odd that we're here, sleeping in tents in the rain, 44 km away from the nearest road to town. We're eco-warriors, and this is yet another in a seemingly endless round of battles about what really is important: ancient wilderness or another logging site – planet or money.

I'm sitting sideways in the driver's seat, door open, facing Bob, who's hunkered down on the sideboard, regarding me with his easy smile. We sit companionably, shooting the breeze about the weather – cloudy; the number of people available to do the next day's action – not that many. He gets me and I, him, and that's both rare and precious.

We chat as we wait for the satellite phone (on loan from Greenpeace – our group didn't have money for gear like that) to ring with a call that could change the course of what we're doing up here, so far from home.

The Owain Lake Ancient Forest in Temagami was the first old-growth stand of red and white pine to be put on the logging block in several years. After a years-long forest management planning process that was supposed to prioritize ecological concerns raised in an earlier forest blockade camp, here we are, back at it again. A group of environmentalists gathered to raise the alarm on yet another round of logging of hundred-plus-year-old trees in an ecosystem that predates the creation of what we call Canada. It was the endless merry-go-round of ancient forest destruction, protest and more "planning" – rinse and repeat.

Bob and I had been here before. He had shown up, camera in hand, to so many of the protests I had been a part of. He was an irreplaceable presence at these events, a unique blend of media and activist; a "friendly," and the only media/eco-defender who knew exactly why we kept showing up to do these actions – because our hearts required it.

Bob and I had been to this forest before too. Months before this logging of Owain's ancient pines had started, our organization had brought up a group of activists to train for protests to protect this place and, moreover, to sound the media alarm that another ancient forest conflict was nigh. Bob and his cameraperson were embedded media, slogging along with us to get the behind-the-scenes story of what we were planning, which they would then share with the world. It was early May, and our itinerant guide had promised we would just make it before blackfly season began, and I, an incurable optimist, believed him. Instead, our arrival day coincided perfectly with day one of the blackflies. We were a blackfly buffet. We spent three excruciating days training people to climb trees and set up blockades, while Bob filmed and interviewed, waving huge clouds of blackflies away from our faces. I went to a nearby town and bought out their entire supply of bug hats and spray, and even that didn't really help. Not a word of complaint from Bob the whole time.

We knew this place, Bob and me. This time, our ragtag group of forest lovers had set up the Owain Lake Forest Defence Camp in late August, during a miserable heat wave. Since then, I had been arrested and held in jail for ten days, only to turn around and head back as soon as I was released. The first team of road blockaders and activists who had made their stand for the forest had been arrested, some jailed, eventually released. There was an invaluable, rather feral group of about 15 to 20 folks who were our core, who stayed rain or shine, sleeping in flimsy one-season tents. October had brought rain, so much rain, and chilly temperatures, but still we stayed, greeting media (even the BBC made it up to visit), new volunteers and regulars like Bob.

The four-hour-plus drive from Toronto kept Bob from coming up as much as he'd wanted, but he did come back, creating story after story to share with the folks who watched CityTV. Because he'd been there for our first blockade in late summer, Bob had made sure he was here for this: the big decision on whether the logging at Owain Lake was legal.

In our efforts to halt the logging of these old-growth Temagami pines, we used every tool in the toolbox: locking people to giant concrete blocks to barricade the road, as well as mounting a formal legal challenge of the government decision making that had allowed this logging to commence. It was this legal decision that Bob, the rest of our crew and I were waiting for. We had been told by our partner legal organization that the logging here did, indeed, contravene the ministry's own legal guidelines, and the odds looked good that the court would find the logging in Owain Lake illegal. Almost two months after we had arrived and set up camp here, we would be able to celebrate a rare victory for Temagami's pines and head home. Home to warmth, real beds and indoor plumbing, secure in knowing that the Owain Lake Forest would stand for at least a while longer.

The satellite phone rang, and I looked at Bob, feelings of hope and worry knotting my stomach. His easy grin and thumbs up as he lifted his camera to film my conversation made it easier to pick up the receiver.

"We lost," came the blubbering voice of someone on our legal team in Toronto, sounding like they were another star system away. "The court said the logging there is legal and even if it isn't, it has already started so there isn't much they can do about it. We're going to appeal, but that will take months. Sorry, Lea Ann..."

I could see Bob's kind eyes taking in the answer we'd been waiting for, and he could see it wasn't good. The rest of our camp denizens were standing together a few metres away, waiting for the news. I looked over and shook my head at them, and several of them began to cry. This legal action and its promise had seemed like such a strong possibility, and now it was gone. The group started to turn to one another, hugging and sobbing.

I could feel tears forming in my eyes and shook my head again, feeling so crushed, finishing the call, putting the phone down. Bob lowered the camera.

"Take a couple of minutes," he said. "I know, this is hard. You're the voice here. You don't get to have a good cry just yet. It's part of the job."

And then he smiled that smile that had reassured me dozens of times that I wasn't nuts. That I was doing the right thing by spending my time doing all of these crazy things to try and bring people's attention to this old-growth forest logging, the wilderness-destroying, even if it didn't stop things at all.

I sat and watched my friends, my big-hearted wilderness lovers, as they grieved the upcoming loss of these old trees we had come to love. We mourned what would have been the best ending for this good story: ancient forest put on chopping block, forest lovers come to the rescue, courts deem the logging in that ancient forest illegal, everyone goes home to rest, knowing those trees still stand. I pulled myself together to give Bob my comment on what had really happened, because that was my job.

"Ready?" Bob asked, lifting the camera, that smile always present. And I was ready. I was ready because I was looking into the eyes of my mentor, my friend and one of the few people who knew exactly what that job felt like, the job of creating those media "mindbombs" that we kept throwing out to people, hoping they would end up caring about the land, the water and the planet as much as we did.

"Okay, let's go…so Lea Ann, what's your reaction to this disappointing news?" and off we went, knitting together yet another story about wild places we loved, hoping other people would fall in love with them too.

A year and a half later, long after we'd gone home (which the hardiest of us didn't do until it was -20 degrees Celsius with almost a metre of snow around our tents), the appeals court found that, in fact, the logging of the Owain Lake Ancient Forest had been illegal…too late to undo the logging already done.

FAITH IN SIGNS

by Paul Ruzycki

ON MARCH 9, 1995, the Canadian fisheries patrol vessel *Cape Rogers* boarded the Spanish fishing trawler *Estai* in international waters. They arrested the trawler's crew and forced the *Estai* to a Canadian harbour. Canada claimed that the European Union factory fishing ships were illegally over-fishing Greenland halibut (a.k.a. Greenland turbot), in the Northwest Atlantic Fisheries Organization (NAFO)–regulated area on the Grand Banks of Newfoundland. Greenpeace supported the "turbot moratorium."

My first campaign with Greenpeace had been in 1988, on the riverboat *Beluga*. The campaign was called Water for Life, and our slogan was "We All Live Downstream." After that, I was firmly in the grip of planet saving. From 1988 to 1995, I sailed steady with Greenpeace. From my first position as a volunteer deckhand, I worked my way up to bosun, third officer, second officer and finally to chief officer.

My father had been a sailor in the Royal Canadian Navy during the Second World War, and I'd spent some high school years staring at the ships transiting the Welland Canal, but the other influence for my choice of career was Bob Hunter of Greenpeace. I had seen documentaries and video of the "early days," particularly the early whale-saving campaigns. I thought I would like to join such a group and put my seafaring skills to good use.

I finally met Bob in 1995, at Bob's local pub, the Rex, near the CityTV offices. Steve Shallhorn, Greenpeace Canada's campaign director at the time, introduced us.

A meeting was set up at Bob's house with Greenpeace campaigners Shallhorn, Kevin Jardine and me. It was called to discuss how to locate a ship to lease, and how to find the Spanish fleet off the east coast of Newfoundland. Bob asked if a friend could join the meeting, and in walked Paul Watson, co-founder of Greenpeace and founder of the Sea Shepherd Conservation Society. Paul was extremely helpful; he gave highly experienced input. His only motivation was that of stopping the overfishing.

After the initial meeting at Bob's house in Toronto, Kevin and I made our way to St. John's, Newfoundland, with all of our GP campaign equipment. Kevin and I scoured the wharves of St. John's, searching for the ideal local vessel to charter. We found a large ex-fishing vessel, MV *Cape Mugford*. It had been retired from fishing due to the lack of fish. There were many fishing captains who had to face the same reality.

As soon as we were all on board and satisfied that all of our equipment was with us, we got underway toward the fishing grounds of the Grand Banks, where the Spanish fishing vessels were known to be.

The North Atlantic Ocean in March is notorious for bad weather, quick-forming fog banks and dangerous icebergs – caution is a constant order. I know that not all of us slept well on that first night on board, due to the pitching and rolling of the ship. Small patches could be seen behind the ears of most people on board. Slow release seasickness medicine, used by many non-seafarers, I was told! Luckily, that scourge has never affected me. Despite the weather, we made fairly good time toward the area where the fishing fleet was said to be.

I started to prepare and paint a simple banner to go across the wheelhouse of the MV *Cape Mugford*. These banners have been a longtime Greenpeace tradition, going back to the first nuclear campaign. Bob talked us into incorporating the peace and ecology symbols – one on either side of the word *GREENPEACE*. It looked like one of the first Greenpeace ship's banners. Cool!! Traditions are important on voyages.

On the second day of the trip, we arrived at the fishing area of Sackville Spur, where we came across five large fishing vessels. These were indeed the Spanish fishing vessels, just outside the 200 nautical mile Economic

Exclusion Zone. The area became busy with shipping traffic. An older Spanish warship was providing protection to its country's fishing fleet. On our side we had military or Coast Guard/DFO aircraft doing "flybys" to assess the situation.

The next day, a military helicopter ordered us to back off from the area and keep two nautical miles away from the Spanish trawlers. That meant we wouldn't have any visual on what was happening due to the distance and the weather setting in. We could only monitor by radar.

On day four, one of the Canadian warships ordered the Spanish trawlers to stop fishing, and they all regrouped near the Spanish warship. The Spanish ships then attempted to approach the 200 nautical mile zone to get a reaction from the Canadian authorities' vessels. Our translator, Ricardo, heard over the radio that the Spanish vessels were asking their government to send more warships!

On day six, outside the 200 nautical mile zone, tensions calmed. We saw a large target on the radar and went to investigate. It was a large factory-processing vessel, registered to Japan. They informed us that they were conducting research under the guise of NAFO, but the heavy flow of blood-red liquid pouring out of the ship's scuppers indicated that she was actually processing fish when we came across her. She later reported to the Japanese and Canadian authorities that a Greenpeace ship was harassing her on the high seas!

The next day, still outside the 200 nautical mile limit, we were closing in on the Spanish trawlers. A few whales breached the surface, and Bob said, "That's what's known as a 'sign.'" It was time to launch the Zodiac. We got the Zodiac in the water, and I had it running with Kevin in the boat with me, both of us waiting for Bob.

As we motored toward the Spanish trawler, Bob stood up and told us to make the sign of the cross with our hands over our bodies. He said, "If the fishermen think we are Christians, they won't harm us!" We all made the sign of the cross, so they could see us. I think some of the fishermen were laughing or smiling.

The weather worsened, but the campaign improved. The premier of Newfoundland joined in as an ally of Greenpeace. The Canadian initiatives, both governmental and NGO, provided support for a state or country's right to take unilateral steps to respond to serious threats to important resources. With this push from the governmental bodies, the tide turned in our favour, and the Spanish fleet was in retreat. This was a winning campaign. It took only a handful of protesters to lead the charge, to highlight the environmental atrocity and to make serious change happen. This was another example of how media is the message. Bob was professional in every manner and managed to get the job done "his way."

After the campaign, I asked Bob if he would do another gig with us in Greenpeace. He said it had been 15 years since he had been on a Greenpeace ship. I said, "Why so long?"

He said, "Nobody asked me."

I said, "I'm nobody, and I'm asking you!"

Bob had signed one of his books for me, and I'd cherished it. He'd written, "To my Lifelong Friend and Guru." When I later told him how French commandos had stolen it when they seized our ship near Mururoa for nine months, Bob gave me another copy and signed it again. This time he wrote, "Paul, To my Guru, Teacher and Source of Inspiration, Bob Hunter 2003!"

That was vintage Bob – he saw his reflection in his friends. He found the best in all people, including me. I am a better man for knowing him.

A COPP OUT

by Todd Southgate

IT WAS A PISSY APRIL MORNING in Ontario. Seasonally dullish and chilly. I arrived at CityTV shortly after 9 a.m. and sluggishly sauntered into what appeared to be a deserted newsroom. My eyes then focused on a distant small light in the dimly lit newsroom. There was Bob, hunched over and reading the morning's paper at his desk.

"So what drags your ass into the office on a Sunday morning, Hunter?" I joked. I knew why he was there. We had already discussed the assignment a day earlier. I was a weekend worker; it was an obligation to make wisecracks at Monday-to-Friday staffers whenever their jobs required them to ruin a weekend.

Bob just chuckled. "Fuck off, Todd."

Bob and I were teaming up to cover the 1995 G7 Environment Ministers meeting in Hamilton, Ontario. For four days, those in charge of drafting fundamental environmental policies for the world's wealthiest nations would gather in Steeltown to discuss everything from biodiversity and the progress made implementing the 1992 Convention on the Conservation of Biological Diversity to climate change, and the recent agreements made a month earlier at COP1 – the first conference of parties on climate change – in Berlin, Germany.

On this Sunday afternoon, a full day before the ministers wrapped up, a leisurely boat tour of Hamilton Harbour awaited international dignitaries, complete with lunch, wine and some Canadian fanfaronade. Hosted by Sheila Copps, Canada's then environment minister and deputy prime minister, G7 environment ministers were given a reprieve from bickering over environmental policy details. They would be pampered and doted on as Copps proudly explained Canada's success in cleaning up a once notoriously polluted harbour.

Greenpeace saw the floating target of wined and dined VIPs as an opportunity and decided to do what Greenpeace does: create a media spectacle to try and pressure global ministers into political action.

Bob and I were going there to do "journalism." Well, sort of.

The plan was for Greenpeace to use Zodiacs filled with banner-carrying activists to surprise and skirt the tour boat, grabbing the attention of ministers and the media. Greenpeace argued that Canada was paying oil companies subsidies while only paying lip service to climate change. Bob would be in a media boat Greenpeace hired for journalists to cover the action from the harbour. Bob loved adventures.

I was "accredited press," meaning security cleared me to board with the G7 ministers. I would film the Zodiacs from the tour boat's perspective and get images of the ministers reacting.

About 40 minutes into the tour, Greenpeace Zodiacs appeared and raced alongside the tour boat, waving banners that read *Cut Co_2 Now* and *Don't COPP out*.

Sheila and the ministers peered out the tour boat's windows at the commotion. Others on board – media and boat crew – also started gathering around to see the excitement. Suddenly, police boats joined the fray. It was all quite exhilarating, at least for a little while.

It took just a few minutes for the curiosity and excitement over the banner-waving harbour pandemonium to peter out. Canada's deputy prime minister laughed at the protest, then ignored it. The ministers got back to their lunches, wine and political small talk.

Bob was tech-savvy. He was the first I knew to own a portable cellphone. His first mobile phone was a humongous brick-like device he lugged everywhere over his shoulder. In 1995, the tech had evolved, and he connected to the world via a more portable white Motorola. It was still a technological novelty at the time; few had them. But it was no longer a massively awkward brick; it could fit into a jacket pocket, albeit uncomfortably. Greenpeace also had a cellphone on this day to help coordinate the action.

Earlier, and just before I headed to the tour boat's embarking area, Bob gave me his cellphone, simply saying, "Keep this close by; we will need to keep in touch." He gave me a wink and finished with "Good luck."

Roger that!

As the ministers started paying more attention to their forks and knives than the Greenpeace Zodiacs buzzing around them in the harbour, the action grew tedious. Suddenly, I heard Bob's phone ring. I pulled myself away from the scrum of cameras and answered.

"What's going on? How does it look?" Bob shouted, his voice raised considerably to a cut above the roar of the Zodiac's screaming engines.

"So-so," I said. "They mocked it. Now, none of them are paying any attention. They're just eating and chatting. It's just kinda, I dunno, boring and anti-climactic."

There was a short pause. "Okay, walk up to Copps with my phone and see if she'll talk with Greenpeace, and I'll put Kevin on the line." Kevin Jardine, Greenpeace's energy campaigner, was standing right next to Bob on the media boat.

"Huh?" I responded. Bob could sense the concern in my responsive grunt. "Put the phone in front of her and see if she will take a call from Kevin," Bob repeated.

I understood what Bob meant. I was also a tad nervous about it. Surrounding the ministers were all sorts of security folks who I imagined were armed. I wasn't sure if I'd get jumped approaching a table full of dining dignitaries with some strange white object in my hand.

Grow a pair, Todd.

I waited for my moment, and with the camera rolling, I sauntered over to the deputy prime minister of Canada while she was cutting into something on her plate. Offering her the phone, I meekly asked, "I have Kevin Jardine from Greenpeace on the phone, and he wants to know if he can talk to you." Caught off guard and noting that the entire exchange was unfolding in front of a camera, the minister was no longer smiling. She begrudgingly put down her cutlery and surprisingly, although hesitantly, took the phone, saying, "Sure."

"Hello, Kevin?" she said into the Motorola.

Bob put Kevin on the line.

I filmed the uncomfortable exchange from my end; it was mostly Sheila nodding while listening to Kevin. Bob's cameraperson recorded Bob with Kevin on the phone on the media boat, with the Zodiacs, the minister's tour boat and police boats in the background.

TV magic. I was unsure if Bob had planned this all along, or if he'd come up with the idea on the spot. Regardless, the whole thing was pure Bob Hunter environmental media genius.

"So there we have it," Bob said in his final on-camera sign-off for the nightly news. "The environment minister of Canada has decided to take decisive action on greenhouse gases, but the Greenpeace people here are skeptical; I'm Bob Hunter at Hamilton Harbour for CityPulse."

Bob stayed in Hamilton to do a "live hit" to introduce the story. I raced back from Hamilton to Toronto to edit a three-minute story for Sunday's evening news. It was such a quick turnaround that the story went to air without any other eyes in the newsroom falling on it; we barely made the deadline as it was.

I waited in the newsroom for the newscast to end, elated and exhilarated. Bob was still making his way back from Hamilton. As the newscast's end credits rolled, the producer entered the newsroom. Her face was red, and she was shaking her head disapprovingly. She thought we had crossed a line. "That's not journalism; that's activism," she scolded. "We'll deal with this tomorrow when Bob's here," she finished, then stormed off.

I guess we did cross a line in traditional journalism – that whole flawed concept of taking a hands-off, impartial view of matters, seeing every issue as a power struggle between two equal opposing sides.

But we had done a fantastic job in advocacy journalism by highlighting an issue of critical importance, and we did so in a manner that was engaging enough for viewers to want to watch it on TV.

CityTV was a progressive TV station back in the day; the fact that they even had an "ecology specialist" was proof. Just as importantly, CityTV always demanded interactivity, or "process," as they liked to call it, from its reporters in their news stories. This news story was pure journalist-driven "process." Bob always exceeded expectations.

I made a quick, discreet call to Bob on his cellphone from the newsroom. "We're in the shitters, Bob," I said.

"Look, don't worry about it, Todd; it was great," Bob reassured me. He was always the optimistic one. Nevertheless, I did sense a tone change from excitement to concern when I broke the news.

As I drove home that night, deflated, my mind raced through all the possible punishments. Suspension. Firing. Assigned to film traffic accidents for the next six months. By far my greatest fear was that the newsroom would ban me from working with Bob in the future. Bob wasn't just great to work alongside; he was my mentor. Bob sparked my interest in the environment. He influenced and helped shape my studies and the direction my entire life would take later. I cherished learning from him and working with him. Bob was also a great friend. I loved having a beer with him.

The following day, Bob and I arrived in the newsroom simultaneously. We cautiously approached the assignment desk, the newsroom's epicentre. Bob reassured me that we had done nothing wrong, though he knew we had pushed the envelope considerably. We did ambush the deputy prime minister of Canada for an environmental group.

Shortly, the news director, Stephen Hurlbut arrived. Stephen ran the show at CityPulse. He was the top dog. Stephen had also been very instrumental in my career's direction. Though a great boss and very accommodating, Stephen was also known to have a bit of a temper and not "spare the rod," so to speak, if an employee strayed from norms or crossed a line.

From the other side of the newsroom, Stephen's eyes focused on Bob; he made a beeline toward us. It was the lurching strut of a man on a mission. Shit, I thought; I looked worryingly at Bob. Then, in a big booming voice sure to be heard by everyone in the newsroom, Hurlbut burst out, "That was the best bit of TV I have seen in a long time!" He started laughing and finished with "One old...one young...one cause!"

Bob looked at me and, with a boyish grin, giggled and said, "You doubted me?"

AT THE REX

by Steve Shallhorn

IN THE TORONTO OF THE 1990S, it seems I was the only environmentalist who hadn't met Bob Hunter. There was hardly a day that went by without my hearing his name: Bob was at such-and-such an event, or "Did you see Hunter's piece on CityTV last night?"

When I started at Greenpeace as a nuclear disarmament campaigner in Toronto in 1987, Bob was still on the west coast. The Nuclear Free Seas campaign against warships carrying nuclear weapons into nuclear-free Vancouver did not go unnoticed by Bob, whose column in the *North Shore News* chronicled those events.

It was a warm, sunny afternoon in February when I finally met Bob Hunter, who became my comrade, mentor and friend. By then, I was back in Toronto as campaigns director for Greenpeace Canada. The City of Toronto had just announced that it was closing all of its outside skating rinks for the season because of the unprecedented warm weather. Bob had called the Greenpeace office to see if anyone would comment. I had a few minutes, so we finally met in the muddy little parking lot. The first thing I said to Bob was "Everybody's been telling me I need to meet you."

His response was "Everybody's been telling me I should meet you." His generosity of spirit was evident from the beginning.

He asked his question; I gave him my best shot. When I was done, he froze. You could see the wheels turning to see if I had given him what he needed for his story. Then a big grin, and a "Yeah, you nailed it on the first take," as he passed the microphone back to the videographer. We agreed to meet later at the Rex.

The Rex is an old-time tavern on Toronto's Queen Street, a former hotel known as an evening jazz club. It was also Bob's "office." Over the next five years, we would spend many a late afternoon plotting the eco-revolution after Bob had filed his daily story at CityTV. The Rex was just a few minutes from the CityTV studios but was not the bar of choice for the CityTV crowd.

I visited Bob a few times in that large newsroom, where he seemed to hold a special place in their pecking order. As it was known for its Fashion Television, everyone else was dressed in style. Not Bob. He was the Eco-Specialist and dressed the part; flat hat, lots of layers and earth tones. Many an eager beaver producer, new to the job, would try to assign stories to Bob. Sometimes he would agree, usually because he was planning on doing the story anyway. But it didn't take long for them to realize that they were not the Boss of Bob.

Those afternoons at the Rex became a hotbed of ranting, analysis and eco-plotting. We were often joined by Kevin Jardine, Greenpeace climate campaigner, and other enviros, Greenpeace or not. It was here that the seeds of many of the Greenpeace/CityTV collaborations were sown. When either of us had a story that needed peddling, the obvious start involved the Rex. Within a month of our first meeting, we put together the plan that saw the Greenpeace/CityTV team take to the high seas off the North Atlantic in defence of the turbot. Two months after that we were in Hamilton Harbour chasing Sheila Copps and the G-7 environment ministers in an early protest to advocate taking action on climate change.

Always the committed ecologist, Bob succeeded in bringing many an environmental struggle to the airwaves. The '90s witnessed eco-battles to save Canadian forests in Temagami, Ontario, and the Great Bear Rainforest on BC's central coast, among others. The US and Canada Greenpeace offices collaborated to hang a humongous Great Bear Rainforest banner off the observation deck on the American side of Niagara Falls. Bob somehow managed to convince the station to let him and a camera guy make the trip to the Niagara border. It was a tough sell to get both countries to agree to let a single camera crew cross the border.

As it turned out, one of Bob's greatest fans was the woman from Canada Border Services who was in charge of the border station that morning. Instantly recognizing him from his early morning TV review of the day's newspapers, she gave permission for him and the camera guy to walk across the famous Rainbow Bridge, warning them not to cross the midline border with the US. But of course he did, and got the money shot that no other Canadian media could get.

Bob's ability to function after consuming "refreshments" that would incapacitate mere mortals is well documented in his writings. On a freezing winter day, he had filed his story and arrived at the Rex before me and was at least a pint ahead. His phone rang; the station wanted him to do a teaser to run at the top of the 6 p.m. newscast. They would send a camera right away. The CityTV truck pulled up, the guy handed Bob the mike with a wide grin. "This is Bob Hunter and tonight on City Pulse I am going to bring you the story of…" I could barely stand, but he was able to deliver the teaser on the first take.

One Sunday morning, I got an unexpected call from Bob asking me to come to his Scarborough home. I arrived, and into the room came Paul Watson, Captain Paul Watson. My surprise would have been evident; I hope my terror wasn't. I knew that Bob did a lot of work with Paul and the Sea Shepherd Conservation Society. Despite their differences, Bob's loyalty to Paul resulted in their being close friends and co-conspirators. But I never expected to meet the guy who seemed to revel in publicly demeaning Greenpeace. We had a wide-ranging conversation, and I came away with an appreciation of the bond between them, a bond of ecology and activism.

By the fall of 2000, I was doing a second stint in Washington, DC, as campaigns director of Greenpeace USA, where I spent three weeks a month. That allowed only one week in Toronto and time to meet at the Rex.

The Greenpeace ship *Arctic Sunrise*, a former Norwegian icebreaking sealing ship, was on the west coast as the 2000 presidential campaign was in full swing. The *Arctic Sunrise* was a major step up from the ships Bob had worked with in the '70s. Not only did it have a heli-deck, it also had an elevator that lowered the chopper into its own below-deck hangar, a heated, enclosed crow's nest, spacious accommodation for the multinational, mixed-gender, mainly professional crew, and a satellite dish for communications. And the Zodiacs had evolved as well. Gone were the soft-bottomed, "blow up" boats, replaced by hard-bottomed beasts with powerful engines, all serviced in the on-board workshops. Being situated in Los Angeles meant it was easy for pilot Paula Huckleberry, flying Tweety, the helicopter donated by Ted Turner, to rent a stabilizing device for the video camera.

With old friends Twilly Cannon, Jesse Reid and Dick Dillman on the team, we awaited a supertanker that was to dock at Long Beach, just south of LA. The plan was to board the supertanker by surprise and hang an enormous banner linking global warming to supertankers. The day before the expected arrival of the ship, Bob held court on the heli-deck, thrilling everyone with his self-effacing eco-credibility and decades of experience storytelling in the name of the Earth.

The action did not go as planned. The tanker had made an unscheduled stop at an oil terminal farther down the coast and had lightened its load. This meant that our boarding ladders couldn't reach the deck of the colossal ship. There was no gangway lowered for the maritime pilot to come aboard the ship, and, worst of all, the US Coast Guard had a whole flotilla of patrol boats to keep us away.

Someone from the Coast Guard had bragged to the newspaper that the Coast Guard had Greenpeace under surveillance and had alerted the tanker well in advance to expect Greenpeace to try to board.

I had a few channels into the upper echelons of the Coast Guard and demanded a meeting with the local commander. A frosty meeting it was. Dick Dillman and I were ushered into a small lounge with a handful of uniformed officers, engaging in chit-chat, when the commander burst into the room. All the other officers stood up and snapped to attention. Dick and I remained seated, and the meeting was conducted with all of them standing, When I recounted this absurdity to Bob, he shook his head sadly, recounting the first voyage to Amchitka, when there had been a near-mutiny aboard the Coast Guard vessel that boarded the *Phyllis Cormack* on her way to the nuclear blast site.

That was the last Greenpeace collaboration between Bob and me. We had a few more pints at the Rex, but work took me to the UK, and Greenpeace took me to Tokyo. I was executive director of Greenpeace Japan when he passed in May 2005. I was honoured to represent Greenpeace at Bob's jam-packed Hart House memorial, joining the podium with Premier Dalton McGuinty, TV mogul Moses Znaimer, and eco-warrior Paul Watson, among others.

I learned many things from Bob. That you can be famous and humble. That generosity of spirit is contagious and, in fact, is an eco-strategy necessity to bring people along the journey to true sustainability. That a few people, equally brave and foolhardy, can cut through the noise and inspire real change. That storytelling is perhaps the greatest weapon of all.

ENDURING INFLUENCE

by Dinah Elissat

GRACE

I AM SINGING "Amazing Grace," or, more accurately, I am screaming, "Amazing Grace!" Screaming because I'm staring down a watery grave as the ship writhes in cyclone-forced seas. I'm in the engine room three floors deep within her, watching the "oh, shitstick" careen wildly to and fro. Here in the most stable part of the ship, the engine room, the motion is monstrous and overwhelming even for me, someone who has endured a wild voyage or two. I "sing" because I can do nothing else. I clamp my eyes shut, trying to keep my feet on the deck plates as another wave pushes us broadside, and then I wait for the rebound that comes much, MUCH too slowly. No one can hear me, no one will save me if the time comes to abandon ship. I am on my own. Lost in the effort of just breathing, my mind takes me to another place, another time – the last time I heard what I now sing.

The piper stood in a field shorn of its growth. Bob and I made our way out onto the wraparound porch and waited. The piper was a farmhand, a minder of wool-bearing sheep. The sun was making its way closer to disappearing into Lake Huron, and the sky was alight with softness. We had come from picking mushrooms – morels, plucked from an undisturbed undergrowth in the provincial park called Inverhuron, just across the road. We had finished shooting a story about farm life lived and worked in the shadow of a nuclear power plant, and a provincial park left isolated and for the most part abandoned for fear of nuclear disaster.

The sound of the bagpipes began as they most often do, unsure of tone or tune. The notes began to swell, the song began to float across the land now falling deeper into shadow. My breath was caught. The sting of tears, the blink, the tightness of my throat made it hard to maintain a level of unresponsiveness. I glanced at Bob, who faced his own struggle with composure. Gently, so as not to disturb, Bob laid his arm around my shoulder, and I wound my arm around his waist. We wept together, silently – and as the notes drifted off into the ether, our tears splashed onto our dusty boots.

I hold both these memories now: one created in a time of unexpected pleasure, and one reached for, to bring comfort in a time of extreme distress. Most of my experiences with Bob were like that. A moment in time created in the past and brought to the future to help me move forward.

THE HIGHWAY

The highway extends into the distance, spotted with dots of white and red. The lights, traffic and population of Toronto are in the rear-view mirror. The truck is warm – nice, considering the frigid grip of a winter's midnight. Bob and I are on our way to Trenton, to the air force base, for a story about food movement and humanitarian goods being transported to a desperate and starving place halfway around the globe.

It is an odd hour to be driving; we chat and joke about missed hours of sleep and what those repercussions will be. There is no coffee shop for miles, and that brings a shiver of concern to both of us. I have never really driven out this far east from Toronto, but the highway is quiet, and the speedometer settles itself at 130 km/h, the truck's sweet spot.

A wall of white lies across the highway that I have trouble understanding. Where did THAT come from? Before too long, I register that it is snow, and not just any snow, but a blinding snow with winds that push at the truck with more intent than I would like. The road surface disappears, replaced by a whiteness that allows for no discerning of lane or ditch. My hands are sweaty on the wheel, my lungs hold my breath longer than they should, my stomach is a knot and my heart hammers into my ears. The highway has completely disappeared, no lights to guide, just white, WHITE! WHITE! WHITE! If I lose control, we will disappear into the abyss, the truck is white, the snow is white, they will find us in the spring. I am off the pedals, off the gas and brake, concentrating on not hitting something in front of me and hoping with all small mercies not to be hit from behind.

Bob is quiet. Not a word spoken, perhaps in solidarity with my need to concentrate. My mind plays footsy with my soul. What if there's a crash and something happens to Bob? Bobbi will kill me, just kill me. And if not her, then Hurlbut. And what about all those who love Bob, love him for his start of Greenpeace, his environmentalism, his writing, his humanity...oh my fuckin' gawd, I will have killed a fuckin' ICON. My mind is flap-doodling. I try to find a moment of calm, but there is none.

I glance at Bob. He is relaxed, lounging against the window. I take a breath... better. I glance again. His face is calm and still in repose. I take a breath... better still. I glance again and begin to realize that he has fallen asleep. I take a breath and exhale... much better. The snow squall rages, but I am soothed as all mind/body distress becomes still. I GRASP that he trusts me enough to sleep, to have faith in my driving abilities, to have faith in me that I will get us through. I drive on, I will get us through; he has faith, and now I do too.

Coffee needs to be found.

THE BEVERLEY

The Beverley Tavern sits across the street from CityTV. A monument to drinkin', storytellin' and pool playin'. Bob and I head over, done for the day. I need to talk, and I dread what I have to talk about. The heavy door swings in, and the welcoming murk envelopes us. All is quiet but for the clink of preparation echoing around the bar. A sticky table tucked into the corner receives the drinks Bob sets down. A few moments of sippin', of settlin', before beginning a conversation that will affect my life for some time to come. Bob knows what's coming – he can read my face, my eyes, my soul. He knows of the torture that I have been dealing with for some months now. I have been altered by an experience. I have been emotionally, spiritually and forever rearranged – and he knows it's all his fault. Our adventure to document the west coast Makah Nation's desire to resume whaling has brought about a massive shift in how I see my place in the world. I know what I need; I need to help stop the killing of whales and marine wildlife. Joining Sea Shepherd will help me achieve that goal. I am at a crossroads.

Bob's face is mirrored in careful thought. A sip and a sigh. I am expecting a certain answer, and I am taken aback when I don't get it.

"Don't do it, just don't do it, don't go, the pain, the anguish, the heartache, the heartbreak will break your spirit."

I am stilled, mystified by his use of those words. A sigh and another sip. The words are slower this time, with a twinkle and a smirk, "You will go, I know you can't stay, doesn't matter what I say."

And I did. And Bob was right. So right in the end.

He wrote of his understanding in an unpublished chapter of *Red Blood*:

When you approach events as stories, you underestimate their undertows. Getting in too deep, you can get sucked under. Been there too. Dinah is going through something I went through many years ago, when I was around her age and felt myself to be in the grip of some larger destiny than mere observation. She was captured by the story, captured by the siren whale. I should have had her lashed to the mast of the ship as we went by. But the boat itself was the Sirenian, wasn't it? There was probably no way of saving her. It's not a story to her any longer. It's reality, and she is a part of it. Her presence begins immediately to be a factor. She is alive now in a way I have never seen her. No longer the chronicler, her Ishmael shield of objectivity has been stripped away. She has been drawn by some mighty current from behind the lens into the evolutionary battlefield itself. A partisan! Dinah – rainbow warrioress-campanero! A fresh volunteer. Or is it...recruit? In which case, who's doing the recruiting? And the answer makes my brain go all mushy. Again. A whale! A whale zapped her!

He and Bobbi sent me off to sea with a splendid bon voyage party, and they were with me when I returned to marry the love of my life, Tibor. And later they celebrated my greatest achievement, our son, Hunter.

I know there is a straight line that travels between Bob and me, a line of strong, softly worn hemp rope that now includes intricate knots of decisions made, a heart opened and followed, and a contented life created... I love and cherish those knots as I do Bob and his enduring influence.

LOST IN ACTION

by Todd Southgate

"BOB'S MISSING?" I interrogated curtly, regretting my tone immediately.

"*Calma*," Coca shot back, shooting out her palm into a crossing-guard "stop" gesture, just inches from my face. "The driver we arranged to pick Bob up at the airport says he wasn't on the plane," she explained in near-perfect English with a thick Brazilian accent. "I'm going to call to see what happened. *Tranquilo.*"

She turned and darted away. Coca's palm was the last of her to disappear from my sight.

I stood there motionless. "There" being in Silves, a tiny island about 200 km east from Manaus, the capital of the Brazilian state of Amazonas, in the heart of the Amazon rainforest. Originally a Jesuit mission in the 17th century, fast forward 300-ish years to 1998, and this sleepy island rainforest community was about to host an international cabal of ecological do-gooders plotting to save the world. Or, at least, conspiring to keep a giant green life-harbouring swath of the Earth away from chainsaws.

I was keen to see Bob. We hadn't seen each other in over a year. After finishing my master's degree in environmental studies in Toronto, I moved to Amsterdam to work as Greenpeace International's senior creative video producer. None of which would have been possible had it not been for Bob.

The incurious and somewhat problematic boy Bob had first met at CityTV in Toronto in 1986 bore no resemblance whatsoever to the man he would be meeting in the Amazon in 1998. To say he played a transformational role in my life doesn't cut it. I have often struggled to explain this relationship. He was a mentor and a friend. Sure. A colleague. A co-worker. Of course. But there was something more.

Our trip to the Amazon was last minute. Bob had a demanding schedule pulling at him to return home to Toronto before even arriving in Brazil. He was an award-winning author, famed TV reporter and gifted speaker/lecturer, and was constantly juggling several projects.

Bob was a workaholic, but he made work look fun and easy. Talented people can do that. They make it look effortless while masking all the actual agony, self-doubt and determination needed to fuel such monumental achievements. What made Bob even more remarkable was that, while his workload was gruelling and he had a family to raise, he still found time to teach, inspire and help mould those around him who were open to the idea of also reaching for the stars, or at least making positive waves in life. He never hoarded his wisdom.

This Amazon trip was also a project from Bob's ever-expanding portfolio. He was the creator of a new TV pilot called *Greenpeace Odyssey*. This show would harness Bob's unassailable life experiences as an environmentalist, his bona fides as one of Greenpeace's founders and his equally profound credentials as a media scholar and communication genius to help convey the urgency of environmental matters today, in an entertaining TV format.

Neither of us had been to Brazil before, let alone the Amazon rainforest. We'd travelled to South America to cover a large Greenpeace forestry meeting in Silves that brought in specialists and scientists from 32 Greenpeace offices worldwide to discuss the state of the world's forests and the Amazon rainforest in particular. The premise of this show.

The majority of the destruction in the Amazon in 1998 was illegal. The consequences of this destruction could be far reaching if allowed to continue. The Amazon is not only a biologically rich cauldron of life, harbouring close to 50 per cent of the world's known land-based species; it is also a critical carbon sink that helps regulate the Earth's climate. Or at least it was. In 2021, given increased fires and deforestation, for the first time in history the Amazon rainforest emitted more carbon dioxide than it was able to absorb, scientists discovered. Bob spoke of climate change years before it was considered the crisis it is today. Bob was always ahead in the game with anything related to the Earth, its ecology and its inhabitants. He saw the importance of the issue and made sure he found the time to help make this episode.

"Coca, any news?" I asked gently.

"You won't fucking believe it." She let out an exhausted huff. "Bob's in Rio de Janeiro! Rio fucking de Janeiro," she repeated, sounding every bit as confused as I must have appeared.

Coca, a Brazilian Greenpeacer, was in charge of our travel logistics. In her pursuit to find Bob and get him to the Amazon as soon as possible, Coca was relentless.

"Okay, I found him. He is on his way," Coca said. "There was a big fuck up." Coca loved gringo expletives, I learned. "The airline is doing everything to get him here ASAP," she finished triumphantly.

I asked, "He will be here when?"

Coca took a long, deep haul on her cigarette and responded less optimistically, "Probably tomorrow afternoon."

Fuck!

I was concerned about Bob's well-being, bouncing around Brazil. But Bob could also handle himself. I know. We were together when a mob of violent marauding sealers stormed the unpoliced streets of the Magdalen Islands in search of environmentalists and journalists to assault. I was his cameraman when a Spanish warship barrelled down on us in the angry Atlantic seas, 200 km from the Canadian coast. Bob stays remarkably chill in feverish situations.

I was troubled that we had a TV show to make and only five days to make it. Strike that, three days. Worse, I had not seen Bob in a very long time. After ten years of working with Bob, I learned to cherish every story, every experience, every joke and every moment. I was looking forward to seeing him after being separated by an ocean for close to a year.

Bob never lectured. He was a storyteller. He could effortlessly communicate abstract environmental concepts in ways that were easily digestible for laypeople, but he did so entertainingly. It never came across as a pedantic harangue, or a preachy academic treatise, or an environmental hippie rant. You were learning without realizing that a master professor was imparting some of the most endearing lessons and wisdom in your life.

It was Bob's theories about media "mindbombs" and blasting people out of their complacency that first got my attention and helped forge my career as a documentary maker. Bob would argue that the world needed a revolution. Not an uprising that relied on bombs and guns taking lives, but a global mental coup where images, science and passionate stories about the interconnectivity of all life on Earth won hearts and minds.

"Mr. Southgate, I presume," Bob chuckled in the darkness as the dodgy aluminum boat used to ferry him across the Itabani River approached.

"Here, it looks like you need these," I joked, handing over two somewhat chilled Brazilian Brahmas.

"You read my mind, Todd." He giggled, dropping his rucksack to free up a hand and grab the beer. "So, this is the Amazon." He chuckled again. "Quite the fucking adventure to get here, eh?" We all laughed.

In Brasilia, Brazil's capital and one of its international hubs, Bob came face to face with Brazil's renowned shoddy infrastructure and service issues of the '90s. Having heard the name "Manaus" crackle through the airport's almost inaudible departure announcements, Bob had made his way to the boarding gate marked on his ticket. He handed his boarding pass and passport to the woman working the gate, asking if it was the correct flight. She took his boarding pass, examined it, looked at his visa, smiled and pointed to the plane while returning Bob's documents. Off Bob went. The attendant didn't explain there had been a gate change, or that she couldn't understand English and didn't know what Bob had asked.

"On the plane, I grabbed a nap, and when I woke, looked out the window expecting to see a forest. I froze with confusion, staring at the bloody Christ the Redeemer statue," said Bob, now laughing almost maniacally. It was an infectious laugh; we all joined in.

There was a lot to do to produce the show. First, Bob needed rest. It was late. We were sharing a cabin. Since the beer had run out, Bob and I traded "good nights," and I turned out the lights to let the forest symphony of chirping insects, croaking toads and frogs and the occasional roar of a howler monkey serenade us. Just before falling asleep, Bob whispered,

"Todd, listen. Here diversity shouts its presence." Bob had arrived; new lessons had begun.

On the last day of filming, it was time for Bob's on-camera show opener. I hit record and barked, "Rolling, Bob."

Bob began. "The Amazon, the mightiest ancient forest remaining on the planet and still the most mysterious with the second-longest river anywhere running through it. Welcome to Greenpeace Odyssey. I'm Bob Hunter, here to chronicle Greenpeace's biggest campaign ever to save a forest that could be reduced in less than a generation, to a shattered wasteland."

"And cut. Perfect," I said.

Little did I know this would be the last time I would focus a camera on Bob. After a decade of working together, this would be our final project as a team.

I have spent the last 20 years living in Brazil and working in the Amazon rainforest. I am still using media and images to convey the urgency of what is happening with this forest, hoping to "blow people out of their complacency" and help usher in a new green "mental revolution." Though nearly a quarter-century has passed since Bob and I last worked together, he's never really left my side – or the Amazon – for that matter. I feel him when I work there; I hear his words. When confronting complicated situations, I find myself rummaging through old memories, looking for a classic Bob Hunter lesson plan to apply.

BAHAMA BOZOS

by Garry Marchant

First published by *Vancouver Magazine* in 1985
With an introduction by Bobbi Hunter and Marnie Mitchell

THIS CHAPTER IS DEDICATED to a rare friendship between two wonderful men: Garry Marchant and Bob Hunter. Their birthdays were two weeks apart. Friends since their teens at Winnipeg's Kelvin High School, both left the 'Peg in their 20s; both became writers. Garry, whose keen interest was travel, became a respected travel writer. Bob became an environmental journalist and advocate and book author. Decades later, Garry had travelled hundreds of countries, with Bob attaching himself to the adventure as often as possible.

They savoured maximum enjoyment on their journeys: luxury barge-touring through England; partaking of beers and Bavarian merrymaking at Munich's Fasching festival; running with the bulls in Pamplona, Spain; boating through France's Loire Valley; enjoying Havana together, with Bob tasting the famous cigars; and celebrating their 60th birthdays together with their wives in Paris and Greece. Garry held a special place in Bob's life: he truly made Bob's world global. Sadly, Garry is no longer with us. He died in December 2017.

For these two companions, travel was often an adventure or a mishap. Garry said that Bob was a resilient companion, accepting the joys and frustrations of travel with equally good humour.

BAHAMA BOZOS

"Adventure is when something goes wrong," says Bob. We would soon experience my old friend's definition of the word.

Nassau is a tourist town, no doubt about it. The day trippers bet on the pasteboards at the Cable Beach Casino and watch statuesque chorines in pink ostrich feathers hoof it to Parisian and Broadway show tunes at the Bahamian Rhythm night club. They stop in marathon-drinking-stained bars like the Poop Deck, over the water by the yacht basin, and English-style pubs such as the Green Shutters Inn.

However, they avoid Rastafarian bars with No Hats No Plaits signs, or the dockside Oriental Cafe, where stevedores are having an impromptu party. They dance on the concrete floor to music made from an ice pick run up and down a carpenter's saw, and beer cans and bottles banged together. It is a different version of local culture than the pirate-with-rubber-sword act performed in many Caribbean hotel lounges.

"We have to get away from this, to relax," says Bob. We plan to island hop among the 700 Family Islands, which bear rousing tales-of-the-Spanish-Main-type names: Man O'War Cay, Morgan's Bluff, Pirate's Well and Devil's Point.

We landlubbers choose to rent low-riding 70cc Honda trail bikes, with knobby tires on wheels like dinner plates. "This a crazy thing, mon," warns the tall Bahamian, lackadaisically gassing the minibikes. "You better be careful."

We ride the 35-mile, grandiosely named Queen's Highway that circumnavigates the island, dutifully stopping at such local sights as Lookout Tower, Devil Tree, Belmont Church, and some abandoned plantations.

But as we race around a sharp curve, doing our best junior Hells Angels routine, Bob's bike cannot hold the road. He plows a tunnel through the thick scrub, vicious thorns ripping at his body. He stumbles out a mess, clothes torn, blood dripping from lines scratched on his face, sunglasses askew. He looks like a cartoon character but does not appreciate my mirth.

Two days later, his dignity regained after the local clinic cleaned him up, we are standing on Prince George Wharf, Nassau. It is 7:02 a.m., and we watch incredulously as the *Spanish Rose*, only 100 feet away, steams toward Spanish Wells, our destination. We had left wakeup calls at the hotel. They never came. And the *Spanish Rose*, on its weekly cargo run, is the only thing I have ever seen depart on time in the Bahamas. According to Bob's definition, this is adventure.

But salvation comes: The flight to Eleuthera leaves in an hour; from there, it is only a short ferry ride to Spanish Wells. So, soon after our seeming disaster, the Bahamas airplane settles onto an island airstrip. We descend the stairway to the waiting taxis.

"To the Spanish Wells ferry, please."

"Sure, mon," the driver says pointing his large limo north.

"How much?" I ask, expecting no more than ten dollars.

"Ninety-seven dollars and fifty cents," the driver answers, thrusting a smudged cardboard rate sheet over his shoulder. This is the most expensive taxi ride in the Bahamas: Rock Sound to Gene's Bay, nearly 100 miles. We got off at the wrong airport on the country's longest island.

We finally reach Spanish Wells, named by Spanish buccaneers who'd filled their water casks here. Here, on the edge of the basically Black Caribbean, most of the 2,000 inhabitants are blue-eyed, blond descendants of early Loyalists. "No problem, my man, right on, all right."

At the North Eleuthera airport, a ferry ride later, we await our departing flight in the Love Your Enemy It Will Drive Him Crazy and Cold Beer snack bar.

The manager of the small Green Turtle Club resort/marina meets the guests in his shorts and leads them to the bar for a Tipsy Turtle, the house drink. The cottages are not even locked.

On Saturday nights, the Rooster's Rest, a steamy, darkened bar with fluorescent signs behind the stage, is jammed with townsfolk gathered to hear the Gully Roosters sing "All Day, All Night, Mary Anne," and "Zombie Jamboree" ("Back to back, belly to belly"). Next door is the more popular Blue Bee Bar, better known as Miss Emma's, a shack with business cards stuck everywhere, T-shirts hanging from the rafters.

The speed limit along Parliament Street is 15 mph. And on this sun-baked day the only people on the bougainvillea-lined streets are a pair of plodding Frostbacks in search of non-adventure.

A POLITICAL WIN

by Will Hunter

GROWING UP, I was always amazed at some of the mind-blowing ideas my dad shared with me, like the morphogenetic field theory, for example. Roughly speaking, it's the idea that when new solutions and new ideas are discovered, or an individual connects to new archetypes, these ideas can be shared with their species through an almost Jungian "collective unconscious."

I thought he learned this concept from magazines or scientific journals. What I discovered recently, when reading "Animal Man 30th Anniversary Deluxe Edition Book Two" by Grant Morrison, was that it was something he learned from a comic book in 1989! Similarly, there was a concept in that *Animal Man* series about how killing whales contributes to global warming. This one is solid science. Go ahead. Google "killing whales contributes to global warming" right now.

Amazing, right? This was 1989. I can't imagine a lot of people were linking these things together back then. Anyway, I noticed that my dad became hot on the issue of climate change in the years after this. I find that interesting. I wonder if it was a little bit of his morphogenetic field at work in a roundabout way.

He never spoke to Grant Morrison. And Morrison never spoke to my dad. So it seems like his "mindbombs" had an influence on Grant Morrison. And Grant, in turn, was influencing my dad. Bob became more focused on and concerned with climate change and the possibility of a runaway greenhouse effect in the years after this. Eventually, this led him to write his magnum opus on climate change – *2030: Confronting Thermageddon in Our Lifetime.*

While he was writing that book, I was working on finding my own ways to try and make a positive difference. The Conservative government of Mike Harris in Ontario had just gone through the Walkerton E. coli outbreak tragedy and seemed to have an anti-environmental bias. So I got involved with the Ontario Liberal Party under Dalton McGuinty, who, on top of sending more pro-environmental signals, also seemed to have the best shot at replacing the government. I was also influenced by my admiration for my dad's friends David Oved and Gary Gallon, who both worked for Environment Minister Jim Bradley in the Ontario Liberal government of the 1980s and helped pioneer the province's recycling programs.

Dad covered the Walkerton tragedy extensively in his role as the ecology reporter for CityTV. The next summer, in 2001, a friend asked if I would be willing to ask my dad to run for the Ontario Liberals in a provincial by-election about to be called in the riding of Beaches–East York. I thought there was no harm in trying. So I pitched him, and to my surprise he said, "Yes!" I was so sure he'd say no, when he replied yes, only half aware, I just continued to try to convince him.

The reason he agreed was because he'd finished his climate change book. With that done, he was thinking, "What do I do now? How do I put my money where my mouth is and put this climate change knowledge to action?" This seemed like the answer, and that "yes" began an intense journey in our lives.

Dad was a popular character in Toronto at the time – he was a television news reporter and had been for a while. So just days after Dad accepted the idea of running, the rumours started to circulate, and the Mike Harris Government dropped the writ right away. The race was suddenly on, leaving our team scrambling to get organized and ready.

Even though my dad had run international campaigns and co-founded a worldwide environmental organization, he had no experience being a local political candidate.

The good news was that the campaign swiftly gained momentum once it got off the ground. Bob Hunter signs were popping up like mushrooms all over the riding. Over time, we appeared to be winning the "sign war." Dad often referred to himself as a "sign salesman," and he did an outstanding job. As our momentum picked up, many elected politicians from the Ontario legislature came to help the campaign. Dad formed new friendships and new bonds with some of those folks. The election was set for September 20, 2001. Momentum was on our side, and then disaster struck. 9/11 happened nine days before election day. The Twin Towers falling was a heavy human and security tragedy. A by-election suddenly seemed beside the point. Out of respect for the victims, all the campaigns downed tools and ceased activity for days.

Beyond 9/11, the biggest shock in the whole campaign for both my dad and me was the behaviour of someone who personally betrayed him. A politician from one of the opposing parties, whom Dad had been friends with for years, attacked him in the most surprising and horrific way. Dad wanted to get into politics to do something about the energy policies in Ontario. He wanted less coal and more green sources of energy like wind and solar. He wasn't a partisan guy, but he generally had progressive views. This politician didn't care about any of that. He was running for a different party. So they took an excerpt from a novel Dad had written about 13 years prior, with underlying themes about deadly sins, and used it to accuse him of sexual deviance. We squashed the controversy with the help of well-known author Barbara Gowdy, whose novel *White Bone* was written from the first-person perspective of an elephant. She spoke at a press conference and explained that she is not an elephant, obviously. And, similarly, a fictional piece my dad wrote wasn't necessarily about him.

Moving on from there, election day finally arrived. When the final tally came in, my mother, sister, future wife Veronica and I were in the back room of the campaign office with Dad when they told him the bad news. He had lost. We all hugged and cried. He had put his heart and soul into the fight, and he'd had things he wanted to accomplish.

We set off to the planned victory party expecting a small crowd and were amazed that there must have been 500 people at the party. There were cheers, excitement, applause, drinks, laughter, and in the end a well-delivered and inspiring defeat speech. Everyone there had such a meaningful experience working with Dad that they wanted to show their gratitude. The media covering the event were flummoxed, as here was this celebration over a loss when the winner's party was a small, dull affair.

Another big, surprising lesson was that losing was not such a bad thing. Ultimately, all Dad wanted to do was to impact provincial policy, and he made great contacts in the party that would eventually form the government. He was able to advocate with much more authority with those folks on many issues, including the increase of windmills in the province and phasing out coal-fired power plants. Most of the things he advocated hard for wound up in the platform of the Ontario Liberals running in 2003. Almost all were all centred around climate change, which he knew would become the most transformative issue of our time. And Dalton McGuinty's Ontario Liberal government made progress on many of those issues. They got rid of coal, which was the single largest GHG reduction measure in North America. That government brought in the toughest drinking water standards in the world; built 1,000 wind turbines; created the Greenbelt and expanded it to nearly two million acres of protected land; and cut smog days in half. I joined the government when it formed in 2003 and worked there for over a decade to help see those priorities become a reality.

The contacts Dad gained, and the positive influence he had on them, helped to push forward some excellent progressive environmental policies, and so, in the bigger picture, I think he would have been really happy with the outcome.

Looking back, if he had won, I'm not sure he would have enjoyed the political life. My dad was not faint of heart. He was a great leader, but he was also a free spirit, and I think he would have found being an elected representative a restrictive way to live. It all worked out in the end. He was able to make a difference, and that's all he wanted. He didn't have to get elected. He ran and lost. But by running, and giving it his all, and fighting honourably, he wound up having an influence on Ontario environmental policy that lasts to this day. And the way he educated people through his activism, his writing, his television work, and even direct personal interactions, has influenced people the world over. Many of them have contributed to this book.

I loved my dad and I still do. I'm one of those people he influenced heavily. His outlook still colours the way I see things. For example, he pointed out that our dependency on oil as an economic engine for civilization was fundamentally sick because, honestly, if you think about it, oil is formed from the remains of marine plants and animals that lived millions of years ago. So our fuel is the dead? Is it any surprise that, by pumping the dead into our air and into our lungs, we're destroying our planet?

The reality is, those softer "hippie" environmental issues – like wanting to stop the killing of whales, wanting to save the trees – have a direct impact on humanity's potential survival. It turns out chopping trees and killing whales and pumping more oil all help to accelerate the climate crisis.

So maybe, rather than seeing these as sweet little tree-hugger, hippie issues, we should understand that they represent a morality test that has real, direct implications for us if we fail.

HAVE YOU OUTLIVED YOUR SOUL?

by Hap Wilson

HAVE YOU OUTLIVED YOUR SOUL? A cryptic phrase scratched with a knife on the wall of the fire tower cabin, perched 120 feet above the ground. The sketchy metal framework of the tower rattled like bones in the wind. Chee-bay-jing, or "place where the soul spirit dwells," known by colonialists as Maple Mountain, had already taken ten lives over the past century: before European interlopers arrived, it was an ancient burial place for the Teme-Augama Anishnabai First Nation. Bob and I looked at each other, silent for the moment, reflecting, almost afraid to make any movement or say anything. It was Bob who spoke first: "Well, that sort of sums things up, doesn't it?"

I first met Bob in 1989 during the logging blockades in Temagami, northern Ontario – the same blockade where soon-to-be premier, Bob Rae, was arrested along with dozens of other protesters. Like most green crusaders, I revered Bob Hunter as the soul of the environmental movement in Canada, a Bob Dylan guru, a Jack Kerouac rebel rolled into one formidable media personality of acclaimed notoriety that motivated the world into ecological consciousness.

As Bob was forging ahead with Greenpeace out of British Columbia in 1971, I had attached myself to the burgeoning environmental movement in Ontario, where clear-cut logging practices were eradicating ancient forests. Eighteen years later, Bob would take up the fight as ecology specialist for CityTV out of Toronto. I looked at Bob then as a warrior brother, born of the solidarity earned through collective action in defence of the trees. But there was a much deeper and more salient character to Hunter beyond the GTA mainstream plug as the resident eco-guy and morning critic of headline news – the wilderness beckoned, and Bob dove into the depths of the dark forest with elation and a newfound sense of creative freedom.

Canada needed help. Corporate bad guys were laying waste to precious natural resources. Rivers were being diverted and dammed, old-growth forests were being cut down mercilessly, wildlife preserves were being deregulated for diamond interests and the mining industry was plundering precious minerals and poisoning the land. For Bob it was a cornucopia of vital material for green action. CityTV would fund nationwide wilderness sojourns that I would research, and Bob would get the message out in brazen attacks against environmental villains. Over the next decade Bob would embark on more than a dozen wilderness trips spanning all four seasons, three provinces and two territories.

These were not your garden variety, sunny day, quiet paddles on a calm river; some of these ventures pushed the limit on endurance and risk, raising the bar on environmental exploration to historic expedition proportion. Within the Canadian wilderness was the very "meat and potatoes" of industrial exploitation and greed that was the essential target of unadulterated eco-action – and he would be the conduit to make people listen.

Bob would take on each trip with zeal and professionalism. I'd locate a destination based on an environmental cause or issue, research was done, and Bob would turn wilderness sound bites into strategic video messages. It became evident that Bob's work didn't stop with the Rainbow Warrior or the "morning guy" critiquing local papers; he was the "real deal" – the man-in-the-field, validating his far-flung broadcasts with almost fanatical passion.

Life on the trail would often get tough; I mean really tough. Where others in the coterie of trekkers would whine about the wind, or the biting flies, or the long carries over rocky portages, Bob's mind was always occupied with the next "stand-up" sound bite, or he'd be sitting on his pack at the end of a trail jotting down memos to self about how to approach the next video segment. The one thing I remember best about Bob was his ability to focus on the raison d'être, the motive for being there.

When it came to learning canoeing skills, Bob's mantra was "how hard can it be?" and this defiance often got him into trouble. But it was in trouble where Bob seemed to be most at peace, and he'd handle adversity with unusual aplomb. On a rather tumultuous rapid on the Hayes River in northern Manitoba, where most of our paddlers had overturned their canoes, Bob was in my bow. Our canoe filled with water but safely edged into shore, while the other canoes drifted by us wrong side up. Todd Southgate, trip videographer, clinging to the barrel that housed his camera, floated by in peril. I had to leave Bob behind in the dense scrub to effect a rescue. I took the wanigan out of the canoe, perched it on shore and Bob calmly sat down on it and rolled a smoke while mayhem unfolded on the river.

The historic Hayes River, running 500 km to Hudson Bay, is a Canadian Heritage River, and with good reason; it was the main thoroughfare for interior exploration and settlement. It wasn't unusual to find old clay pipes, trade knives or other centuries-old relics at stopping points along the way. But instead of preserving the river in its natural state, Manitoba Hydro had plans to divert the flow into the already dammed Nelson River to the north in order to pump up the overall power output of its dams. Now here is where Bob was a genius, a strategist of uncommon dexterity. Whereas most mainstream eco-leaders would proffer up prime Canadian wilderness during boardroom discussions, Bob would pry open the back door and, with a hammer blow, nail the head of the problem with a brilliant stratagem. Bob knew when boardroom banter, civil disobedience, even ecotage failed to alter the direction of a campaign. In the case of the Hayes River, it was as simple as creating an ad hoc committee. The "Preservation of the Hayes River Society" was born, albeit with only his closest mates to sign on to the declaration; but in effect, it was all it took to sway bureaucratic minds and put the fear of "Greenpeace Bob" into the machinations of corporate intentions.

Learning skills to manoeuvre canoes through bony rapids or command a team of dogsled huskies was incidental (sometimes accidental) to Bob's purpose, and that resolution ascended from a higher purpose. Bob's methodology was purely Machiavellian, and he'd sometimes work the environmental angle by the skin of his teeth and shine the more for it for his stalwart bravery. Except when it came to bears. That was Bob's Achilles heel.

After campfire social hour, embedded in his tent, Bob needed to know where Hap and the 12-gauge shotgun were located. "Where's Hap's tent?" he'd ask his tent partner. Then he'd practise taking the safety off the bear spray, unsheathe his hunting knife several times, making sure to locate the spot in the tent where he'd cut himself free of an attacking bear. Once settled, he'd be fast asleep in a matter of minutes; a herd of muskoxen stampeding by his tent couldn't have wakened him.

Near the coast of Hudson Bay, we had a close encounter with a polar bear. It rattled us all, and with good reason – it's the third-fastest land animal on the planet and can swim faster than we could paddle. Where the Caribou River disappeared under a morass of boulders and scrub willow, we were forced to portage our loads over long distances – in thick polar bear territory. Bob wasn't happy unless he carried the gun. I relented but never told Bob that the cartridge magazine was empty. That was for our own and the bears' safety.

Everyone has their own idiosyncrasies that make them human. Bob's quirks were well defined, and he admirably wore them on his sleeve. When it came to environmental scrutiny, the art of the man was impeccable. His stories were gritty, shot from the hip, and he never missed a target. The one most valuable thing I learned from Bob, after hundreds of wilderness miles and many campfires, was the fact that the Earth could no longer afford the rich.

GOING DOWN THAT ROAD

by Bobbi Hunter

WE WERE DRIVING INTO TOWN to spend an evening with friends in the spring of 2000. Life was finally on a steady course, even though Bob was still trying to get his all-important book *2030: Thermageddon* out of his head and onto the page. It took about seven serious attempts to get the book to emerge for all to read. Thoughts of global warming were always with us, day after day, and would be until his thoughts were finally in print, and even then, ever after.

Bob seemed distant and sad. I was confused, as there did not seem to be anything to feel down about. Then out of the blue he turned to me and said, "I need to tell you something, but before I do, I want to assure you that it is not a problem." I knew him so well, I could tell this was just said for me; inside he was in turmoil.

I was driving, so I couldn't gauge his demeanour accurately. So I just waited. He said in the lightest, most nonchalant tone he could muster, "It seems that I have prostate cancer."

My insides heaved. My hands shook, my soul shattered in a million pieces. He was being so brave that I had to do my best to control myself. I took a few moments, then I said to him, "How do you know this?"

He said, "You know how you told me I should check it out, well, I did, and the results came back this morning."

I paused and then as calmly as possible, I said to him, "We will fight this. Your mother had cancer three times and beat it each time. We will get the best doctor, and you will be okay. Let's not worry about it, you will be okay!"

We dropped it, didn't dwell on it, trying to make life look normal on the surface; we didn't tell the kids or friends. Temporizing the situation, not wanting to disturb, and wanting to retain as much normalcy as possible as long as possible, we went into a short avoidance stage.

At the same time, quietly we decided to go down the Western medicine route. Bob went to every specialist that was suggested to him in Toronto, discreetly asking people who the best doctors were, looking for leads all the time. He talked to three top-notch oncologists in three differing disciplines, one a surgeon, one a chemotherapist and another a 3-D conformal radiologist. Each doctor assured Bob his solution would work, but each one scared him when they talked of the side effects. In the end, he went with the radiologist at the renowned Princess Margaret Hospital. Partly he chose this route as it seemed the highest-tech, but also because he was informed if it didn't work then he could always try the chemo or surgical routes, whereas if he did surgery or chemo, there was no other option afterward. He also was amused by how paradoxical it was that he should start his destiny by protesting radiation and here he was seeking it. All this analysis, testing and finding various doctors took years, and Bob was being measured all the time. It was a huge wait-and-see game and a slow, steady decline that he rarely burdened anyone but me with.

He was still feeling good and continued to work, go on canoe trips and travel, and he finished his magnum opus, *2030: Thermageddon*. We didn't know it, but we were living on borrowed time.

The kids by now were aware, as were some friends. Bob started the radiation and suffered. His numbers got worse. Just in case things continued that way, we took out our retirement savings and went on a family vacation with Bob's two older kids, Conan and Justine, along with their spouses and his grandchildren, plus Will, his girlfriend Veronica, and Emily. This was the only time we were all together for a trip, and Bob was thrilled.

We also took Will and Emily and went on a whirlwind European vacation on Eurail passes. We charged through France, visiting with Garry and Marnie, then carried on to Italy, Spain, and of course back to see Walt and Cleone in England. We had a wonderful time being vagabonds with our kids.

Bob didn't have a bucket list. His life was always unplanned, and he had had so many adventures he really would not have known what he felt he had missed – other than that trip to outer space. We continued to live in a serendipitous fashion.

After years of tumultuous anxiety and false hope, the radiation did not work, whereupon we then went and consulted the surgeon and the chemotherapist about next steps. They both said, "Well, you would have been an excellent candidate, but now that you have had the radiation, you don't qualify." It was too late; we had marched down the wrong road.

We visited a respected naturopath, and he suggested a clinic in Tijuana that had had some successes. We put our life on hold and flew to our last desperate hope, traditional doctors having given up on Bob. We were met at San Diego airport and driven by a chatty and upbeat taxi driver named Jose. The clinic was in Rosarita Beach, south of Tijuana, off the main road and down several hugely rutted dirt roads. The clinic was small, with the typical pastel pink exterior and hefty rawhide-covered furnishings in the large interior reception area. When we arrived, there were patients waiting in line for their herbal meds. A friendly staff member took us up to our room on the second floor. There were only about 12 rooms, and we had a nice bright one with a view of the ocean. We were given the tour later and then settled in. The patients were varied and interesting folks, and the staff were attentive and kept the facility immaculate. Bob was given a holistic program to follow, mainly herbal supplements, relaxation, health food and chelation therapy, a cleansing of the blood. I'm not certain if any of the therapy helped, but for Bob and me the lack of stress and the moments together were a tonic. This was the first time we had ever spent any serious, unbroken amount of time alone in all our years together. It was just the two of us. We walked, ate and painted together and did what Bob loved best, and that was having me read to him for hours. After a few months Bob did improve. He looked and felt much better, and numbers reflected that. We decided we could go home.

Bob being Bob, ever the optimist, announced to the world that he was cured. I begged him to not tell people that, as something made me feel uneasy, and I didn't want him to have to suffer the sadness of later having to say he was wrong. My instincts were right, and within a few months he started to fade. We got a call from Dr. Donsback of the Rosarita Clinic, who was checking on Bob. As with all people who connect with Bob, he loved him by this time. He encouraged him to come back at no cost to us.

We felt deep despair and cried often. We didn't know if we should stay and live in the warmth of our home life or keep fighting. Then for several tearful sessions we took out the I Ching. Bob always consulted the I Ching at life-changing moments. Throwing the dice on our bed, first him and then myself, until the final throw that would describe the direction we should take. We got Hexagram 24, Return, after a time of decay comes the turning point. We chose to carry on fighting. He still had good work to do in this lifetime.

We went back and spent the winter months in Mexico. Bob put his last effort in, but he was slipping away. He suffered a stroke and had some clots in his brain and was nearly unconscious. The doctors suggested that Bob could have brain surgery to remove the clots, or I could take him home and he could be put on meds to alleviate his pain and let him die in so-called peace. I didn't have the money for the brain operation as the six months in the clinic had drained us financially. But I promised to fight, and fight I did. I sent an appeal letter out to his friends to see if they would help. I was overwhelmed with letters of love and with financial help.

We went to a great modern hospital in Tijuana with Justine, Will and Emily at his side. The operation was tense, as he could have died on the table. He made it through. Afterward he hugged his kids and talked to them all separately. A few days later we flew home to Canada as Bob wished. Within days of arriving home, I had to call 911. Bob could not stop heaving. He died in hospital a few days later, on May 2, 2005.

Ten years later, Will, Veronica, Emily and I are standing in front of a plaque that is dedicated to Bob in the centre of Bob Hunter Memorial Park. It is his birthday, and every year we make a pilgrimage to this spot for a celebration of his life on the weekend closest to October 13. We stand in front of a photo display plaque that has that famous photo of Bob doing his mighty power salute on the mast of the *Phyllis Cormack*. We all hold a glass of wine and talk about him and his impact on our lives. We always pour a glass for him on the earth, and every year, in a manner that is so truly Bob, an eagle circles above our head, just as one did the moment he died. It spirals into the sky and disappears.

The park makes me feel connected to Bob. Every year our family grows, and we have a few more Hunter children to bring with us, and every year the trees behind the plaque grow larger. Life goes on, and we must all complete our course, and while doing so we must love ourselves, love each other and love this planet. That was Bob's strong message.

FAREWELL BUT NOT GOODBYE

by Pat Demco

ONE ALWAYS FELT a sense of energy and enlightenment in the air when Bob was around. The conversation around the dinner table was informative yet entertaining. He was such a great storyteller and would really draw you in. I remember my kids and I listening, questioning and really learning from this knowledgeable man. He played the role of a prophet sitting at our table teaching life lessons. I was proud to have such a remarkable person as a member of our family.

In the early fall of 2004, I hosted a reunion for many of Bob's closest friends and original Greenpeace members at our home in Vancouver. In my mind I wanted this event to be a Celebration of Life for Bob, except we would be fortunate enough to have Bob present with us. Bob was already terribly ill on this trip back to Vancouver, but his drive couldn't be held back, and he still wanted to participate in radio interviews scheduled a few days before the party. He rallied himself for those public times and especially rallied on the day of the party. I remember being very worried on that day that Bob wouldn't have the strength to come out and see his friends. He was very weak and had to rest most of the day. Bobbi and I asked him if we should cancel the party, but Bob being Bob insisted that we carry on. Thankfully, he became his old social self once people started arriving.

By this time, Bob was relying on a wheelchair. That evening, seated in his wheelchair, he moved through the crowd of his friends and family, talking, laughing and greeting everyone with love and affection. It was so good to see the cheerful, lighthearted Bob present that evening. I was amazed by the strength he showed both physically and emotionally.

There were about 20 of his closest allies and friends around the dining table, talking and enjoying their dinner. Everyone else was gathered at tables close by, socializing and beginning their meals. Slowly, people began to stand up and speak to Bob about their favourite memories of him. The whole process was very powerful.

Finally, Bob stood up and spoke. I hadn't seen him stand during his whole stay at our house. But there he was, standing tall and speaking bold, and as always making jokes throughout and chuckling to himself like he always did. Everyone in the room knew that this was the last time they would hear him make a speech and probably the very last time they would ever see him.

Bob was the bravest person I have ever known. Throughout his life he was ready for any challenge and fought tirelessly for the causes he believed in. His final battle with cancer was so difficult and painful, but Bob bravely fought till the end.

HOW LONG DOES
A BUTTERFLY LIVE?

by Emily Hunter

WE KNEW THIS DAY WAS COMING for years, but in the last few months death seemed like it was knocking on our door. We thought we'd almost lost him several times over, and yet miraculously he survived. But today I knew in my gut that this was the day. This would be the day my father – Robert Hunter – would die.

It all seemed so surreal and so deeply tragic to me. Here was a man who had given so much of himself to the world, only to be poisoned by the very thing he was trying to stop. For the very things that we humans do to our planet Earth – extraction, pollution, consumption, biodiversity extinction, to name just a few – are like a cancer on the planet. The very cancer my father relentlessly tortured his mind and body trying to stop. Yet that globally perpetuated cancer leached into his own tissue and bones, perhaps in the form of exposures to toxicity, as he was diagnosed with prostate cancer that spread to the rest of his body over the course of years.

My parents hid the truth for a long time when I was young, shielding me from so much of the hardship they had to endure. In my late teens, and in my blissful ignorance, I decided to take a "gap year" and backpack around Asia. My father was beaming with pride at my adventures, as he had always been my biggest fan in seemingly everything I did. I think there was a touch of the "sacred" in him in the way he treated me, his daughter, and our everyday moments together as gifts.

In our overseas correspondence we spoke deeply about the world, philosophy and the cosmos. He was always that kind of dad – by that I mean an entirely unique human being – who was more concerned about the existential conundrums of life and our relationship with the world around us than everyday matters of the current political and social affairs of the day. Despite being a journalist, he knew innately that much of what was called "news" is just noise and distraction. Instead, he felt that we ought to be using our consciousness and life's energy for the big stuff – love.

That's right. I am a hippie's daughter after all, so I said it – love. My father taught me a lot about the macro stuff that matters – the planet's well-being, our collective well-being, independent thinking and interdependent relationships – but most of all he taught me to love. To love is not simply to love one another in the human "anthropocentric" sense of the word, but to deeply love beyond yourself, your ego and your attachments to the human world. Instead, he taught me to love a blade of grass, to love the swaying tree ruffling in the wind and the oxygen it generates, to love the newly hatched birds chirping for their mother in a fragile cycle of life, and even to love the interconnected web of existence that is mostly invisible to us humans, yet all around us.

He taught me that to love yourself was to see yourself as part of this web of life – not the centre of it – but one cog in the wheel. To love the human world – despite our many flaws – was to know that a gathering of these cogs in the wheel could turn the course of humanity around into the world that Charles Eisenstein describes as "the more beautiful world our hearts know is possible." But to love something or someone so deeply that you know you have to let them go is the hardest love lesson of all. A lesson I am still trying to learn today...

———

On this frightful day, I was standing in a cold, sterile hospital room with my father nearing the end. I could see the life draining from his body as he became paler and weaker than in days past. It's so painful to see a body that once held the person you loved so dearly and watch their spirit slowly leave that same body. In those final days and hours, I would have sacrificed everything to have given him the death that he wanted. For he wanted nothing more than to leave this hospital room and return back home to pass away peacefully in his own bed surrounded by his loved ones.

Yet we were powerless against the Canadian medical system's bureaucracy. We had tried for days to get him sent home to die, but the people who took care of such transitions didn't work on weekends. Of course, he wasn't being treated as a "hero" that day; they didn't care about his many accolades, or even the founding of Greenpeace. Nor was he being treated much like a human being in this system at all. Instead, he was being treated as a number.

For anyone who has lost such a pivotal person in their life, they know how horrifying it is to watch that person being "put through the system," even in death. Something that is such a sacred act – death – has no place in our economic machinery, and yet we perpetuate that system in everything we do. But if there was one lesson my father imparted to me, it was that if you are lucky enough to not be born in a totalitarian system, then you can choose the system you are participating in.

We can choose to participate, and therefore perpetuate, the institutional structures of the current destructive empire. Or we can choose to spend our life in gratitude for the world around us and each other by participating in deconstructing that system, or even building something new. Given the right space and time, a collection of individuals working toward this alternative world might just create the threshold moment that flips the current world order on its head.

I have heard stories about my father my whole life, from a small group of individuals who start Greenpeace to stop nuclear testing to the man who helped started Sea Shepherd, a movement to save the lives of countless beings in the oceans. In fact, I have lived some of these stories myself, having been inspired by my parents. I saw the climate movement take down pipelines, and I joined social innovators in challenging economic growth models with circular economy models in community spaces. I've seen what my father always told me about the old world being deconstructed, piece by piece, and I've started seeing the new world breathing life into itself. We are in a great time of metamorphosis, but like any butterfly, you believe you're almost dying before you're reborn.

———

In that moment in the hospital, though, all I could see was death. Here he was lying on his deathbed in the hospital room. It was at this moment that we decided to take matters into our own hands, literally. We took each other's hands and decided to all connect with his breath, and in this way, connect with his spirit in his final hour. In this un-sacred, sterile hospital room, we morphed it into a sacred space.

I saw my mother Bobbi, my brother Will and his wife Veronica, my sister Justine, my Aunt Pat, my Uncle Don and myself in the room. It was his family all surrounding him just as he'd wished. We could give him this one part of his dying wish. Because we all knew innately he was about to go, this was our last moment to show him how deeply we loved him and show him the meaning of love, just as he'd shown us. Which, in this moment, was a sacrificial kind of love, a love that meant lovingly telling him it was okay for him to leave this world.

We all took a deep breath in and exhaled out. We took another deep breath and exhaled more slowly next time. We soon followed his pattern of breathing ,which was long and shallow deep breathing. At times it was hard to follow his pattern. The breathing became slower and shallower. We held hands as hard as we could with each other, palms wet but firm. We each ceremonially took turns speaking to him and telling him what our love for him meant and gave him permission to let go of this plane of existence.

I remember my mother talking about their 30th wedding anniversary, which had just passed a few weeks earlier, and saying she'd always be his soul mate. I remember my Uncle Don, my father's brother, saying he looked forward to seeing him on the other side, even though neither of them was religious, which really meant he just wanted to see him again. It was clear nobody really wanted to let him go, but we also knew we had to.

I told him that he was more than my father, he was my best friend. He was the person in my life who most understood me and could see with great clarity the person I would become. Some people never get to have that kind of person in their life, as they never feel fully seen by another person as who they genuinely are. I told him that growing up I knew I was one of the lucky ones, not because of wealth or fame – we were mostly scarce on these things – but because I had a father who truly saw me and allowed me to explore my full potential. That made it all the harder to let him go. But I told him that wherever he was going, I would always try to live by his example and never give up on the "good fight" for our sacred planet Earth.

Then that was it. As my mother held him, kissed him and whispered into his ear, he emitted one last breath. One last slow exhale. Nothing more. He was gone.

For some people the Earth stands still when a loved one passes in this way. But the Earth did the opposite that day. Suddenly, we could see through the window that the outside world was rapidly changing. From a blue-sky day to a large and dark ominous cloud taking over the sky and pouring rain ferociously down. It then quickly turned into snow, hail and pounding winds, almost a cyclone. It was like all the seasons in one day, in a time when this wasn't the new normal. Then, in the blink of an eye, the cloud cracked open and the sun poured through. We watched an eagle fly past the hospital window and spiral upward into the opening in the sky. Off in the distance was a rainbow. It was an otherworldly moment, as if the world wept for him and yet simultaneously opened some kind of portal for him to pass through. If stuff like this doesn't make one spiritual, I don't know what will.

———

The truth is, ever since that day I've carried a hole in my heart. Over a decade later I still carry this gaping hole in my heart. But, inspired by my father, I have continued the "good fight" for the planet in his name. I jumped aboard the Sea Shepherd vessels to the Antarctic Ocean in order to directly intervene, even crash into other boats, in order to save the lives of whales. I joined Greenpeace in climate campaigns that were redefining the way they made change. I allied with a Musqueam First Nations woman, Audrey Siegl, along with thousands of people joining us in a virtual protest, to block Shell's Arctic oil drilling rig called the "Polar Pioneer." I even moved to New Zealand to lead a new fight in protecting the Pacific Ocean. But all along my adventures and battles, I still always carried this hole in my heart. For nothing could fill the gaping void he left in me. Or so I thought...

Because somewhere along the line I fell in love. His name is Ryan Dyment, and he is a man who also wants to change the world. He wasn't wounded like me, and he had a bigger vision for another world possible, just like my father. In Freudian-think, this was terribly attractive! Ryan and I first battled police barricades at anti-austerity protests and slept in a tent in the Occupy Movement of Toronto. He later blossomed a new organization into being – the Toronto Tool Library – that challenged economic growth through local grassroots organizing. Plus, he believed in me – the same way my father did. Ryan left everything behind to join me in New Zealand for my passion pursuits. It was there in New Zealand that we got pregnant – another sacred act. But it was Ryan and this pregnant belly of mine that made that hole in my heart feel a lot smaller – smaller than it had ever been since losing my father.

The day I was heading to the hospital to give birth, I often thought of my father. Hoping he could be there with me in some way. But the birth didn't go to plan; it took many days and approaches. My natural birth plan – like many other women's – fell by the wayside. My son was tiny and getting malnourished inside me from a placenta that had stopped working, and he was beginning to show signs of distress. The doctors had to intervene. But being on a surgical table – just like my father on his hospital bed – seemed to take the "sacredness" away. All I was holding onto in that moment was that my baby would survive. I didn't know if the baby was a boy or a girl; we didn't care. We just wanted our little human being to be alive and survive this moment.

———

When I heard that first tender baby cry, suddenly the sacredness all came rushing back to me. I cried and screamed again as loud as my vocal cords allowed. This time it was pure joy – my baby was alive and safe. The doctors announced, "It's a boy," which was no surprise as it was something I innately knew already. But when I looked at his perfect little face with those wondrous dark eyes, it was like an old friend staring back at me. Or an old soul I had somehow known before, now somehow wrapped up in this tiny little baby's shape.

When I held my son for the first time in my arms, I could feel our souls infusing, like that invisible web of life my dad always talked about.

Or, in this case, the invisible umbilical cord that would always connect our two souls together – mine and my son's. But what was perhaps even more spiritual was that another invisible connection was happening. For in all the commotion of the past few days of my birthing experience I had barely paid attention to the date of my son's birth.

Ryan took my hand and asked me, "Do you know what day it is?"

It suddenly hit me like a shot to the stomach. I replied, "No, you can't be right, this is not that day." He told me it was "that day," and my mother – who was patiently waiting outside in the hospital lobby – confirmed the date. The day my son was born – May 2 – was the exact day my father passed away 14 years earlier.

———

Remember the butterfly analogy? Well, it seemed the caterpillar may have died, but the butterfly was being born. Now I don't mean to say my son is my father's reincarnated soul. I don't believe my father is still here. Instead, I believe my father's spirit had to pass from this realm, perhaps into another. Yet I can't deny that there is something here – something bigger that my father's spirit was a part of, that is instilled in me, and now is instilled in my son.

Maybe it's just DNA that I'm speaking about, but maybe it's something more. I don't call it "God," and I don't call it the universe, or even the Earth. Instead, it's all of those things and more. Yet what I do know from my father is that, in being part of that larger web of life, we can either be on the side of history that works toward making creation and healing the larger collective we are all a part of, or we can be on the other side of history that continues to destroy that larger collective.

Today, above all days, I was on the side of creation and healing with my son's birth. But while there were many strange coincidences that happened that day, what was perhaps more serendipitous was the name we chose for our son. We had decided on his name several months prior to his birth, before we could have ever known that he would be born on the same day my father passed away.

We named him Phoenix. A symbol of rebirth in many cultures, it represents a bird that rises from the ashes into a new life and form. For me, his name meant the birth of a new world. Of course, I didn't initially intend for my son's name to connect with my father in this weird and miraculous way, but the name seemed to take on an entirely new meaning. Like the eagle that flew past the hospital window and spiralled into the opening between the clouds. Now our little bird in our arms had risen from the ashes, from his own near-death experience, and was born (or reborn) into this world.

Something Phoenix has taught me is that rebirth is an essential part of the life cycle. For the world we know today is dying. The sooner we accept that and lovingly let it go, the better. But in that same breath, a new world is being born (or reborn).

It is the world my son will begin to know in his lifetime. It is the age of adaptation to a warming world. It is a world that must shed the skin of the old world's ways and structures to morph into a new being. It's a world where new possibilities may lie, and where "the more beautiful world in our hearts" may exist. But this will only come to pass if we learn my father's lesson once and for all. That we must choose that alternative path of creation and healing, despite the world crumbling around us. To let go of fear and hate in our most turbulent moment, and to lean into love. Not for ourselves, but for the sake of our collective web of life. Only then can we be reborn.

To Phoenix: may you always know your grandfather in your heart.

FOUR
SOLIDIFYING

THE PROMISE

by Carlie Trueman

ONCE UPON A TIME, long, long ago, I had a conversation with Bob Hunter. It was a very short conversation, perhaps five minutes, or maybe ten at the outside. We didn't plan to speak. It was just one of those spontaneous talks that people have as they pass by each other, going about their own business.

A casual conversation. Except, it wasn't.

It has stayed with me ever since, and I have had the same conversation with others over the ensuing decades, except now, I take Bob's part.

———

I was working for Greenpeace, and studying law at the University of British Columbia. I was broke. I was thinking about quitting law. I was extremely unhappy, and exams were coming up. I was experiencing a lot of stress.

One day Bob and I were getting ready to leave the Greenpeace office. Bob was on his way out when he walked past me and spoke. It wasn't probing or even inquisitive. It probably didn't even warrant anything other than a non-informative, noncommittal reply. A grunt would likely have sufficed.

He'd asked how things were going for me.

I repeated my standard joke about wanting to step in front of a bus. Even to my ears there was too much bitter truth in it to fool anyone.

Bob stopped. He gave me his full attention. And then he said this:

"Carlie, you can kill yourself anytime you want. No one can stop you. It is entirely your decision. But I want you to promise me one thing. Before you actually do it, you have to write down the names of all the people you know, and you have to invite them to a going-away party. And, at that party, you have to explain to them exactly why you are going to kill yourself."

I was startled. I started to laugh. My legalistic mind kicked in, and I said, "Right, what possible effect could such a promise have, when it is given by someone theoretically contemplating suicide? A promise? Don't be silly."

He replied that he really didn't care what I thought about it, but I had to promise him, and, if it was such a stupid idea, it shouldn't be hard to do. I laughed at how ridiculous the whole scenario was. And then I promised. It was the only decent way to end a difficult and unexpected situation, and that's the only reason I promised him. We left the office. We never spoke about it again. I'm not even sure he remembered it, but I never forgot it.

It is surprising how powerful that promise is.

I started a guest list in my head. At times, over the years, I actually wrote out some names. It is strange. As another name gets added to the list, it becomes obvious how they're just not going to see the situation, whatever it is, the same way I do. A whole roomful of people like that makes throwing a party rather ridiculous.

It is also a very good reminder of how connected we all are, even when we feel alone.

Oddly, I became a student of suicide, because suicide permeates criminal law. I have come to believe that it's not the temporary problems that cause suicides. It is the belief that there is no solution and that there is never, ever, ever going to be a solution. Not now. Not ever.

And what do we do when someone tells us they are contemplating suicide? We become confused. We want to make sure we say the right thing. We want to help. We offer advice. We try to solve the problem. Then we wonder if what we said, or did, was the right thing. We have taken the responsibility for another's life onto ourselves. We have taken on a responsibility that was never legitimately ours. Not now. Not ever.

Bob did not give advice. He did not offer condolences or sympathy. He offered no solutions. Indeed, he didn't even inquire into the nature of my distress. Instead, he simply spoke the truth: "You can kill yourself any time you want. No one can stop you."

That is actually quite empowering. I can act. I do have power. No one can stop me. I can affect my reality. But it also conveys exactly where the responsibility lies. Bob was telling me not to rely on him for help. He was telling me that my life was my responsibility, not his.

But he never said that.

He gave me agency over my own life, and then he told me to use that new-found agency – and the resources I already had – to deal with it. And, if it didn't work out, no one could stop me from killing myself, so I might as well give it a good try.

And how did he enforce my being held accountable for my efforts? He extracted a promise. I have probably extracted the same promise over 20 times in the years since.

Like Bob, I don't have to figure out what to say anymore. But, like him, I do have to figure out if and when to speak. And those quick conversations are great. No history, no follow-up needed or expected. Autonomy. Information. Empowerment. Reality. And there are good reasons for sticking around a little bit longer, while the situation around you changes because you engage in changing it.

How does one change this reality? By writing up a list of your true friends. By talking to them. By being truthful about yourself, to yourself and others. By listening to different people. By being part of a community. And then we all live happily ever after. Or not. Not all suicides are grounded in external circumstances, and even Bob's comments cannot save everyone. But, even then, his comments can make a difference.

Community. That's what Bob was really talking about.

THE RIPPLE EFFECT

by Marlayna Demco

ALTHOUGH THE NUMBER of interactions I had with my Uncle Bob were few, the impact that they have had on my life has been tremendous. Bob Hunter was not someone you forget, and the time I was fortunate to share with him has influenced the path I have taken in life.

When I was growing up in Vancouver, BC, my Uncle Bob, Aunt Bobbi and cousins Will and Emily would visit about once a year from Toronto. I distinctly remember one visit where I had the chance to sit and talk alone with Uncle Bob. He was sitting at the head of our ten-foot table, suitable to feed our family of nine, sporting rainbow suspenders and a long ponytail. With a big, crooked smile, Bob told me stories of his adventures as an eco-warrior, saving whales and seals. He definitely found it a bit comical and ironic that his last name was "Hunter."

There is something spiritual about this particular memory of Bob. He was the crusader, and I was his burgeoning disciple. I sat in awe of his feverous passion, his humour, his selflessness and his desire to protect Mother Earth.

It was in this moment, at such a young and transformative age, I began to realize the meaning of my life. Live your life with purpose. Dedicate your life to something more important than yourself. As Bob spoke, I was filled with excitement as I felt a shift inside of me. It was as if my destiny was made clear: to carry on my uncle's fight for the environment.

Ever since then, my most significant life choices have been influenced by my Uncle Bob. I went on to study environmental science in university. Since graduation, I've dedicated my professional and personal life to being part of solving the climate crisis. I am passionate about using business as a force for good and believe this is how we are really going to move the needle on the climate crisis. Although my path is still evolving, my intention remains true and is a direct result of being Bob Hunter's niece.

Bob has continued to live on in my soul and be a mentor to me, even though he is no longer physically here with us. Bob was not your usual mentor who helps define your goals and advise you on the right career moves to climb the corporate ladder. What Bob provided was far more psychologically significant to me. I've spent much of my career struggling with the dynamics of organizational politics, but I've found peace in knowing that my Uncle Bob also struggled with the concept of power. Just as he didn't play the game, I remind myself that I don't need to play the game either. This validation has been so important to my emotional well-being. Whenever I try to discuss these struggles with others in my life, I'm often told, "That's just how it is." This answer doesn't work for me, and I'm grateful to Uncle Bob, and find comfort in knowing my mentor would understand my position. Bob led from a desire to inspire those around him with his passion and to make everyone feel valued. This is the type of leader I strive to be.

Bob has also taught me that it's okay, or perhaps even a good thing, to question authority. I've been told that in the workplace I often ask the tough questions that no one else wants to ask, and that I hold those around me accountable for their actions. I find courage from my Uncle Bob when I stand up for what I believe in. It may sound silly, but when I'm speaking up to my superiors, I think about my Uncle Bob standing up in front of seal hunting ships to protect the seals, and I feel proud to wear my heart on my sleeve and stand up for what I know is right. Bob taught me the importance of standing up for what you believe in.

Bob has been the single biggest influence on my life. What's remarkable is how much Bob has shaped the direction of my life, even with the few times I spent with him as a child. Bob's passion has had a ripple effect into the next generation. I'm so grateful for the impact he's had on the person I am today, and I'm honoured to carry on his eco-crusade.

HAIL TURTLE ISLAND

by Cathy Anderson

A FRIEND AND I were driving along a six-lane highway when we were stopped by a red light at a busy intersection. We were the first car in the left lane. While we waited, I looked over to the left and noticed a turtle making its way across the middle of the intersection; it had only reached the far lane of the oncoming traffic but seemed determined to cross all six lanes.

Traffic was way too heavy for the turtle to make it across alive, and before I could stop myself, I jumped out of the car and ran, waving my arms and pointing to the turtle until I was standing right beside it. The light had changed, and my presence had stopped traffic from all directions from hitting the turtle. Luckily, the car that was headed right toward the turtle had stopped, and the driver was out of her car, astonished a turtle was there.

I said it needed, for reasons of its own, to go all the way across the six lanes of traffic. She said, "I'll pick it up, you stop traffic." By that time, another car had come forward and stopped beside her car to protect us from getting hit. Soon, every driver at the front of each lane followed suit to hold back the traffic, even as cars far behind started honking. I had no idea which lights were green and which were not, but we got the turtle safely across the intersection and placed far away from the road. Even as we'd left the intersection to drop off the turtle, every single car stayed put until we ran back to our cars. The highway was backed up more than a kilometre, and transports down the way were honking, but all the drivers at the front had stayed put. We waved and smiled at each other as we drove on.

I realized that the drivers who stopped had chosen to take a compassionate role in the success of one turtle's safe crossing. I see this spontaneous cooperation as a positive sign; many of us realize our ecology is in crisis and wonder what one person can possibly do. Well, the answer is pretty much anything that needs doing.

My own action was an effect of coming to know Bob Hunter through working on the pieces you have been reading in this book – it deepened my instinct to be on the side of protecting nature in any single moment, even if I'm the only one acting on it. In one little insignificant moment on a busy highway, I was one person, just doing one thing, taking action for one wayward turtle. Then others joined in as they saw fit, and together we made sure the turtle safely got where it was determined to go. At a time when people are struggling with isolation, separation and division, this was a profound moment of connection on many levels.

After I told my friend, Dinah Elissat, about the incident with the turtle, she had a good chuckle, as if it were an inside joke. When she asked, "When do you ever find a turtle crossing the middle of an intersection? This was kismet!" I remembered how Bob had taken a stand in situations far more dangerous than crossing six lanes of traffic. Thank you, Bob, for inspiring me to take action.

A GREEN TRIBUTE
TO BOB HUNTER

by Jim Robb

WHEN I ATTENDED UNIVERSITY, I learned about Greenpeace actions to stop atomic bomb tests on Amchitka Island in Alaska. I saw the media coverage of Bob in a Greenpeace Zodiac bouncing on rough seas in front of a rusty Russian whaling ship. I saw the deadly harpoon and its cable fired dangerously close to the Zodiac. I saw the violence as the harpoon struck the whale and the slow, bloody death of this magnificent creature whose species was being driven toward extinction. Although I didn't know it immediately, these images created a "mindbomb" that changed me – just as Bob and his Greenpeace activists had hoped. I realized that knowledge without action is useless. I knew I wanted to use my scientific knowledge and passion to be an ecological activist.

A few years after graduating, I joined the "Save the Rouge" movement on the northeast doorstep of Scarborough, Ontario, near the beautiful bluffs of the Rouge River's Finch Meander, just north of the Toronto Zoo. With mentors like Lois James, and the support of thousands of baby boomers, and a few visionary politicians, our team of activists helped to create the 42 km² Ontario Rouge Park, which has evolved into the 79 km² National Rouge Park, which extends from Lake Ontario to the Oak Ridges Moraine.

I first met Bob in 1989 at a Save the Rouge Rally for the Valley. Bob had retired from Greenpeace, and he attended the Rally for the Valley as a CityTV reporter whose experience as a writer, activist and philosopher helped him capture the essence of environmental stories. Bob took the time, off- and on-camera, to understand and communicate environmental issues in a way that reached many minds and hearts.

Bob distilled our messages into a great CityTV news story about a coalition of environmental activists and community groups that were working to "Save the Rouge" from urban sprawl. After the interview, I said something that downplayed the influence of developers over polit-icians. Bob gave me some jovial but sage advice, which I've never forgotten: "If you're not skeptical about developers and politicians, you're not paying attention."

Bob connected with people from many walks of life. After my in-person encounter with Bob, I recalled a conversation with my Uncle Harold about Greenpeace. My uncle was a Second World War Canadian Navy veteran who lived in Victoria, BC, and worked at the Navy dockyards after the war. Because he was twice the age of most Greenpeace activists, I wondered if my uncle thought of them as idealistic "hippies." He did not. He had witnessed the terrible losses of war and the destruction of old-growth forests on Vancouver Island. He supported the work of Greenpeace activists like Bob.

After the Second World War, a new generation of children (baby boomers) grew up in a world imperilled by atom bombs and ecological ignorance about such things as the widespread use of toxic pesticides like DDT. In the 1960s, we were told to hide under our desks when the air-raid sirens screamed. We suppressed our fear during these foolhardy tests of our "readiness" – as if children could ever be ready for a nuclear war. I remember my mother worrying about giving us milk because the radioactivity from a US atomic bomb test was accumulating in dairy cows.

Since my first meeting with Bob, there have been times when I have felt overwhelmed by the power of the proponents of development. At these times, I recall the courage and actions of activists like Bob and Dr. Martin Luther King Jr. Their examples have given many activists the courage, the hope and the inspiration to continue the battle for ecological and social justice.

When Bob died in 2005, I felt a deep sadness. Bob's family and friends lost a loved one, and our planet had lost a catalyst for environmental progress that we all desperately needed. Like many baby boomers, Ontario Premier Dalton McGuinty admired Bob, and he looked for a way to create a lasting green tribute. The creation of a park was considered, but some bureaucrats suggested inappropriate parcels of land. Eventually, government staffers, including a former Save the Rouge volunteer, suggested the creation of Bob Hunter Memorial Park (BHMP) on a 500-acre wedge of public land between Box Grove Forest and Rouge Park in Markham. Greenbelt activists were ecstatic because they had been advocating for the protection of this land as part of our proposal to "Link Lake Ontario to the Oak Ridges Moraine" by expanding Rouge Park to 100+ km².

With the help of Bobbi Hunter, Bob's wife, and the Rouge Park Alliance, Friends of the Rouge Watershed (FRW) were given the honour of restoring forests and wildflowers on approximately 65 hectares (161 acres) of Bob Hunter Memorial Park. Between 2008 and 2013, FRW involved more than 10,000 students and community volunteers in the planting of more than 200,000 native trees, flowering shrubs and wildflowers in BHMP.

Each planting would begin with an informational tribute to Bob and Greenpeace. Most of the young volunteers were surprised and inspired when they learned about the courageous and effective environmental actions of Bob and his colleagues. Like me, they were proud that Canadian activists, with some help from our American neighbours, gave birth to an international activist movement that halted commercial whaling and atom bomb testing, and continues to work to combat climatic change and ecological exploitation.

Today, when the volunteers who planted in BHMP return, they see young forests and wetlands flourishing and biodiversity returning. They can see many of the 1,700 species of plants, birds, butterflies, fish and animals that live in the Rouge. They can see sycamore, hickory, and tulip trees, which are native to the Carolinian Forest Zone, one of the most endangered eco-zones in Canada, and the home of 20 per cent of Canada's species at risk.

Ecological restoration helps to restore human optimism as we see the Earth heal, with some human help, after centuries of unsustainable deforestation and wetland destruction. We know that, as the forests grow, carbon dioxide and pollutants are being removed from the atmosphere to combat climate change and protect air quality and human health. We know that instead of quickly running off and causing flooding and erosion damage, precipitation is being directed underground by tree roots and being stored and filtered before it slowly emerges as cool and clean water in our streams, lakes and drinking water sources.

In the minds and hearts of many Canadians, Bob Hunter and his Greenpeace colleagues hold a special place. Looking back, I clearly see and appreciate the catalytic effect that Greenpeace had on the many people who stepped up to help Save the Rouge, as a park, instead of an endless wall of invasive urban sprawl. In 2005, Premier Dalton McGuinty listened to Ontario activists and citizens, and he created Ontario's 8000 km² Greenbelt to curb urban sprawl.

The next generation of environmental activists, like Bob's daughter, Emily Hunter, and Greta Thunberg, face formidable climatic and eco-logical challenges, but they can and will succeed. They have strong roots, good role models and growing scientific and public support.

HIGH PRAISE

by Bobbi Hunter

Bob Hunter Greenspace – David Onley

TWO QUITE DIFFERENT MEN were hired at CityTV in 1989. On the surface these two men seemed to have little in common. One man was, by all appearances, a gentle, respectable, tolerant man who emitted a steady aura of beneficence. The other man was tall, slim, confident and bold, with an edgy uniqueness that demanded attention. He emitted a quick wit and infectious laughter. These two unique beings would spend the next 16 years in the same newsroom.

David Onley and Bob Hunter worked with CityTV as reporters and news specialists. Over the years, David moved into different roles at the station. He was the weatherman, education reporter, Breakfast TV reporter and held the science and technology beat. Bob was titled the Ecology Specialist and later branched into a couple of news analysis segments called *Paper Cuts* and *Hunter's Gatherings*. It was a fast-paced environment, but the two men knew well how to tune out background tensions and absurdities and maintain their own personal rhythms.

CityTV was a crowded newsroom full of large egos and equally large talents. Even though David and Bob were considered two of the giants among that diverse crowd of alpha personalities, they were both completely humble and unassuming. Their innate strengths of character would lead them to be strong admirers of each other. They acknowledged one another's intellect and held each other's abilities in kind regard. Although their schedules did not often afford them much time together, they were of the type who could instantly find common ground.

Over time, viewing each other at arm's length, they slowly got to know one another – not only learning that there was much to admire in the other but also learning there were many similarities. These two men had a passion for science fiction and all things extra-planetary. They were both noted and accomplished authors. Both men held strong spiritual beliefs. They had a drive to be involved in politics in order to bring about positive change in the areas of their lifelong concerns.

After Bob passed away, there were many tributes awarded to him. Huge among them was a 400-acre park in the Rouge Valley Park system. They named it Bob Hunter Memorial Park. This was a provincial initiative.

Even though the huge Bob Hunter Memorial Park had been announced, David felt he wanted to honour Bob with a second smaller but significant park. He knew of a piece of city-owned land south of his home in Scarborough. This land was vulnerable to the growing onslaught of developers. Saving this land in Bob's name became not only a tribute but also a campaign David knew his respected colleague would welcome. It would be a physical expression of their shared conviction to respect planet Earth.

David also has a unique personal connection to this piece of land. Inside this 17-hectare site is a small piece of flood land that is filled with local history. In the middle of winter, his boys, as youngsters, would skate on the frozen pond hidden in the centre of that forest. It was a special enchanting spot for children.

David approached me in 2007, and we put together a proposal to present to Toronto City Council. Happily, in due course this beautiful 17-hectare parcel of city land was named Bob Hunter Greenspace, and David Onley officially dedicated it to the memory of Bob Hunter.

David Charles Onley went on to great things and became the 28th Lieutenant-Governor of Ontario from 2007 to 2014. His seven-year term makes him the longest serving Lieutenant-Governor of Ontario.

I recently asked David if there was anything special he took away from his friendship with Bob. This was his answer: "Express your beliefs with strength of conviction, respecting others who may disagree. Your opponent is not your enemy."

Archives, Lectures and Scholarships – Dr. Thomas Hart

Another person who has taken a keen interest in studying and heralding Bob's life's work is Dr. Thomas Hart, the brother of Will Hunter's wife, Veronica. Thomas did not meet Bob, yet he feels as if he's known him for years. Thomas has a PhD in philosophy and teaches at Ryerson. Upon hearing all the family stories about Bob, the scholar in Thomas was eager to know more. I had placed all of Bob's writing and research in the University of Toronto Robarts Library at the Media Commons Archives, on the wise counsel of the chief archivist, Brock Silversides. Thomas began to pore through those treasures and read all of Bob's books.

His interest in Bob was piqued when he was asked to give a lecture at the School for the Environment at the University of Toronto at the annual Bob Hunter Scholarship event. From then on he has been instrumental, alongside Will, in organizing many of the annual Bob Hunter Lectures, such as the ones given by John Bennett and Dan McDermott (co-founders of Greenpeace Toronto); Elizabeth May (former leader of the Green Party of Canada); Dalton McGuinty (leader of the Ontario Liberal party during Bob's run for office in 2001); and culminating in a capacity crowd at the Isabel Bader Theatre in Toronto, given by 350.org co-founder Bill McKibben.

Dr. Thomas Hart has been putting his efforts into another tribute – a book that brings to life how Bob was many things, high among them a philosopher. Thomas has studied the books that Bob has left behind (there is a list of Bob's published books at the back of this book). Thomas and I suggest that you read some of them: they just might change your life's path.

BOB IN FRAGMENTS

by Jerry Rothwell

I FIRST MET BOB HUNTER in negative. A small roll of 16mm film rattled through a film edit deck, a set of images miraculously teleported from the first Greenpeace anti-whaling campaign in 1975. It was just one of more than a thousand reels of rushes from that period that had recently found their way to the Social History Museum in Amsterdam. On the tiny screen, in celluloid reddened by age, Bob stood to attention facing the camera. He was uncharacteristically wordless, because the sound for this clip was somewhere in a stack of unopened suitcases full of quarter-inch audiotape, on the other side of the room.

Several months later – the footage now synced and digitized – Bob "introduces" himself. "Oh Christ," he says. He's gesturing at the extraordinary green coat he's wearing in the footage, designed and made by a costumier for the "leader" of the forthcoming expedition.

"That's for when you go visit the captain of a whaling ship," says someone from behind the camera. "It'll blow his mind," replies Bob. He shows an evident discomfort at the proceedings. But his embarrassment at the hierarchies and status the coat seems to confer fights with his sense of the unsolicited generosity of whichever supporter made it.

"Oh Jesus, look at these buttons," he says. "Imagine the work that went into this thing."

"Are you actually going to wear it?" replies a fellow crew member, handing him a cigar to chew on like a psychedelic General Patton.

"Well, I don't know, I've paid my price in terms of human dignity for this organization time and time again. But you're presenting me with a moral dilemma," says Bob diplomatically, seemingly looking for the moment when he can take off this uniform.

I love this piece of footage because I think it says so much about the man: his immediate grasp of the craftsmanship of the costume, his distrust of the authority it might be seen to represent – and his delicate ability to negotiate that duality with humour. Later in an essay, he remembers it: "wrought out of green and navy-blue corduroy, with epaulettes the size of bricks, gobs of gold tassel, gold colored silk lining, extra-large size brass anchor buttons, absurdly flared trouser hems a la John Lennon, with huge pirate style cuffs featuring enough officer's stripes to rank me as the commander of some imaginary NATO." Recalling this period in *Warriors of the Rainbow*, he writes about the anxiety that leadership brought him: "Having always hated leaders it was close to nauseating that I was now leader and group father myself." The coat seems to confront him with a question: Is he a leader, or is he parodying leaders, or can he do both at the same time?

We started working on our film about the Greenpeace founders, *How to Change the World*, in 2007, some eight years before its final release. Bob had passed away two years before, though we didn't really understand how pivotal that was to any idea of what the film would be.

It's a strange process getting to know someone in their absence, through the traces they have left in writings, images, audio recordings or fragments of film. In the intensity of research, I relentlessly consume everything I can find that might be relevant – and in Bob's case this is a gargantuan feast. Thirteen books, ranging from the novel *Erebus* in 1968 to the climate change prophecy of *2030: Thermageddon* in 2002, hundreds of thousands of words of journalism, diaries, notes, interviews, and the hours and hours of taped interactions with friends and comrades record-ed by film crews on the early Greenpeace voyages. And then there were the memories: reminiscences of those who had worked, drunk, loved and debated with him over 50 years.

For the filmmaker, research compresses a lifetime into a few months, and then an editing process tries to distill that experience into an hour and a half. Despite what the fly-on-the wall documentarists might say, a film can never straightforwardly represent the real. It's always the result of a collision between reality and the filmmakers who pursue it. You can become haunted by its subjects. The strange process of listening to endlessly repeated snatches of dialogue, paying attention to a slight gesture, the flick of a pair of eyes, sunlight glinting on the hairs of an arm, as you find the right moment to begin and end a shot in a way that adds meaning to the whole. To make a film can be to experience a kind of possession – the people in the frame sit on your shoulder and talk back to you, judge your decisions and inhabit your dreams. I've had nightmares of being held captive by contributors to my films, of them ripping me apart or vice versa, or of discovering at a big premiere that they have completely recut the film. It's a kind of dialogue in absence, you feel close to them, bound up with them, responsible to them; a virtual, one-way relationship. But if they're no longer around, you'll never sit in the pub with them and share a drink. You don't know them in a way a friend or even a casual acquaintance would, and even if they're alive, they hardly know you.

And so it was with Bob. What I loved about his writings on Greenpeace was their honesty, a poetic self-critique much more powerful than propaganda and quite unlike most writings about political campaigning. I realized soon after starting to read them that they should be laced through the film, so that we see the boldness and certainty of the young activists through the countercurrent of Bob's doubting, self-deprecating, funny stream of consciousness. His words manage both to maintain a critical distance and to remain in the service of the movement, pointing to the things we could learn and do better.

Talking to his friends and those who worked with him, I realized how the characteristics of his writing were part of the man. He had an ability to bridge the inevitable tensions in a tightly knit group, listen and think about why people did the things they did and what part they played in the whole picture. The mantra that Greenpeace needed both mystics and mechanics was made a reality because he could show that both were valued. "He wasn't an organizational man," says Rex Weyler in the film, "but Bob embodied what I think of as real true leadership. He was visionary, he could look into the future and imagine things that didn't yet exist, and he could inspire and empower people to contribute." I wonder who else could have held such diverse personalities as those aboard the *Phyllis Cormack* in 1975 in a single movement for as long as he did.

Key to that achievement was his understanding of performance – of media as drama and of campaigns as a story. There's a moment in the footage of preparations for the whaling voyage when Bob looks up at the mast. "Can we get a Greenpeace flag up there – I mean, this is theatre," he says – and then with a jaunty apology to the camera – "ahem, sorry, this is reality." Bob believed that, like a film, an activist campaign tells a story that provokes others to think about ideas, in which they can relate to other peoples' – or creatures' – experiences. This is the function of the mindbomb: to shift the centre of gravity in consciousness. It is not that stories change the world – but that the best stories raise questions that require us to answer and act on them in the real world, away from the text or the image or the stage.

Bob was a master at provoking those questions. But he also understood the difference between the performance and the detailed strategic work from which change is built. He could recognize performance as a tool in seeking truth or change, without mistaking it for truth or change.

As we spooled through those many hours of film shot in the 1970s, I would come to realize that when Bob finally managed to take his coat off in front of the camera that day before the launch of the whaling expedition, it wasn't the last time he wore it. Sometimes it would appear, inhabited by its increasingly bedraggled owner, in that voyage and on over the years of campaigning. And it seemed that it came out in moments of crisis, the moments that needed performance. So, after two months of searching for the whalers, on a boat with two days of fuel left and a food supply polluted by diesel, surrounded by a big empty grey ocean, the crew are faced with a decision – to go on, or to turn back – and Bob appears in his coat.

It's now five years since we finished our film *How to Change the World*, but I still catch myself wondering what Bob would do in a given situation. He confronted the dilemmas of principles and strategy with a generosity and a desire to synthesize different world views, cultures, personalities. It's a talent at odds with these times, where increasingly we seem to exist in silos of those we agree with. Those silos are also full of stories – but we easily forget the difficult, messier reality beyond them.

THE MAN WHO HUNTED RAINBOWS

by Captain Paul Watson

IT WAS BILL DARNELL who coined the word "Greenpeace," in response to someone leaving the meeting and flashing a peace sign, when he said, "Why not make it a green peace?" I believe it was Bob who recognized the significance of that catchy passing comment and said, "That would be a great name for the boat." Greenpeace was simply the campaign name for the boat.

Although the official history of Greenpeace states that there were three founders of the Don't Make a Wave Committee in 1969 – Irving Stowe, Jim Bohlen and Paul Cote – they, along with Bob, me and a few other concerned friends had formed the Don't Make a Wave Committee, specifically dedicated to stopping the nuclear testing at Amchitka. Paul was the lawyer who filed the papers, and Irving and Jim, both Quakers, signed the incorporation papers. The fact remains that our Don't Make a Wave Committee was not Greenpeace. To say that they were one and the same is to say that the Don't Make a Wave Committee was the Sierra Club or the Society of Friends, to which the three signatories also belonged. Of the Don't Make a Wave Committee trio who filed the incorporation papers, only Jim Bohlen sailed on the first voyage. The lawyers Irving Stowe and Paul Cote did not.

There were 13 crew members on the first Greenpeace 1971 voyage to Amchitka, all men, and Bob was the most passionate of that motley bunch. After a few weeks of bad weather and personality conflicts, Jim Bohlen and Ben Metcalfe opted to throw in the towel and retreated from Amchitka before the bomb was detonated. They'd had enough of the internal feuding, bad weather and clash of the alpha personalities. Bob, Bill Darnell, Terry Simmons and Richard Fineberg all wanted to continue but were overruled by the others.

I was crewing on the *Greenpeace Too*, sailing to replace the first Greenpeace vessel, so Bob proposed a third option. To keep the story alive, they should hold off announcing the return of *Greenpeace* until the *Greenpeace Too* arrived to take on the forward momentum.

I had met Bob at the Don't Make a Wave meetings before the voyages, and we met again briefly when my ship, heading north, and his ship, heading south, met to transfer the flag.

The US government had delayed the atomic test prior to the first Greenpeace vessel arriving, and they detonated the bomb while the *Greenpeace Too* was battling severe weather crossing the Gulf of Alaska.

When the *Greenpeace Too* returned, Bob was there to greet us. He had turned 30 just two months before on the day of Bohlen's decision to retreat from Amchitka. Although both voyages seemed like failures, the publicity, much of it instigated and nurtured by Bob, led to a decision by the US Atomic Energy Commission to abandon all further tests in the Aleutians.

With that decision, the Don't Make a Wave Committee, established expressly to stop the testing at Amchitka, was dissolved and the Greenpeace Foundation was established.

Not many people are aware that when Bob named Greenpeace as a foundation, he did so in honour of science fiction author Isaac Asimov. He had said many times that whereas Greenpeace was the Foundation, Sea Shepherd was the Second Foundation. Although we could never decide if the Mule was Patrick Moore or David McTaggart.

The newly incorporated Greenpeace focused on addressing France's atmospheric nuclear testing in the South Pacific. Media master Ben Metcalfe took the leadership position, backed solidly by Bob's progressive media skills; Greenpeace boldly struck out on a new campaign.

In 1973, Ann-Marie Horne photographed French commandos beating Greenpeace captain, David McTaggart, near the French nuclear test site on Mururoa Atoll, in the South Pacific. She was able to smuggle the film back to New Zealand, despite being searched by the French military, and sent the film to Bob. McTaggart insisted the photos not be released until his release from the hospital and French custody. But Bob understood that if they waited, the story would be old and no longer urgent and relevant. He released the photos along with a statement that exploded in the international media. Despite the huge public outcry, McTaggart was furious because he was not available to speak to the media in person. He threatened to sue Bob.

When the French warship *Jeanne D'Arc* paid a visit to Vancouver harbour in February 1973, Bob asked me to skipper his friend Hamish's vessel the *Maddie* to protest the ship's arrival. It was a game of chicken, and although the huge helicopter carrier could have easily crushed us, they decided to change course to avoid us. Bob weaved the story into a classic David versus Goliath drama, arranging for Rod Marining to bomb the French warship with a cascade of mushrooms and marshmallows as the vessel passed under the Lions Gate Bridge.

In March 1973, David Garrick and I journeyed to Wounded Knee to support the American Indian Movement, which was in conflict with the US government. Bob risked his job at the *Vancouver Sun* by openly supporting our alliance with armed and righteously angry Native American militants.

Bob's defining decision in 1975 to protect whales allowed Greenpeace to move in a completely new direction. It was a decision that laid a solid groundwork for the growth of a global Greenpeace movement. Needless to say, the Quakers were not amused.

Because of Bob's vision of the Cree prophecy of the Warrior of the Rainbow, I suggested that we paint the rainbow stripe on the *Greenpeace V*. Later, the name *Rainbow Warrior* would be emblazoned on the bow of the most famous Greenpeace ship, the vessel that was mined and sunk by the French Navy in Auckland Harbour in 1986.

The organizing of the first two Greenpeace whale campaigns was enormously stressful and took an emotional and physical toll on Bob's health. He was not a seaman, but he was leading a seagoing campaign and he made mistakes, most of which were quite forgivable. A couple were not.

Bob wanted to be seen as part of the crew, so he appointed himself as the keeper of the heads. As part of his duties, he decided to paint the floors and the walls of the two latrines in the bow of the ship, one side red and the other side green to represent the port and starboard sides of the ship. He was pretty damn proud of his work, so proud that I didn't have the heart to point out that he'd painted the port side green and the starboard side red.

Despite a few eccentric moments, he was our collectively unopposed leader. We recognized that it was not seamanship that was driving the campaigns, it was media strategy, and there really was no one who could have replaced him, even if we had wanted to do so. He also knew how to juggle conflicting personalities on vessels overrun with big egos.

But it was on the radio and with the typewriter that he was crafting both strategy and tactics, dramatizing the events of each day and firing up the imagination of the public. This, more than anything, established the Save the Whale movement as the essential crusade to save the oceans.

In 1977, Bob and Bobbi Hunter trekked across the monotonous, dusty, hot Nullarbor Plain of Australia to lead a campaign against Australian whalers, a campaign where they successfully faced down a gang of bikers on land and harpoon vessels at sea, the beginning of the amazing transition of Australia from a whaling nation to the leading nation defending whales before the International Court of Justice.

When I left Greenpeace, Bob and Bobbi supported the establishment of the Sea Shepherd Conservation Society and even put up their house as collateral on a loan to purchase the *Sea Shepherd II*. Years earlier, they'd convinced Bill Innes, Bobbi's father, to put up the family home as collateral to fund the first whale campaign. Bob and Bobbi did for Sea Shepherd what Bill had done for Greenpeace.

In 1979, after I'd hunted down, rammed and ended the career of the pirate whaler *Sierra*, I wrote the cover article about the campaign for the *Greenpeace Chronicles*. This was just two years after being voted off the Greenpeace board. Patrick Moore by then had replaced Bob as the new president of Greenpeace. Bob and Rex Weyler featured the story in the *GP Chronicles*, which proved an embarrassment to those who were opposed to my "violent" tactics.

Bob Hunter was fully aware that my tactics were non-violent and agreed with my strategy of "aggressive non-violence." He was of the opinion that there was a place for this approach, and that led him to invite me to a meeting where he laid down the foundation for what would become Greenpeace International. It was that meeting in 1979, coupled with the sinking of the *Rainbow Warrior* in 1986, that firmly established Greenpeace on the world stage.

If I had one very strong criticism of Bob, it's that he should have kept a firmer grip on the controlling reins of Greenpeace. He had the power to do so, but it was his generosity and his tendency to delegate that unfortunately placed the authority over Greenpeace in the hands of those who did not share his generous perspective, nor his incredible media philosophy and skills.

In 1987, *Sea Shepherd* anchored off Amchitka Island during a campaign to investigate and oppose Japanese drift net operations in the North Pacific. Bob was not with me when we stepped onto the island for the first time. However, his eldest daughter, Justine, was on the crew and, like her father, she was there as a journalist.

In 1992, a Japanese fisherman threw a knife while Bob was being interviewed on board the *Sea Shepherd II* during a drift net campaign. The knife flew over his shoulder and landed on the deck. Bob picked it up, looked at the camera, chuckled and said, "I got a souvenir."

In 1995, when a mob of angry, drunken sealers assaulted me in the Magdalen Islands, Bob was there documenting the drama and standing up in the face of this unruly, unpredictable mob and their demands for him to turn over his video footage. He gave them some blank tapes after having hidden the recorded ones in a snowbank.

In 1997, when I was arrested and detained in the Netherlands on an extradition demand by Norway for the sinking of an illegal whaling vessel, Greenpeace supported the request for my extradition, stating I was not one of the founding members. Bob flew to the Netherlands and held a media conference in the prison, declaring that I was indeed a founding member.

We had our differences, but we never allowed those differences to alienate us from each other. I was always captivated by his wit and his unique sense of humour, and the fact that he was always able to be serious without being arrogant or dismissive.

After Bob passed away prematurely, Sea Shepherd named a ship in his honour, and I was incredibly happy that his second daughter, Emily, sailed on board that same ship to challenge the illegal operations of the Japanese whaling fleet in the Southern Ocean.

Emily and I scattered Bob's ashes across a huge flattop iceberg off the coast of Antarctica.

As the helicopter pulled away from the iceberg, Emily and I looked down on the greyish dust that was blowing across that flat, white surface. The words of the song by Kansas sprang to mind: "Dust in the wind, all we are is dust in the wind."

As that noble dust swirled within the bitter vortex of the wind, it tumbled over the jagged, blanched edge of that monumental berg, cascaded through the cracks in the cobalt blue ice and drifted across the cold white rim of the frigid sea, some 20 metres below.

Bob was gone, merged into a sea of life he had toiled to defend for decades, leaving behind a legacy of service, passion, courage and imagination that launched a global movement for the future of us all.

Bob Hunter taught me the true nature of media and demonstrated through his writing and his actions that each of us has the power to profoundly change the world for the better.

THE WHOLE EARTH CHURCH

by Bobbi Hunter

AFTER MORE THAN 30 YEARS of marriage, raising children, stepchildren and a nephew, career changes, financial ups and downs, hard knocks fighting for what is right for the planet, building an international organization only to have it turn on us – after much joyful travel and several books published, and a new and successful career in TV, I was holding Bob for the last time. He was emaciated from his difficult, five-year battle with cancer. We had tried everything, and we had lost. He was leaving us. In a large room at the hospital everyone had a one-on-one, private goodbye. Immediate family, children, sisters, brother and friends told Bob it was okay; he could go now. He had been released. Yet he hung on for a few days. I looked deeply into his eyes one last time, and I realized what was holding him back. Our leader, the man who would go first in face of adversity, that huge soul, looked back at me. I could see that he didn't know where to go. I held him in my arms and whispered in his ear, "It's okay, Bob, you can go now. I'll meet you on the *Astral* in our next lifetime." And then, with one great sigh, he was gone from our everyday. On that day I lost a huge part of me, but to this day his soul remains with me in many forms, but none so powerful as in his children.

Our children, Emily and Will, were raised in a non-conformist, free-spirited, adventurous environment. But within this non-traditional upbringing there were some interesting nods to tradition. Although the kids never attended any formal church, unbeknownst to them they were raised by the grand pooh-bah of the Whole Earth Church – their dad – and one of his early disciples – me. Their parents were spiritual leaders of an early Earth-loving religion.

In 1969, their father was on assignment in San Francisco, as a reporter for the *Vancouver Sun* newspaper. He was there to check out the scene at Haight-Ashbury when he ventured into a storefront and happened upon the Church of the Good Earth. He listened to the New Age teachings by the bearded hippie priest and was impressed by the idea of a church that focused on love of planet Earth and not on a divine being or saintly human. After his return home to Vancouver, Bob was busy helping get all the elements together for the first anti-nuclear campaign of the fledgling Greenpeace organization, when he discovered that it was an easy task to register a church. So, soon after that, the Whole Earth Church was created, with its purpose being as a side arm and a fundraising vehicle for Greenpeace, as well as a bold New Age statement that Planet Love should be the emphasis and focus of religion.

Nothing happened with the church for years, as Bob and I were too involved with the day to day of putting together Greenpeace whale and seal saving campaigns and looking after the office, its staff and finances, as well as hammering together multiple musical and fundraising events.

Then, around the time Emily was born, a couple who were friends of ours asked Bob if he would officiate at their marriage. Bob did such a wonderful, joyful ceremony that, before you knew it, he was asked again and soon had performed seven marriages, one child welcoming and a farewell ceremony for a beloved dog.

In a typical marriage ceremony, Bob would stand with the I Ching in hand, and he would have the couple throw the coins that would then indicate a reading that was found in the ancient Chinese text. Bob would proclaim that this reading would be the divine guidance for the couple through their married life together. He would then have the couple share a beverage and break some bread and would talk to them about the importance of sharing in a strong relationship. He would look to everyone present and tell them that they were the witnesses to the couple's desire for the melding of their two lives, and that they, the friends and family who witnessed the ceremony must actively be supportive in making the union grow. Then he would ask all present to lift their right hand and point to the couple, and in unison and loudly they were to proclaim, "Zap! A flower is your brother." He would then say that, with the powers bestowed on him as a crusader for the planet, he now pronounced them a bonded couple and a new force for the good of our Mother Earth.

The ceremony was simple but oddly appealing and memorable. That Zap! was special, as it sent a jolt through you and made you feel connected to all the people who attended the happy event.

Since Bob's death, the church has been resurrected two more times. The first time was for a celebration of life in Vancouver at Jericho Park where Bob, John, myself and many others had launched the Greenpeace whale campaign over 30 years earlier. I was asked to be a key speaker at the memorial. I felt it was the perfect time for the Zap! ceremony in remembrance of Bob and two of our good friends, Lyle Thurston and David Gibbons. I gathered the approximately 60 people present in a circle, and we all held hands and zapped the loved ones of the men who had left us all too soon. I did my best to honour these great men and to emulate Bob's original intent in my ceremony. It was a healing event as well.

I had thought that that ceremony was to be the last Whole Earth Church ceremony, but recently I invoked the Zap! once again at a very special occasion – our daughter Emily's wedding. We were on an island, beside the water, the sun was shining, and an osprey flew overhead as they exchanged their heartfelt vows.

I asked the officiant to speak of the history of the ceremony and to have everyone stand up, point to Emily and Ryan and, on the count of three, say, "Zap! A flower is your brother." Bob would have loved that. He is ever present to this day.

Image and symbolism resonate through time.

A LIFE BIGGER THAN LIFE

by Elizabeth May

IT IS HARD TO ACCEPT that so many years have passed since we lost Bob Hunter. In sitting down to write an afterword to this wonderful collection of tributes to Bob, I was shocked to realize that he died before I became leader of the Green Party of Canada in 2006. I remember as though it was yesterday attending his memorial in May 2005 in Toronto, hearing tributes from everyone from Premier Dalton McGuinty to Bob's old friend, Paul Watson.

Bob's genius, his wit and his sense of humour made him impossible to forget. And that indelible imprint makes me feel that he is with us still. I can imagine his laugh and his talents as a raconteur. The wonderful story of his near brush with Queen's Park, where his bid to be a Liberal MPP was thwarted by a nasty NDP smear campaign. The punch-line of the story was on election night, when his brilliant partner Bobbi said, "There's more bad news. I know you wanted me to cancel those tickets for a vacation in Greece, but I forgot." I'll never forget the picture Bob painted of himself a few weeks later, floating in the Aegean Sea and wondering why he had ever thought he would want to be in politics.

I was a big fan of Bob's run on CityTV with Moses Znaimer, another one of those to deliver a eulogy at that packed memorial. Later, environmental journalist David Israelson would write that "for would-be journalists, Bob's perspective was more useful than a few years of journalism school." Pure Bob. Pure genius.

But it was Bob's climate work where we most closely conspired. His book *2030: Confronting Thermageddon in Our Lifetime* was published in 2002, just as Canada was coming down to the wire to ratify Kyoto.

In his reflections looking toward 2030, he framed the time in terms of his then-youngest grandson, Dexter. Now we are uncomfortably close to 2030. How did Bob know with such certainty that 2030 was to be a do or die moment? A threshold to the point of no return?

He wrote, "In the years that I have been studying and writing about climate change, I have noticed a pattern of reaction when the subject is introduced – and the consistency of the pattern fills me with deep unease. I have seen it in many different countries. If I suggest to someone that the climate crisis could be upon us within thirty years – that is, around 2030 – instead of the century-or-so they have grown accustomed to hearing about, I see them immediately running one key calculation through their heads: how old will they be by then? Will they be around to face the music? If it happens to be a person fifty years old or older, the automatic response, usually accompanied by an apologetic grin (but still a grin rather than a frown) is: 'I'll be gone by then.' I call this the NIML Syndrome, meaning 'Not in My Lifetime.'"

Youth activists have seen this clearly. In the lead-up to the Paris negotiations, as the year 2050 was used as the next big milestone, the youth T-shirts read "How old will you be in 2050?" It was a stab through the heart to the older diplomats ploddingly negotiating when urgency was required.

2030. Bob was the inventor of the "mindbomb." This was a key aspect of the book's power. 2030 was far in the future when the book came out in 2002. But it was uncomfortably close compared with 2100.

I was executive director of Sierra Club of Canada and promoting the book like mad. One day, one of our young staffers came to me and said, "There's this old lady on the phone and she says she wants to buy a copy of Bob Hunter's book for every MP. I think she's serious. Do you want to talk to her?"

Dorothy Cutting, who left this Earth in August 2021, became my adopted mom in 2003 with my own activist mom's death. She was calling from Salt Spring Island in British Columbia. She was so powerfully impacted by Bob's book that not only did she buy copies for all 301 MPs; she bought an electric car to drive across Canada to deliver them. She had emblazoned on the bumper "I am driving this electric car to give my grandchildren a future." She met her hero, Bob Hunter, when she got to Toronto, and he joined her in Ottawa to meet with MPs and press for Kyoto. He personally inscribed all the books with "Please ratify!" And we did.

Of course, within six months of Bob's death the minority government of Paul Martin fell (undone by a pact between the Conservatives, the Bloc and the NDP), Stephen Harper's Conservatives formed a government following that election and, within weeks, cancelled our Kyoto commitments.

Canada has continued to have the worst environmental record in the industrialized world. We approach 2030 knowing that the Intergovernmental Panel on Climate Change, which Bob quite accurately explained had an overly conservative view of the speed with which we were hurtling toward climate chaos, has said that without more than cutting Canada's greenhouse gas emissions in half, and the world as a whole halving emissions, we will shoot past an increase of 1.5°C global average temperature increase. That is tipping well into a danger zone from which we may never emerge. I am torn between feeling it a blessing that Bob did not live to see Stephen Harper as prime minister and bemoaning cruel fate that he was not with us to bring Harper down and move to climate action.

Absolutely every word he wrote about the threat of climate crisis was true, and now it is much, much worse. I am so sorry, Dexter, but your grandfather was right: "I mark the year 2000, the year of your birth, the year we found out the Arctic ice cap was 40 percent gone, as the point where history will say the greenhouse 'fingerprint' became visible enough for policy changes to begin, for someone somewhere to start changing course."

I write these words in 2021. More than two years after the IPCC warnings that we must move aggressively and immediately to cut global emissions in half by 2030 – or face unacceptably high risks of losing human civilization. We still have a chance, but the odds are increasingly against us.

Thankfully, we still have Bob. I still hear his laugh. I can pick up his books, reread his warnings and remake his pledge to Dexter. Our house is on fire. And Greta Thunberg and other young activists are holding all of us to account.

We need Bob. We need a mindbomb. We need an eco-warrior for our time.

Time to reboot and demand that we, who love whales and love our forests and know how to love our friends, recommit to doing what it takes. Non-violently. Relentlessly.

Kick ass to save the Earth.

THE HERO REDEFINED

by William E. Jackson II and Bob Hunter

From Jackson's book *Once Upon a Greenpeace: An Eco Memoir*.
Infinity Publishing, 2010

BECAUSE THERE WILL BE no further words from Bob now that he has passed, this interview is included. By rights, his words – his arguments, stories, jokes, visions – and that infectious laugh should be on a *Best Hits of Planet Earth* album headed for deep space...just in case that isn't where he went!

We chatted on, as Hunter was wont to do, idly, seemingly, but always pushing at a critical point. We rolled a bomber, and somehow the old subject of eco-heroism came up:

HUNTER: The whole hero thing grows from already obsolete models, eh – perhaps wholly mythic models that never worked as conceived, but still rule today. Classically, the "real" heroes were the giant Greek gods, since then it hasn't been a good career choice. The only hero left now is the anti-hero, the expatriate, the anti-patriot. The insurgent. But he is as flawed as the hero he replaced. He's an impossible figure. What matters is that heroes were at one time or another able to effect meaningful change in the order of things, which by the way, is usually called progress...until it hits the brick wall of limitation as a human concept.

We call people who do this, who happen to be in the right place at the right time, our heroes.

WILL: With the goods...and the vision.

HUNTER: Careful. Maybe not the vision.

WILL: The ability, somehow, to see what exactly is necessary, and then doing it.

HUNTER: Whoever has the tools, yes. A side question is: How were those tools acquired? Through thought, or rote repetition?

WILL: The old school-or-life conundrum.

HUNTER: Well, almost. But we also pervert that perversion: we call movie stars our heroes – people who are by definition faking it! Hello Iron Buffalo, you were right to change your bio.

WILL: From actor to acter.

HUNTER: Yes. So, he could be an anti. But we idolize our stars – because they role-play our issues for us.

WILL: That's what theater is for – a representational acting-out.

HUNTER: Granted, but is that really healthy? To suppress yourself – make oneself subservient to pretense – to avoid reality? Is that why we don't reward our teachers as heroes? Teachers make glacial changes in the world every day, yet we pay them shit. Hardly a positive reinforcement. Yet our fake heroes get millions. Planetarily, that ramifies exponentially, daily.

WILL: But wait – you rail against teachers and schools all the time – traitors, tools of oppression!

HUNTER: Particularly when I'm drunk. [laughs]

WILL: Deeply seated resentment. So where is the real...?

HUNTER: Heh heh...You see, the older one gets, the more hypocritical one becomes – by necessity, mastering the dubious art of compromise. And that incorporates learning, wisdom, native knowledge, happenstance, and good old hard knocks.

WILL: Good old Existentialism.

HUNTER: As far as isms go, yes. Sartre's label for what was already happening – is always happening – in the human psyche, at the core of it all. Feeling, action...hence the tendency to react and respond relatively, to stay viable in an ever-changing environment.

WILL: Adapting.

HUNTER: Exactly. At the heart of evolution and ecology, eh. All things living must fit in, by definition negating those who don't...

WILL: The unfit.

HUNTER: Getting old is a bitch, Uncle Will.

WILL: So is being poor.

HUNTER: And ugly.

WILL: That one hurts.

HUNTER: And stupid. Being stupid is the worst. God...

WILL: Precisely. So, is God the survivor of the fittest? Or the survivee...?

HUNTER: The one who fits the circumstances best holds sway over who God is, it seems.

WILL: Now you've gone too far.

HUNTER: Over who gets to be God. See? It's a human construct. So, people have to be in agreement, and take turns appointing each other. Unfortunately, they have no other way of getting through life.

WILL: Like being stuck in a ghetto.

HUNTER: The power ghetto. A very lonely place, eh.

WILL: Ghetto of the Gods. Sounds crowded.

HUNTER: But that's where we put our heroes! That's the proverbial pedestal. It's really a prison. Fuck that...!

WILL: Is that an order?

HUNTER: Trapped by yourself, competing with yourself, even more than with others. They're just excuses, foils, the set-up men. [smile] We are most brutal on ourselves, in the end. Even the big shots. But see, that pressure forces compromise and selection as an equally important part of the process as, say, morality, ethics, conscience, humanity. Cruel as that may sound, it is the primary model of Earthly life. And it puts existential relativism – indeed hypocrisy and waffling – right at the epicentre of life force.

WILL: Et tu, bruté.

HUNTER: I told you so.

WILL: So, it's like the New Dark Ages, where nonalignment becomes an adaptive mindset...

HUNTER: Precisely. Thus, Greenpeace flying the UN flag right beside the Prayer flag...heh heh...

WILL: If one remains rigidly loyal, then, to the wrong idea, evolutionarily, existentially, one is soon gone.

HUNTER: I present Richard Nixon.

WILL: Extinct.

HUNTER: By one's own device. One and all!

WILL: Very democratic, really.

HUNTER: No, fascistically tyrannical.

WILL: A glass half empty?

HUNTER: Like an endlessly irreducible point. Heh heh...like pi.

WILL: A glass full of pi.

HUNTER: So, what is being hypocritical, when it comes to succeeding?

WILL: That depends on what you consider success.

HUNTER: Ah! In a game of sport – not too threatening...or war, which is inherently threatening – deception is a crucial tactical element of correct strategy; yet it is a lie, the same way being unfaithful or concealing a fact intentionally – lying by omission – is a lie. Hiding baby Moses was a deceit. And ignoring Jesus' eastern travels, dismissing the whole learning period of his life – those were deceits. Telling the Nazis your Jewish kid isn't a Jew was a lie. Telling your mom being a Hitler Youth is all about camping and singing was a lie. All's Quiet on the Western Front...

WILL: Wrong war.

HUNTER: Same country, same culture, same ideologies...

WILL: Same wars.

HUNTER: The D-day invasion of Normandy was successful precisely be-cause it was built on a lie – great plywood and balloon armies – whole fake divisions – amassed to "invade" at Calais.

WILL: So were Hitler's invasions of Poland and Czechoslovakia.

HUNTER: So is the claim that America is impenetrable. Heh heh...burned down the White House.

WILL: Why did you burn your brother's house down?

HUNTER: What's that?

WILL: Jimi Hendrix.

HUNTER: Ah, yes.

WILL: Learn instead of burn, hear what I say.

HUNTER: So, the question is, what is success? One burned capital does not mean doom, obviously. Unless you're in Alexander's day. There was a hero, who flamed out at thirty-three...

WILL: Six years older than Hendrix.

HUNTER: Hm, never looked at it that way...who would?

WILL: I'm culturally limited.

HUNTER: Heh heh...

WILL: World conquerors have issues.

HUNTER: Indeed.

WILL: I hide in caves.

HUNTER: Yes – caves are good, the birthplace of culture.

WILL: I would argue that when the libraries of his Alexandria were burned, it was doom for human society – about two thousand years of dark ages and counting.

HUNTER: If only we didn't know it. I wish ignorance really could be bliss. But that's not evolution.

WILL: You have an excuse, you're a Luddite.

HUNTER: And thus, fallen behind the biological curve. [Stares at his big blocky computer]

WILL: Obsolete?

HUNTER: Like a typewriter. ·

WILL: I miss your portable.

HUNTER: So do I. The physicality of it. Made me know I was really writing. Kind of a heroic feeling. [Points to computer] Can you imagine having this thing on the *Cormack*? [Taps a key] No balls, no heft.

WILL: (Not) like a gun. Or a guitar.

HUNTER: Yes. Or a printing press.

WILL: *Yes.*

HUNTER: Something that drives you to use it.

WILL: That computer doesn't drive you?

HUNTER: It has too many limitations – bugs and quirks. I'm sure it will someday. It's the future, eh...beyond me.

WILL: You sound like an Old-World journalist.

HUNTER: I am. This [computer] is completely passive, neutral. A typewriter isn't passive. It makes you tap on it, even just walking by one.

WILL: Mechanical fascination. Heavy metal symbolism. It's personal.

HUNTER: Yes! Computers, by comparison, are overwhelmingly indifferent. A typewriter loves to punch paper. This computer gives you your own ideas back virtually in a state of pre-existence...in endlessly masturbatory cycles, without creating anything tangible at all! You can write till you're blue in the face, but nothing happens.

WILL: Sounds like a personal problem, its very presence.

HUNTER: Yes! Write the entire Greek opus, the library of Alexandria, if you will...and erase all of it with the bump of one little plastic button! There will come an age of great mediocrity in language because of the evolving word processor. The language will become unrecognizably base.

WILL: Sounds like what they said about Shakespeare.

HUNTER: Heh heh...

WILL: Or the genius muse shifts, back to the oral...

HUNTER: Yes.

WILL: This rap music culture. And now cellphones. Sampling. Audio recycling, digitally, with no real musicianship anymore...

HUNTER: Virtuosity will lose all its value. But maybe that's a good thing.

WILL: The homogenization of art and culture?

HUNTER: A good analogy is the continents, and what reshapes them from below, or folds them back into oblivion. Homogeneous lava plays no favorites.

WILL: Creative, but completely impersonal. Almost cruel.

HUNTER: Perhaps that's the only answer to our corporate-hero, fat-cat syndrome.

WILL: Cosmic recycling.

HUNTER: The seemingly sleeping rainforest.

WILL: When people ask me if I'm a tree-hugger I tell them, "Hell no! I hug the whole damn forest."

HUNTER: It really does work, doesn't it – embracing nature?

WILL: And here we sit, in a cheesy motel.... What is natural?

HUNTER: For what it's worth, that is nature: the not knowing.

WILL: No wonder you hate school.

HUNTER: I don't hate school, I hate mind factories – that and things that aren't flexible, like schools.

WILL: Of course. But is that hatred unwavering?

HUNTER: In stone.

WILL: Like lava?

HUNTER: Heh heh...

WILL: Great. Now we need a library for your stones. Nuggets of wisdom. Call it Hunter Hall.

HUNTER: Lacks a certain ring.

WILL: At the University of Toronto maybe? Hallowed ground.

HUNTER: At a school?

WILL: Sorry, Bob, but no worse than a Hunter S. Thompson School of Gonzo Journalism...or a Mick Jagger Library in the London School of Economics.

HUNTER: Nothing is sacred. Even the stones change.

WILL: Like presidents.

HUNTER: I'm talking about erosion as power.

WILL: Ah. How euphemistic. Not to mention esoteric.

HUNTER: Heh heh...the anti-heroism of corruption.

WILL: The nemesis of purity.

HUNTER: Thus, I give you...humanity.

WILL: Bob, remember when I wrote you that the popcorn was getting stale?

HUNTER: Yes. And it was. So, I eventually left the theater, too.

WILL: But then you tried to get back in.

HUNTER: Well, anti-heroism is addicting. But the whales intervened.

WILL: So, what is the moral of the story, the punch line?

HUNTER: Heh heh... Dear Mother Earth: How do I love thee? Let me count the ways...

Published Books by Robert Lorne Hunter

Erebus. McClelland & Stewart, 1968.

The Enemies of Anarchy: A Gestalt Approach to Change. Viking, 1970.

The Storming of the Mind: Inside the Consciousness of Revolution. McClelland
& Stewart, 1971.

Time of the Clockmen. Georgia Straight, 1972.

To Save a Whale: The Voyages of Greenpeace. Douglas & McIntyre, 1978.

Greenpeace III: The Journey into the Bomb (with David McTaggart). William
Morrow, 1979.

Warriors of the Rainbow: A Chronicle of the Greenpeace Movement 1971–1979.
Holt, Rinehart and Winston, 1979.

Cry Wolf (with Paul Watson). Shepherds of the Earth, 1985.

On the Sky: Zen and the Art of International Freeloading. McClelland & Stewart, 1988.

Occupied Canada: A Young White Man Discovers His Unsuspected Past (with
Robert Calihoo). McClelland & Stewart, 1990.

Red Blood: One (Mostly) White Guy's Encounters in the Native World. McClelland
& Stewart, 1999.

2030: Confronting Thermageddon in Our Lifetime (also known as *2030:
Thermageddon*). McClelland & Stewart, 2002.

The Greenpeace to Amchitka: An Environmental Odyssey. Arsenal Pulp Press, 2004.

A Long Way to the Horizon: A Bridge on the Prairie. iUniverse, 2020.

Contributor Biographies

CATHY ANDERSON is an artist, designer, art director and writer. When she's not using her creativity to problem solve for her clients, she's using alchemy to create glass works of art and running a program that utilizes neurology and creativity to cultivate resilience.

ALINE CHARNEY BARBER is an ex-pat American who joined the protest to shut down the Cheynes Beach Whaling Station. She met and later married Tom Barber, and together they became wind farm pioneers in California.

DAVID BERNER founded X-Kalay, Canada's first residential treatment centre for addicts, alcoholics and ex-inmates in 1967, and served as executive director. He was a *Vancouver Province* newspaper columnist, and in 2013 he published his first book, *All the Way Home*, chronicling the history and theory of his addictions work.

JIM DEACOVE and his wife Ruth are the owners and inspiration for Family Pastimes, a successful Canadian cooperative games enterprise. Jim is a talented artist, a back-to-the-land advocate, socially conscious forward thinker, kind soul and lifelong friend to Bob Hunter.

MARLAYNA DEMCO is an emerging sustainability professional who aspires to make an impact in the area of corporate sustainability. She was a founding team member of the Los Angeles Cleantech Incubator and is a passionate young leader who has vowed to dedicate her career to solving the climate crisis.

PATRICIA JEAN DEMCO is Bobbi Hunter's older sister and the eldest daughter in a family of five girls and one boy. She is the mother of seven children. She received her education degree at UBC and had a fulfilling career as an elementary and English as an additional language (EAL) teacher. Her husband,

Dr. Alan Demco, was a medical school classmate of Dr. Myron MacDonald, Bobbi Hunter's first husband.

DINAH ELISSAT is a former senior cameraman at CityTV. After years of being an "accomplice" to Bob, she quit her job, chucked her first marriage, sold her house and joined Sea Shepherd, becoming 3rd engineer/ship's manager and full-time seafaring, marine-life-loving activist. She eventually returned to Toronto, where she married and had a son named Hunter.

JANINE FERRETTI is an environmental and social expert with over 16 years of experience in policy making, design and implementation of development operations for both the private and public sectors. She is currently a professor of the Practice of Global Development Policy, Pardee School of Global Studies, at Boston University.

BILL GANNON trained as a cost accountant, earning the designation CPA (chartered professional accountant). He opened his own practice in 1976 and offered his skills gratis to Greenpeace in its fledgling years of the mid- to late 1970s. Bill is an accomplished musician and lifelong environmental activist.

DAVID ("WALRUS") GARRICK was educated as an anthropologist-archaeologist. He is the author of *Shaped Cedars and Cedar Shaping: A Guidebook to Identifying, Documenting, Appreciating and Learning from Culturally Modified Trees.*

DOUGLAS GIBSON is a Canadian editor, publisher and writer, best known as the former president and publisher of McClelland & Stewart. He has edited the works of many illustrious authors, including Robertson Davies, Bruce Hutchison, Jack Hodgins, Alice Munro and Morley Callaghan. In 2011, Gibson published his own memoir, *Stories about Storytellers: Publishing Alice Munro, Robertson Davies, Alistair MacLeod, Pierre Trudeau and Others.*

JEAN PAUL FORTOM-GOUIN financed the 1977 Australia whale campaign and brought in Bob Hunter to deploy the famous Greenpeace tactics. He infiltrated the International Whaling Commission by being appointed the representative for Panama.

BOBBI HUNTER was treasurer, co-founder, main fundraiser, office coordinator, strategist and constant facilitator for the Greenpeace Foundation from 1974 to 1978. She was extremely happily and proudly married to Bob Hunter for 31 years and is the mother of his two children, Will and Emily Hunter, and stepmother to his daughter, Justine, and his son, Conan. Bobbi lives in Toronto.

DARREN HUNTER is the second son of Bob's only sibling, his brother, Don Hunter. Darren raised his son on his own, and they live on a rural property north of Winnipeg. They operate a trucking company together. Darren and Bobbi have remained close through the years.

DON HUNTER'S 50-year career in photography included being a newspaper photographer, a CBC film cameraman, an IATSE camera operator and finally a cinematography instructor.

Don is Bob's only sibling and author of *Have Camera, Must Travel*. Bob read an early draft of the book in his final days. His encouragement was instrumental in keeping Don writing for years.

EMILY HUNTER is a second-generation environmentalist and the author of the book *The Next Eco-Warriors* (2011). As the last child of Bob Hunter, she fully accepted his influence and guidance and has worked over ten years in the environmental field. She directed and produced several short TV documentaries on MTV Canada, as well as her own short documentary titled *Activism 2.0*. Currently, she is completing her master's in environmental studies at York University and a graduate diploma in climate action leadership at Royal Roads University. She resides in Toronto with her partner, Ryan, and their son, Phoenix.

JUSTINE HUNTER has covered news, business and politics for the *Vancouver Sun* and the *National Post*. She has also reported for the CBC. Currently, she is a reporter with *The Globe and Mail*. She lives in Victoria, BC, with her husband, Darryl, and their two children, Rhys and Gwynn.

ROBERT LORNE HUNTER (October 13, 1941 – May 2, 2005) was a Canadian environmentalist, journalist and author of 14 books. Named one of *TIME* magazine's ten eco-heroes of the 20th century in 2000, he was a lifelong multi-media activist and advocate for the environment.

WILL HUNTER got his honours BA at the University of Toronto and became a senior speechwriter for the 24th and 25th premiers of Ontario, Dalton McGuinty and Kathleen Wynne. Will is currently the senior communications officer/writer at the Ontario Ministry of Labour, Training and Skills Development. He is the devoted husband to Veronica and doting father to River and Rocket Hunter.

STEPHEN HURLBUT started his career in broadcast journalism as a news cameraman at CityTV and five years later he was director of news. Later, he became the VP of news at CityTV Toronto and VP/GM of CablePulse 24, a 24-hour local news channel. Stephen was the driving force behind the news at CityTV Toronto for 25 years. He is an avid outdoorsman, and after he retired he opened his own yoga studio and changed his pace in life.

THERESA (TERI) MARIAN INNES is the fourth child of the Innes family and the sister of Bobbi Hunter. She recently lost her husband, Andre. Together they had one son, Tommy, who was named after his uncle he never got to meet.

WILLIAM EDWARD JACKSON II was a musician, activist and author of *Once Upon a Greenpeace: An Eco Memoir* who served with Greenpeace in its early years (1975–1977), as a crew member on the first anti-whaling expedition. He was the founder of Greenpeace San Francisco (the first GP chapter after Vancouver, BC). A pioneer synthesizer player, Jackson was part of the media campaign to demonstrate whale intelligence. Sadly, he died in 2019.

JIRI (GEORGE) KOROTVA was born in the Czech Republic and grew up under Russian occupation. He took part in a student march, was arrested and spent years mining coal in Russia. He bravely escaped to Sweden, and eventually arrived in Canada in 1968. He joined the Greenpeace Save the Whale ship in 1975, and in 1976 became the captain on the vessel *James Bay,* on the second Save the Whale campaign.

LEA ANN MALLETT is an activist, author, speaker and ENGO professional. In her activism journey, Lea Ann has travelled from direct action wilderness activist to non-profit leader, from sitting in an ancient cedar for three days to protest clear-cut logging to leading forest protests to creating thriving organizations as a non-profit executive director.

GARRY MARCHANT was a travel companion and lifelong friend of Bob and Bobbi Hunter. He was a columnist with *Vancouver Magazine* from 1977 to 1989 and a freelance writer whose work appeared in several anthologies, including *Away From Home: Canadian Writers in Exotic Places*; *Our American Cousins*; and *That Reminds Me*.

ROD MARINING became involved in the Don't Make a Wave Committee in Vancouver, BC, and then in the fall of 1971 he sailed to Amchitka on both the Greenpeace vessel *Phyllis Cormack* and *Greenpeace Too, Edgewater Fortune*. He later sailed with the 1975 and 1976 Greenpeace campaigns to protect the whales. Rod was the vice-president under Bob Hunter. Since then, Rod has sailed on numerous Sea Shepherd expeditions. Rod has been a lifelong environmental crusader.

SANDRA ELAINE MASKELL, née Innes, is the fifth child born to the Innes family and a younger sister of Bobbi Hunter. Sandy has had a long and successful career as a registered nurse. She is an animal rights advocate and a devoted mother and grandmother to her children, Mark and Sara, and her grandchildren. Sadly, her husband Dave passed away recently.

ELIZABETH MAY is one of Canada's best-known parliamentarians and is a lifelong environmental advocate. Prior to running for elected office, she worked as a lawyer and a governmental policy advisor and was for 17 years the executive director of Sierra Club Canada (1989–2006). The ninth leader of the Green Party of Canada (2006–2019), she was the first Canadian Green to win election in 2011. She is currently the parliamentary leader of the Green Party caucus, representing the Vancouver Island riding of Saanich–Gulf Islands on the territory of the W̱SÁNEĆ Nation. Elizabeth is the author of eight acclaimed books. She lives with her husband, John Kidder, in beautiful Sidney-by-the-Sea, in the heart of Saanich–Gulf Islands.

DR. MYRON MACDONALD was a general practitioner in West Vancouver and served as a medic on the first 1975 Greenpeace whale campaign. He sailed the world and briefly helped with the Greenpeace 1976 whale campaign in Hawaii. He was Bobbi Hunter's first husband and remains a lifelong friend of Bob, Bobbi and their family. He passed away in 2022.

JOYCE MCLEAN is an environmental activist, writer, photographer and lecturer who was a driving force in expanding Greenpeace in Eastern Canada in the 1980s. Her Greenpeace experience led her to a senior political role in the office of the minister of environment from 1990 to 1995. She was the first green energy manager at Toronto Hydro.

PETER O'BRIAN is a Canadian film producer, broadcast executive and chair of TVOntario. His company, Independent Pictures, won 19 Genie Awards in 1977. He later produced *The Grey Fox, Outrageous!, John and the Missus* and *My American Cousin*. He took a sabbatical from producing in the 1990s to run the Canadian Film Centre, where he met and became friends with Bob Hunter.

CHRIS PASH is an award-winning journalist in Australia and author of *The Last Whale*, which recreates the final days of Australia's last whaling station and chronicles the 1970s Save the Whale campaign.

WALT PATTERSON is a UK-Canadian physicist who arrived in the United Kingdom in 1960. Since 1991, he has been a Fellow of the Energy, Environment and Resources Programme at Chatham House in London. Walt Patterson has published 14 books and hundreds of papers, articles and reviews. His latest book is *Electricity vs Fire*.

RON PRECIOUS was a professional cinematographer for 40 years. In 1977, he co-produced *Greenpeace: Voyage to Save the Whales*, a Genie Award–winning documentary based on the first Greenpeace whale campaign. He documented five Greenpeace campaigns while working for the CBC (1980–1985) and then worked as a cameraman and director of photography for Hollywood North. He was one of the co-founders of *Sea Shepherd*.

JIM ROBB is the general manager of Friends of the Rouge Watershed, an award-winning charitable ENGO. Jim and his colleagues have been guardians and instruments for positive change through the creation and implementation of the Rouge Park, Greenbelt, Great Lakes Water Quality and Watershed remedial action plans.

JERRY ROTHWELL is a filmmaker whose work includes the award-winning feature documentaries *The Reason I Jump, How to Change the World, Sour Grapes, Town of Runners, Donor Unknown, School in the Cloud, Heavy Load and Deep Water.* His work has won numerous accolades, including two Grierson Awards, a Sundance Special Jury Prize, an RTS Award, the IDA Pare Lorentz Award and a BAFTA nomination.

PAUL RUZYCKI was the captain and former chief mate on the Greenpeace vessel *Arctic Sunrise.* Born in 1965 in Port Colborne, Ontario, he was a seaman on the Great Lakes before joining Greenpeace. He was captured and taken into custody in Russia during a protest against Arctic oil drilling. He served two months in Russian jails. A friend of Bob Hunter's since the 1990s, he has been involved in numerous seagoing protests, including the Turbot War campaign with Bob.

DR. STEPHEN BEDE SCHARPER is a professor, author, editor, journalist and public scholar with a special focus on regenerative sustainability and values. He is an associate professor at the School of the Environment and Anthropology (UTM) at the University of Toronto. Stephen lives in Toronto with his wife, novelist Hilary Scharper.

STEVE SHALLHORN was hired by Greenpeace in 1987 to work on the Nuclear Free Seas disarmament campaign in Toronto. Greenpeace work led to living in Washington, DC, London, UK, Ottawa, Tokyo and Sydney, Australia, the last two posts being as head of those Greenpeace offices. Steve has been director of the Labour Education Centre since 2011, where he developed the Working Green program.

TODD SOUTHGATE is an award-winning environmental documentary film-maker and cinematographer. Much of his filmmaking is advocacy-oriented and focused on issues in the Brazilian Amazon. Todd is the director of photography for Animal Planet/Discovery's award-winning series *Biggest & Baddest*, with Dr. Niall McCann. Today, Todd lives on a small subtropical island in the south of Brazil.

PETER SPECK has been on the boards of Greenpeace, Family Services of the North Shore (11 years), Lower Mainland Publishing Ltd., Business in Vancouver, and the Memorial Society of BC. He was president of the BC and Yukon Community Newspaper Association (103 members) for a term. He started the *North Shore News* in 1968 and retired in 2001, still as publisher. He is a retired sailor and farmer, and a dog lover and lifelong non-fiction reader. Peter has been awarded the Queen's Medal twice.

PAUL SPONG is co-director, with his wife Helena, of OrcaLab, a land-based whale research station on Hanson Island in British Columbia (www.orcalab.org), and president of the non-profit Pacific Orca Society.

CARLIE TRUEMAN is a retired judge, trial lawyer and outreach trainer for the Monroe Institute. Before being chosen to be on the first Greenpeace whale campaign in 1975, she was a professional diver and worked for a firm of nautical engineers in Victoria, BC. She completed her law degree and practised in Prince Rupert, where she was ultimately called to the Bench of the Provincial Court of British Columbia. She lives in Vancouver with her long-time partner, Gareth Llewellyn.

CAPTAIN PAUL FRANKLIN WATSON was born in Toronto in 1950 and raised in the New Brunswick fishing village of St. Andrews-By-the-Sea. He served as director, campaign leader and first officer with the Greenpeace Foundation from 1972 until 1977, when he left to establish the Sea Shepherd Conservation Society. He continues to work as the chief consultant for strategy, communications, and operations for Sea Shepherd Global. Captain Watson is also the author of many acclaimed books.

LINDA WEINBERG was a special education teacher in the Langley School District for 20 years. Her husband, Hal, has a PhD in neurophysiology and is an emeritus professor at Simon Fraser University. He was the first mayor of Anmore.

REX WEYLER is a Pulitzer-nominated writer, ecologist and co-founder of Greenpeace International. He currently writes the *Deep Green* column at the Greenpeace International website. He was a director of the original Greenpeace Foundation, the editor of the organization's first newsletter, and a co-founder of Greenpeace International in 1979. He is the author of *Greenpeace*, an acclaimed account of the birth and early years of Greenpeace. He is the proud father of three sons, and he lives on Cortes Island in British Columbia with his wife, artist Lisa Gibbons.

DAVID "HAP" WILSON is a Canadian naturalist, canoe tripper, illustrator, author and photographer. He worked for several years in the Temagami District as a park ranger, later as an outfitter, and was co-founder of the environment group Earthroots. He has authored 14 books, and his writing has appeared in *Canadian Geographic, Cottage Life, Explore, Canoe & Kayak* and *Outdoor Canada*. He is an International Fellow of the Explorers Club, and Royal Canadian Geographical Society recipient of the Bill Mason Award for Lifetime Achievement in River Conservation.

MOSES ZNAIMER is best known around the world as a Canadian media pioneer and the co-founder of CityTV, MuchMusic, CP24, Bravo!, Space, Fashion Television and a dozen or more popular television channels and stations. He now combines media, content and advocacy to champion the needs and interests of Canada's rapidly expanding over-45 population, as the founder of ZoomerMedia and president of CARP, Canada's largest Advocacy Association for Canadians As We Age.

Acknowledgements

This book came to me through an amazing spirit whispering in my ear that I should use my lonely COVID days to some great purpose. I had just completed self-publishing Bob's book *A Long Way to the Horizon*. I thought, *Why not write the story of Bob and share this writing experience with his respected circle?* So I thank Bob first of all, for his enduring influence.

I thank my best friend, my daughter Emily, who had edited an anthology some years before called *The Next Eco Warrior*. She was my inspiration and guide.

I can't thank Paul Watson enough for being the first to respond to my request letter with a resounding "Yes!" I thank him for his lifelong friendship with our family, his perseverance, his bravery and steadfastness for Mother Earth, and his true brotherhood with Bob.

Thank you to our friend Elizabeth May for taking the time away from her important work to write about Bob's most urgent message. Elizabeth has been an advocate for environmental sanity for her entire lifetime.

Thanks to Stephen Schaper for guiding souls to the spiritual aspects of being a crusader for environmental sanity.

I thank Captain Ryan Jackson for allowing me to bring to life words from his father.

I thank Cathy Anderson, our style editor. She is much more than an editor, she is an artist, and since putting her magic touch to this book, she is now a Bob Believer.

And, most importantly, many thanks to all the wonderful friends, family and colleagues who took the time to write and sometimes discuss their experiences in order to make this a remarkable book about an unforgettable Canadian.

—Bobbi Hunter, Toronto, 2022

We would like to also take this opportunity to acknowledge the traditional territories upon which we live and work. In Calgary, Alberta, we acknowledge the Niitsítapi (Blackfoot) and the people of the Treaty 7 region in Southern Alberta, which includes the Siksika, the Piikuni, the Kainai, the Tsuut'ina, and the Stoney Nakoda First Nations, including Chiniki, Bearpaw, and Wesley First Nations. The City of Calgary is also home to Métis Nation of Alberta, Region III. In Victoria, British Columbia, we acknowledge the traditional territories of the Lkwungen (Esquimalt and Songhees), Malahat, Pacheedaht, Scia'new, T'Sou-ke, and W̱SÁNEĆ (Pauquachin, Tsartlip, Tsawout, Tseycum) peoples.